GOLF'S IRON HORSE

GOLF'S IRON HORSE

THE ASTONISHING, RECORD-BREAKING LIFE OF RALPH KENNEDY

JOHN SABINO

Skyhorse Publishing

Skyhorse Publishing books may be purchased in bulk at special discounts for sales promotion, corporate gifts, fund-raising, or educational purposes. Special editions can also be created to specifications. For details, contact the Special Sales Department, Skyhorse Publishing, 307 West 36th Street, 11th Floor, New York, NY 10018 or info@skyhorsepublishing.com.

Visit our website at www.skyhorsepublishing.com.

10 9 8 7 6 5 4 3 2 1

Library of Congress Cataloging-in-Publication Data is available on file.

Cover design and photo-illustration by Tom Lau
Cover photo credit USGA

Print ISBN: 978-1-5107-1347-5
Ebook ISBN: 978-1-5107-1348-2

Printed in the United States of America

Contents

Introduction ix

Chapter 1: **Beginnings** 1

Chapter 2: **The Van Cortlandt Park Golf Course ("Vannie")** 9

Chapter 3: **Bitten by the Golf Bug** 21

Chapter 4: **The Quest Begins** 35

Chapter 5: **The Media Discover Red Kennedy** 51

Chapter 6: **The Winged Foot Golf Club** 73

Chapter 7: **El Gran Jugador de Golf** 86

Chapter 8: **Golf Nomad King** 103

Chapter 9: **Down Magnolia Lane** 126

Chapter 10: **Kindly Cancel My Subscription** 142

Chapter 11: **Old Man River** 153

Chapter 12: **Golf in the Great Metropolis** 171

Chapter 13: Golf in the War Years 191

Chapter 14: Motoring out West 201

Chapter 15: The Next 500 Courses 221

Chapter 16: The Glamorous Traveler 230

Chapter 17: The Final Leg 245

Chapter 18: The Legacy 259

Epilogue 277

Appendix—The Golf Courses of New York City, Past and Present 284

Acknowledgments 286

Bibliography 287

"Modern golf is a stiffer test of a player's skill, but it has robbed the game of its charm as an adventure of the spirit."

—Robert Browning, A History of Golf, *1955*

Introduction

THE AMAZING FEAT OF A golfer with extraordinary stamina has been tucked away and largely forgotten in suburban New Jersey. Although located less than fifty miles from Times Square, the oasis that is Far Hills is a community of rolling hills, wide open spaces, and old-money estates. Home of the United States Equestrian Team, an Englishman would be comfortable in the idyllic borough, with its anachronistic steeplechase races, white three-rail fences, and country houses with cute names. Favored by the landed gentry, the Forbes family had an estate nearby at one time, as have governors, senators, and cabinet members. Far Hills is also the home of the United States Golf Association (USGA) and houses their headquarters, museum, library, and archives. The building that serves as the centerpiece of the USGA museum was at one time a private mansion, a Georgian Revival-style house designed by John Russell Pope, who also designed the National Archives building in Washington D. C. Behind a locked door in the stacks of the research library sits the story of Ralph Kennedy, overlooked for the last sixty years, but well preserved in the temperature-controlled environment. I stumbled upon Ralph's story while researching my previous book, *How to Play the World's Most Exclusive Golf Clubs*, and became enthralled reading through his unique life story.

A member of the New York Athletic Club, Ralph was one of the founding members of the Winged Foot Golf Club in Mamaroneck, New York. He holds a distinction in amateur golf as noteworthy as Lou Gehrig's 2,130 consecutive game streak in baseball: Ralph played golf on 3,165 different courses during his forty-three-year love affair with the game. He played in all forty-eight states, nine Canadian provinces, and a dozen different countries. Ralph had an iron constitution and was tireless in his pursuit of the game. Playing 3,165 courses would take 8.6 years if a golfer were to play one course every day. In addition to the 3,165 *unique* courses he played, the unrelenting Kennedy also played golf a total of 8,500 times over his lifetime, the equivalent of teeing it up every day for twenty-three straight years. By comparison, Gehrig's career in pinstripes spanned seventeen seasons.

Gehrig was obviously covered widely by the media; Ralph Kennedy was, as well. The latter was featured in hundreds of newspapers and magazines on five continents for a period of over thirty-five years and appeared on the cover of the *Saturday Evening Post* twice. He was also featured in *National Geographic,* and in Ripley's *Believe it or Not* three times. Coincidentally, the indefatigable Kennedy lived almost all of his adult life within three miles of Yankee Stadium, in Upper Manhattan. During their overlapping life spans—although Gehrig's was sadly much shorter—they lived in virtually the same neighborhood for a period of time, less than two miles apart. Both men had a banner year in 1931. Gehrig played every inning of every game during that 155-game season; Kennedy played golf on 160 *different* courses around the country. Their ability to rack up impressive single-day feats is another incidental parallel: Gehrig hit four home runs in one game in 1932; Ralph played six different courses in one day in 1936. Gehrig hit twenty-three career grand slams; Ralph once played four different courses in four states between sunup and sundown. Ralph's decades-long achievement was all the more impressive because golf was only a hobby for him; he held down a full-time job as a traveling salesman.

Ralph was a stickler for detail and documentation and kept every scorecard of the courses he played. Not only did he save every scorecard, but he also had someone from the course, usually the professional, sign the card to attest to his round. His cards were then carefully stored in a safe-deposit box in a Manhattan bank branch. He donated all the cards and six scrapbooks documenting his journey to the USGA in 1957, providing a complete record of his quixotic journey. The USGA called him a legend in the golfing world, and its executive director sent him a letter after receiving the treasure trove, telling him it was one of the most significant collections in the *Golf House* museum. Francis Ouimet, the 1913 U.S. Open champion and one-time captain of the Royal & Ancient Golf Club of St. Andrews, called Kennedy's feat "One of the most remarkable performances I have ever heard of, and a title he should hold forever."

One of Ralph Kennedy's six scrapbooks chronicling his journey. (*Photo courtesy of USGA)*

It was a newsworthy event when Ralph left for a new trip: the *New York Times* announced when he traveled to Canada or Upstate New York, the *Los Angeles Times* when he set sail to play in South America. Local newspapers throughout the country proudly announced when he was in town and sought his opinions of the courses he played. The headline writers had a myriad of descriptions for him including golf marathoner, itinerant golfer, galloping golfer, golf glutton, link trotter, champion peripatetic golf player, wanderer of the country's fairways, renowned golfer, golf hobbyist, champion rambler of golfdom, nomad of Yankee golf, divot digger, tramp golfer, roving Ralph, globe-trotting golfer, noted vagabond of golf links, rambling golfer, the man of a thousand golf courses, the energetic American, champion tourist golfer, golfing gadabout, the Dr. Livingstone of Golf, and golf's Lou Gehrig. He was followed by the leading sportswriters of the day, including Grantland Rice, who helped popularize sports in the 1920s. O. B. Keeler of the *Atlanta Journal*—who chronicled Bobby Jones's ascent to the top of the golf world—wrote about Ralph frequently and dubbed him "Ralpho of the Iron Arm." While not exactly as well known as Gehrig's "Iron Horse" moniker, it is an apt comparison.

Ralph's story is worth telling for a variety of reasons. First, the will and stamina required to achieve such a difficult feat is impressive. Second, his lifetime spanned some of the most impactful developments of the last two centuries, from the Victorian Era to the atomic age, and taking a deep dive into his life provides an interesting lens through which to look back and see how quickly and dramatically the world changed in the late nineteenth and early twentieth centuries. His accomplishments began in a world of horse and buggies and extended until the advent of television and commercial jet travel. Third, examining Ralph's life provides an unparalleled look at the game of golf and how it has evolved from its early days in the United States, through to the emergence of our modern era. When Ralph entered college, Harry Vardon was U.S. Open champion, and by the time of his death, Arnold Palmer was the reigning Masters champion.

Kennedy's meticulous recordkeeping of scorecards is a priceless documentary record of hundreds of courses that have been lost to history, and as a result of his foresight they have been preserved for future generations. In some cases, his cards are the only record remaining of courses that no longer exist. The routines and customs of the game also changed dramatically over Ralph's life, and his story provides a detailed and nostalgic look back at them, including the use of sand tees; clubs named mashie, spoon, and niblick; "cops" as hazards; courses with sand and cottonseed-hull greens; company-owned golf courses; and different rules of the game. He played in a world of unruly caddies, when bogey was the standard measure of a score, when courses were built by hand, and when they were maintained without automatic irrigation systems.

His story highlights some forgotten details regarding the evolution of the game, including the unexpected role that slot machines played

A sampling of newspaper coverage highlighting Ralph's journey. *(Author's Collection)*

and the virtues of nine-hole golf courses. During Ralph's lifetime, professional golfers made only a modest amount of money playing the game, and both match-play and amateur competitions were held in high esteem. The thousands of sequentially numbered scorecards he left in Far Hills provide a thought-provoking thread by which to look back through golf history.

Ralph took up the game in 1910 when he was twenty-eight, playing at the first public course in the country, Van Cortlandt Park in New York City. He played "here and there" for a number of years, but his quest began in earnest in 1919 when he met a widely traveled golf fanatic who told him that he had played 240 different courses. Ralph's competitive spirit kicked in, and he set himself on a path to play more courses than anyone has ever played, working at it diligently over the coming decades. Of special interest in a biography of Ralph Kennedy are detailed looks into his historic first course, Van Cortlandt Park, and Winged Foot, where he was a founding member. The extensive collection of newspaper articles that were saved in his scrapbooks have enhanced the story of his journey. He had extraordinarily good press connections, and he was able to leverage them throughout his life.

Ralph's home city also provided the perfect backdrop for his adventure; he lived in New York City during an exciting period and saw the rise of many of its iconic buildings, including its most important Beaux-Arts structures and the great Art Deco skyscrapers. As a resident, he experienced firsthand the emergence of the Jazz Age in the Roaring Twenties and saw his fair share of ticker-tape parades. During the prime of his life, boxing, horse racing, and baseball characterized the sports era, and he had a front-row seat to the New York Yankees dynasty that included the feared Murderers' Row. Since Ralph was a New York City resident, his records also provide an unprecedented look at urban golf there in the first half of the twentieth century. As difficult as it is to envisage today, the city was once teeming with courses. Ralph played twenty-three courses in the metropolis that no longer exist.

The onset of suburbanization, the building of interstate highways, and poor economic times exerted an intense pressure on golf courses, leading to the demise of hundreds of them nationally. Among the courses Kennedy played that no longer exist are several that hosted the U.S. Open and PGA Championship, and courses designed by some of the game's premier architects, including Alister MacKenzie, Seth Raynor, A. W. Tillinghast, Donald Ross, Devereux Emmet, Stanley Thompson, Harry S. Colt, Tom Bendelow, Willie Park Jr., and Charles Blair Macdonald.

Consider only a handful of the changes that occurred during Ralph's life span: America had thirty-eight states and no golf courses when he was born; life expectancy was forty-five years for a male at his birth and sixty-seven at his death. During his lifetime, man introduced electricity and the automobile into daily life and advanced from being flightless to engaging in regularly scheduled air travel. He witnessed dramatic advances in medicine, including the adoption of penicillin and antibiotic drugs, the emergence of fast food, and the beginning of the consumer age. Over his lifetime, there were thirteen

U.S. presidents, two world wars, and countless other significant events. Train travel was the dominant mode of transportation, and America began to exert its influence around the world when he was in his prime years. He lived during a time when there were so many developments and trends that many are named epochs: the Great Depression, the machine age, the Dust Bowl, and the beginnings of the atomic age and the jet age. "May you live in interesting times," the expression goes, and Ralph certainly did.

He lived most of his life during a time when Americans resided in cities or rural areas, before suburbanization and air conditioning, and when women could not vote. His endeavor serves as an interesting backdrop to examine golf's history and progress through the life of an "ordinary" (if obsessive) citizen. He played at a time when equipment was not as consistent as it is today, when the game had half-par holes and a different-sized ball, before golf carts, when there were no rakes in the bunkers, and when an opponent could block their competitors' ball with a stymie. He used hickory-shafted clubs and played in a world that was mostly exclusionary to people of color. It was the world of Ma Bell and Frank Capra. Of bootleggers and bank robbers.

The variety of courses Ralph played ranged from the worst public and municipal courses up to the apex of the golf world, including Augusta National, Cypress Point, Muirfield, and Pine Valley. He played a substantial number of nine-hole courses and a full spectrum of urban, rural, desert, mountain, parkland, moorland, links, and heathland courses. No course was too insignificant or far away for Ralph to pursue. Late in his journey when he traveled to Great Britain, the *Times* (London) said about the persistent golfer, "Nearly everybody collects something . . . Sherlock Holmes collected murders. Kennedy is a golf course-collecting champion. Metaphorical trumpets should sound and drums be beaten for such a conquering hero."

The *New York Herald Tribune* called Ralph's accomplishment the most hopelessly unassailable record in sport. An early twentieth-century Forrest Gump, Kennedy had an uncanny knack for appearing in the most unexpected of places, and along the way he met Bobby

Jones, Walter Hagen, Tommy Armour, Gene Sarazen, and Byron Nelson, and was sought out by movie stars. The *Washington Post* said about Ralph, "He collects courses the way some people collect stamps." Even the urbane *New Yorker* followed Ralph's travels and called his feat the "coziest athletic record we've heard of in some time."

The well-dressed Kennedy in his usual golfing attire. *(Photo courtesy of USGA)*

Much of golf history has focused on the game's stars, competitive tournament play, private clubs, or golf course architecture. Less has been written about what an average (if fanatical) golfer experienced as they played the game. Telling golf's story through the eyes of an implacable amateur golfer and his historic scorecards can help to close that gap just a little. O. B. Keeler twice promised to write a book about Kennedy but died before doing so. Ralph talked about writing a book himself, and he was once approached by a publisher, but the project never materialized. So without farther ado, herein lies the story of a golfer with bulldog determination, a self-described peripatetic golfer. Current and future historians of the game owe Ralph a great deal of thanks for preserving such a complete record.

Prepare yourself to live vicariously and follow the peregrinations of an obsessed and entertaining golfer.

CHAPTER 1
Beginnings

Ralph Anderson Kennedy was born in Hopkinton, Massachusetts, on June 16, 1882, twelve years before the USGA was founded. As was typical at the time, the house he was born into was lit by candle power and oil lamps, and was without central heating and running water. Hopkinton is located thirty miles from Boston and since 1924 has been the starting point for the Boston Marathon. As someone who would grow to love the game, Ralph could not have been born at a better time. The first permanent golf club was established in the United States in 1888, six years after he was born, at the Saint Andrew's Golf Club above New York City, about twenty miles from where Kennedy ended up residing for the majority of his life. His mother, Ilda May Kennedy (née Hayward) was a native of Hopkinton, born there in 1860. His father, Samuel Anderson Kennedy, was also a Hopkinton native. The 1870 census lists Samuel as a farmer, but by the time the couple's marriage license was issued in 1881, his occupation is shown as a bookkeeper. The Kennedys were of Scottish descent, having emigrated from the Ayrshire region.

Chester A. Arthur was president when Ralph was born, elected the year before, on the sixteen-year anniversary of the end of the Civil War and four years after Reconstruction ended. As a child of the Gilded Age, Ralph was born at a time of unprecedented technological advancement:

three months after his birth, the first large-scale test of Thomas Edison's electricity system was conducted in Lower Manhattan; the following year, the Brooklyn Bridge opened; the coming decade witnessed the invention of radio and the X-ray, the gasoline-powered car, and the first subway in America. Kennedy's contemporaries, also born in 1882, included some distinguished men who would go on to achieve great things in literature and politics, including James Joyce, A. A. Milne, Fiorello La Guardia, and Franklin Delano Roosevelt. In "base-ball" news, on the day Ralph was born, the New York Metropolitans beat the League nine of Cleveland at the Polo Grounds in New York.

During Ralph's formative years, basic golf equipment that we take for granted today was evolving. The first golf bag appeared in 1890 and the first steel shaft in 1893. Golf clubs during this period were transitioning from custom implements that were crafted by local professionals to those manufactured by newly formed equipment companies. The gutta-percha ball was the standard used in the late nineteenth century (gutta-percha is a latex-like substance derived from the sap of a tree). When Ralph was sixteen years old, Coburn Haskell of Cleveland designed a golf ball using a gutta-percha cover wrapped around a center

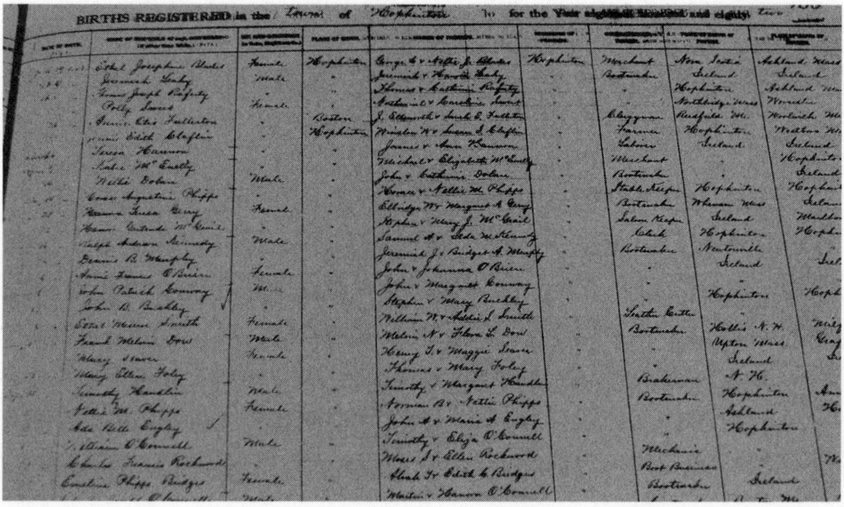
BIRTHS REGISTERED in the Town of Hopkinton for the Year eighteen hundred and eighty two

The birth registry is Hopkinton, Massachusetts, the month Ralph was born. *(Author's Collection)*

of evenly wound rubber "string." Haskell and a friend patented the wound-rubber ball, which, for the average golfer, flew an additional twenty yards farther than a ball made solely of gutta-percha. Although the gutta-percha was eventually replaced by balata (the sap of a different tree), the same basic design would be the standard ball used during Kennedy's entire lifetime. James Foulis of St. Andrews, Scotland, made significant contributions as the sport's equipment evolved. In addition to designing the bramble patterning for the Haskell ball, he and his brother designed the first mashie-niblick club, the equivalent of today's 7-iron, when Ralph was twenty-two.

As golf was still an emerging pastime, there were very few courses in the country at the turn of the century. To get a sense of early golf in America, the *Harper's Official Golf Guide* of 1899 paints an enlightening picture of a fledgling game. It lists a total of 585 courses, highly concentrated in the Northeast, with 52 percent of all courses in New York, New Jersey, Pennsylvania, and Massachusetts. Ten states had no courses at all listed in the *Guide,* including Mississippi, South Dakota, and Nevada. Louisiana, Arkansas, Delaware, and West Virginia had one course each listed.

Mirroring the development of golf in the British Isles, early American courses sprung up close to railroad stations. In its directory, the *Guide* conveniently listed which railroad was nearest to each course. Courses in Atlantic City, New Jersey, boasted that they were within easy reach of "all the large cities by the finest Pullman trains." California had only twenty-six courses at the turn of the twentieth century. Golfers could take an electric car (trolley) to reach the Los Angeles Country Club, which was organized two years earlier.

Eighteen-hole courses were not the dominant course type during this time; many were nine holes, although early clubs were also experimenting with courses of different formats, as well. Denver's Overland Park Club—reachable by the Santa Fe Railroad—featured a nine-hole course for men and a five-hole course for women. The game's nascent stages were evident in the Orlando Golf Club, a rudimentary six-hole course in Florida with crisscrossing holes routed over multiple ditches.

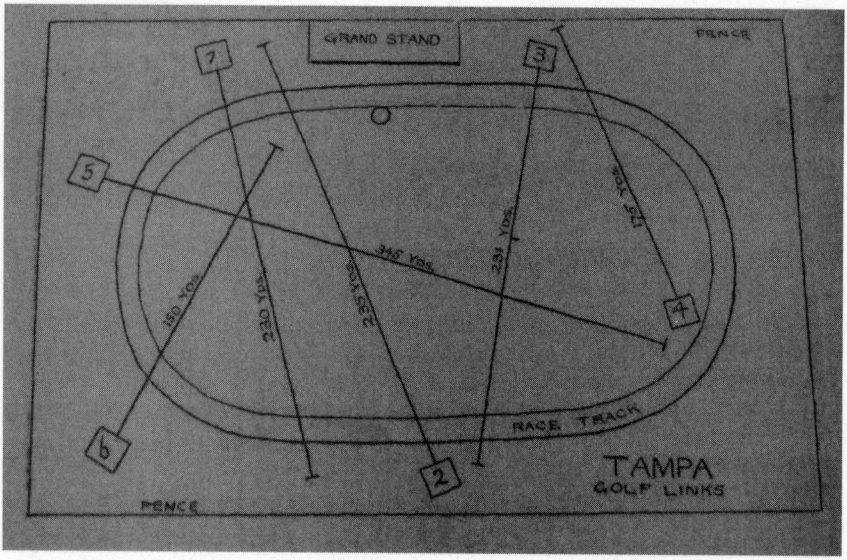

Image of an early, rudimentary golf course layout. *(Author's Collection)*

The Tampa Bay Hotel Golf Club had a full eighteen-hole course designed by John Dunn, which replaced a six-hole course played over and around a local racetrack.

As golf was emerging, Ralph entered high school, in 1896, in Mansfield, Massachusetts, located roughly thirty minutes equidistant from Boston and Providence. He was admitted to Amherst College in Massachusetts in 1900, a small, all-male, liberal arts school with 412 total students. Amherst's curriculum was weighted toward a classical education with studies in Latin, Greek, the romance languages, rhetoric, mental and moral philosophy, logic, and public speaking. While there, Kennedy studied Greek for one year; Spanish, Latin, and French for two; and German for four. He took public speaking classes all four years of his studies, steadily improving, raising his grade from a less-than-stellar sixty-five to a respectable eighty-five.

Founded in 1821, Amherst was originally established to educate indigent men of piety for the Christian ministry; twenty-six "college preachers" were among the faculty when Ralph attended. Ralph prospered while there. He ran the one-mile race on the track team, joined the Phi Delta Theta fraternity, and wrote for the college newspaper. Amherst had a nine-hole golf course when he attended, which was built in 1896. Although quite active on campus, golf would not be among his pursuits.

During his years of study at Amherst, many significant events occurred that changed the course of history. Oil was first discovered in the United States in 1901 in Beaumont, Texas, at the Spindletop well. President McKinley was assassinated the same year, and Teddy Roosevelt took over the presidency. Three years later, work on the Panama Canal resumed under American supervision. Nineteen hundred and three was a momentous year; not only did the Wright Brothers first take flight in North Carolina, but it was also the year Lou Gehrig was born.

A good indicator of the general poor state of health at the turn of the century can be found in Amherst's approach to physical education, which prided itself on making sure that all its men engaged in physical activity. Students were attended to by two physicians who gave them advice on their personal care and "bodily needs." Amherst's student handbook detailed how important exercise was: "While hygienists affirm that, as a general rule, the health of a young man from fifteen to twenty-five years of age is apt to decline, the reverse rule is found to prevail with students here." During Ralph's collegiate years, heart disease was the leading cause of death for Americans; the second and third leading causes of death were pneumonia and influenza, followed by tuberculosis.

Amherst did not yet offer specific degrees with a major; Ralph received their standard liberal arts degree, a Bachelors of Arts, graduating *cum laude*. A solid "B" student, his average grade over the four years was eighty. The handsome, broad-shouldered, 5-foot-10 Kennedy, nicknamed "Red" for his strawberry blond hair, weighed 171 pounds when he entered the world with his degree in hand, full of promise, in 1904.

While Ralph was attending Amherst, his family moved to Providence, Rhode Island. His younger brother, Robert H. Kennedy, went to Providence High School and also attended Amherst, graduating in 1908. Ralph joined his family in Providence after graduating and met the future Mrs. Kennedy, Mary Alice Barber, who was born in Arcadia, Rhode Island, on February 19, 1883. They were married on October 19, 1907, when he was twenty-five and she was twenty-four. After marrying, the couple moved to New York City, where Ralph started working in sales for the Eagle Pencil Company, which was based on East Thirteenth Street in Manhattan. Although they wanted to, Ralph and Mary Alice would never have children.

The 1910 census shows the couple resided at 549 West 144th Street in Manhattan's twelfth ward, part of West Harlem. Ralph's occupation is listed as a "traveling salesman," and the apartment he and Mary Alice rented was shared with his brother, who was in training as a physician at Presbyterian Hospital in Manhattan. The census provides an interesting look at the ethos of the time, and the census enumerator asked Ralph and Mary Alice if they were "Deaf and Dumb?" as well as "Blind (both eyes)?" and whether they were a "Survivor of Union or Confederate Army or Navy?"

Ralph's first foray into golf was on a rainy Sunday, September 25, 1910, when he was cajoled into playing for the first time. He says he was reluctant to try, but a friend, "Irishman" Michael Burke, was persistent and took him to New York's Van Cortlandt Park Golf Course in the Bronx. Located six miles from his apartment, the popular course kept its fairways in good playing condition using horse-drawn lawn mowers, and golfers played for free. Wearing a hat to keep his head dry, Ralph launched a little white orb into the air for the first time as the Edwardian Era was ending. Although industrializing, America was an isolated country, and Europe was still dominated by interrelated dynastic monarchs: George V was the reigning King of Great Britain, his cousin Wilhelm II was the German Emperor, and another cousin, Nicholas II, was Russian Emperor. Ralph was twenty-eight at the time, and it was several years before the Great War erupted.

Air racing was all the rage in 1910, and on the day Michael and Ralph played, the local newspaper was aflutter about ten aviators who entered a New York-to-Chicago air race. Aviation pioneer Glenn Curtiss was among the contestants competing for the $25,000 prize. The contest was to take place over seven days, and the organizers trumpeted that "the race will be the greatest aeronautical event since the art of flying heavier-than-air machines was founded and developed." The contestants were expected to fly between fifty and sixty miles per hour in their biplanes and monoplanes to cover the 960 miles.

Baseball was still in full swing at the end of September, and on the day Ralph first golfed, the broadsheets informed fans that the New York Giants beat the Chicago Cubs at the Polo Grounds. At the time, the Gehrig family was residing at 2266 Amsterdam Avenue, on West 173rd Street, not far from the Kennedys. Their apartments were near Hilltop Park (home of the New York Highlanders—who would later become the Yankees). Occupying one of the highest pieces of ground in Manhattan, Hilltop Park was located in Washington Heights, overlooking the New Jersey Palisades.

Pennsylvania Station formally opened two months after Ralph's first golfing foray, on November 27, 1910. The towering Beaux-Arts structure on Manhattan's West Side was the centerpiece of the Pennsylvania Railroad's expansive network and would be used frequently by the traveling salesman as he ventured out to cover his large territory. The colonnaded building was clad in pink granite, and its soaring interior had 150-foot high vaulted glass windows in the ceiling, allowing sunlight to stream onto waiting passengers. An architectural critic described the grandeur of Pennsylvania Station in religious terms when he said, "one entered the city like a god." The 355-pound William Howard Taft, the first golfing president, was in office when Ralph first took up the game, having succeeded Roosevelt in 1909.

Kennedy's first round was not pretty. Flubs, whiffs, shanks, chunks, foozles, skulls, chili-dips, hooks, and wild slices were among the flurry of shots he hit. New York's state animal is the beaver, which is wholly appropriate, since the first-time golfer dug up turf the size and shape of beaver pelts on that fateful Sunday. One of the intriguing and mysterious aspects of the royal and ancient game of golf is how a first-timer becomes hooked after such repeated initial failure. It is the unexpected magic of that one exceptional shot that snares the unsuspecting newcomer: the straight ball that sails in a perfect arc off the clubface at its intended target.

Ralph took 146 strokes using hickory-shafted clubs on his first try at golf, and in his own words, he became "fascinated" by the game, buying his own set of clubs a week later and encouraging Mary Alice to take up the game immediately, as well.

CHAPTER 2

The Van Cortlandt Park Golf Course ("Vannie")

Although Ralph played the Van Cortlandt Park Golf Course in 1910, the first scorecard he retained for collecting purposes was from a subsequent round played at Van Cortlandt Park in 1911. What ended as a string of 3,165 signed and attested scorecards starts with course number one at Van Cortlandt Park. Ralph typically only wrote his initials, RAK, in the space on the scorecard designated for the player's name, although on his first card, "Kennedy" is scrawled across the top. His cards were not numbered contemporaneously; years later, after he completed his quest, he went back and numbered all the cards, and across the top of the fragile, century-old brown card from the Bronx is "Course #1."

He chose a steamy summer day on which to begin his marathon, picking a course with a total distance of 5,340 yards, playing to a bogey of seventy-five and a par of sixty-eight. Sunday, July 9, 1911, was a day of discomfort: eighty-eight degrees with high humidity and bright sunshine. New Yorkers were feeling the oppressive heat because there was a shortage of ice in the city. During this pre-air-conditioning era, ice was cut from lakes and stored upstate in the winter, then was shipped down the Hudson River to weary city dwellers to provide cooling relief during the summer. At one point, there were 135 large ice houses

A Clare Briggs illustration featuring icemen and golf. *(Author's Collection)*

located on the Hudson River between Albany and New York City. Because the city was in the middle of a hot spell, "ice wagons had none to spare," according to the *New York Times*. In Washington Heights, it was so hot that people were being forced out of their apartments to sit on their stoops, or on "camp stools" to cool down. Thousands took the train out to Coney Island so they could be near the ocean.

The continued emergence of aviation was also news of the day. The *New York Times* had a special "Aeronautics" section and front page articles about flyers who were trying different feats or new aircraft designs. John D. Rockefeller was front page news also, for no other reason than celebrating his seventy-second birthday at home in Cleveland, although they did note that he played golf to celebrate it. The automobile was an emerging form of transportation but had yet to achieve dominance, particularly in the city. In news related to a more prevalent mode of period transportation, the newspaper noted that the driver of a beer wagon died while ferrying his load across Queens, creating a hazard as the unattended horses continued to race through the streets.

The first "Road Conference" was in the planning stages in 1911, to be held in Richmond, Virginia. A group was convening to map out a plan for extensive improvements, since most roads were in abysmal condition. Two years later, the Lincoln Highway opened, traversing the country from Times Square to Lincoln Park, San Francisco, the road extending for 3,389 miles through thirteen states. That same year, in Ralph's home city, one of the most beautiful buildings ever to be built was finished in Lower Manhattan. The imposing Cass Gilbert-designed Woolworth Building was the tallest in the world when it opened on April 24th. Designed in a neo-gothic style and finished with terra cotta tiles, it was dubbed "the cathedral of commerce." President Woodrow Wilson, who pushed a button from Washington, D. C., turned on the building's lights that evening. An inordinate thirty-four elevators were among the sixty-story building's key features.

The sportswriter Grantland Rice arrived in New York from Tennessee earlier in the year, moving to the big city to pursue his passion for writing. He came to the right place, as there were fourteen daily newspapers in the city. Many young people come to New York seeking fortune and fame. Rice would find both.

Ralph took the new subway to play at Van Cortlandt, the Interborough Rapid Transit (IRT) train having been extended three years earlier up to 242nd Street, where the course is located. He disembarked on the last stop of the elevated line's subway into a sparkling new Victorian gothic station house. Ralph's day out was inexpensive. His subway fare was a nickel, and the course was still free: the city issued "permits" that allowed golfers to use the facility at no cost. Enthusiasts of the burgeoning game laid their bags down by the first tee to establish the order of play. The rules printed on the back of Ralph's scorecard indicate that keeping order might sometimes have been a challenge: "No player shall be permitted to preempt a place in bag line by laying single clubs." And since the game was in its infancy and people were not widely familiar with the rules "bags must not be carried on the putting greens" and the rather obvious "Women are not allowed to play on course with high heel shoes" were also stated.

Ralph played Van Cortlandt with Clare Briggs, a well-known cartoonist. Briggs had a nationally syndicated column in the *New-York*

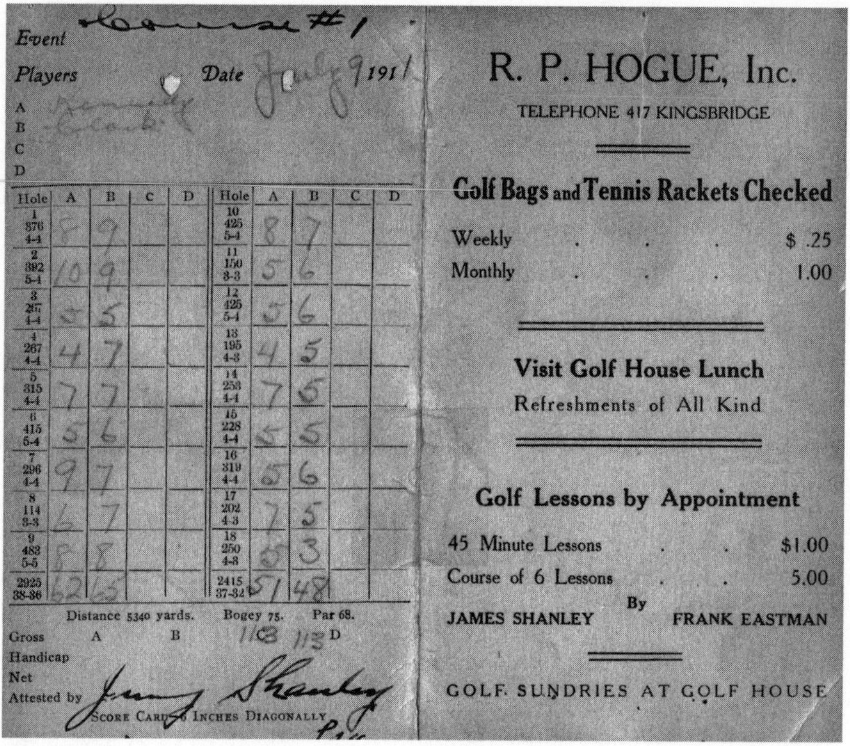

Ralph's first scorecard from Van Cortlandt Park. *(Photo courtesy of USGA)*

Tribune, and his Sunday cartoon "Mr. and Mrs." was carried by hundreds of newspapers across the nation. Both Ralph and Briggs each shot a 113, the only respectable score on the card being a three that Briggs recorded on the final hole, a 250-yard par-3. The professional at Van Cortlandt was the dapper, bow tie-wearing James Shanley, and he signed the card at the bottom to attest to the fact that Kennedy played there, a custom Ralph followed for the next forty-two years. He had obviously been practicing since his initial round one year before, having shaved thirty-three strokes off his maiden score.

Van Cortlandt Park was created in 1888 when the city purchased more than one thousand acres from the Van Cortlandt family, settlers of Dutch heritage. George Washington and his troops used the land the park occupies during the Revolutionary War, and Washington slept in the Van Cortlandt house. The golf course was created in 1895 at the urging of a group of prominent men residing in Riverdale, a nearby neighborhood in the Bronx. The group approached parks commissioner James Roosevelt for permission to play golf in the park and to establish a private club there. There was some initial resistance to the idea because of the cost of constructing and maintaining the course. Harry Brownlaw (H. B.) Martin recounts the story in his 1936 book *Fifty Years of American Golf*: "The ground to be used is covered with a rank growth of wild carrots and hay. To keep it short enough mowing machines would have to be in constant use. This would be an expensive matter. It has been suggested to Mr. Roosevelt that a large flock of sheep might keep the grass short."

The biggest resistance to the early golfers' proposal was allowing part of a public park to be used for private purposes. The Riverdale group pushed back on Roosevelt's initial resistance because they were dismayed at the prospect of the course becoming too crowded. Ultimately they conceded that it could not be for their private use, and they had to take a more inclusive approach if they wanted the course to be built. The affluent businessmen ultimately made a case for building the course on broader grounds, writing to Roosevelt with consent to include the middle class, "The game appeals to all who seek recreation, tramping over the meadows and hillsides on half holidays, as it can be played without any systematic training. The park links should be popular with business men, clerks, and mechanics, when they learn the benefits of golf." (At the time, Saturday was described as a half holiday, since the typical worker worked five full days and half a day on Saturday.)

Roosevelt was eventually persuaded, and a nine-hole course opened in July 1895. T. McClure Peters—one of the Riverdale golfers who clamored for its creation—laid out the original course. The founders played as part of the "Mosholu Golf Club." Although the course was public, the founders were initially granted exclusive use two afternoons a week.

The course had some initial growing pains, and the city made attempts to put it in better condition the year after it opened. Since golf was not a widely known pursuit, some of the fixes were rather obvious, including telling workers who were delivering concessions to the clubhouse not to drive their wagons over the greens, where they left deep ruts. As initially designed, Van Cortlandt was a real test of a player's ability. Its 9th hole was an extreme 700 yards long, one of the longest ever designed. Not only did the hole have an absurd length, but the golfer also had to hit over two stone walls and two small brooks. *Harper's Round Table* described the hole: "It is possible to clear the first wall on the drive and a brassie [the equivalent of today's 2-wood] shot will bring the ball near the second wall. The best record for this hole is seven, which is remarkably good." Since the entire course measured 2,561 yards, the 9th hole was almost one-third of the total distance. Martin correctly noted that since early players were using gutta-percha balls, it would not have been uncommon for them to hit their brassie three or four times from the fairway.

Van Cortlandt attracted well-known golfers from its early days. In 1896, John Reid, president of the St. Andrew's Golf Club in Yonkers, organized a tournament at Van Cortlandt—the first public tournament played in the United States. Walter J. Travis, who would go on to win three U.S. and one British Amateur championships, was among the entrants. Unfortunately, the weather was frightful and the competitors were "wet to the skin" due to the rainy conditions at the end of November. Travis's score in the tournament was 110, which put him in ninth place. He took a ten and a thirteen on the demanding 9th hole in his two loops around the course.

The course grew in popularity and became overused in its initial years. The *Golf Guide* described the management of the original course as "wretched" and stated that a golfer risked their life playing there due to the crowding, although they noted that the course itself was quite lovely: "The turf is good and the nine holes are fairly well laid out." They were, however, highly critical of the bag carriers, noting, "The caddies are extortionate and very badly trained, and the course is always badly congested with players." They also wrote that although players were supposed to first obtain a permit, "this is

Van Cortlandt Park Golf Course. Note the starters tent on the left, a mounted policeman keeping order on the right, and railroad tracks along the rear. *(Author's Collection)*

never done." The Mosholu Golf Club members eventually moved on to other courses, having been pushed out of Van Cortlandt by the swelling influx of middle-class golfers, or "the Philistines," as the founders called them.

Although crowded, the course was a pleasant place to play the game. *Outing Magazine* described Van Cortlandt in idyllic terms in 1899, saying that it could scarcely be more artistic, "A long, flat valley, all grass, with wooded hills coming down on one side close, and on the other a lily-covered lake and park like uplands, in close a moving panorama of color-dotted players, who, in variety of costume, give to the pasture an effect not to be equaled for brilliancy and life on any links in the world. A Saturday afternoon on the old nine-hole course is one of the sights no citizen, much less a golfer, should miss."

Scotsman Tom Bendelow was brought in that same year to revamp the course. The total acreage he was given was expanded from 55 to

120 acres, and he was able to extend the course to eighteen holes. Bendelow did an admirable job, even though Van Cortlandt has always existed on a challenging piece of land wedged between railroad tracks and roads. Bendelow's changes were well received and *Golf* magazine noted that the expanded course was better in many regards, especially for a player's health, specifically noting that "it was now possible for a player to make the round without the risk of a broken cranium."

The course continued to gain in popularity, and people enjoyed its beautiful wildflowers, open meadows, and tall grasses. The early course was so charming it even earned the nickname "the Meadows." Bendelow stayed on and became greenkeeper and professional for two years after designing the course. He also instilled discipline in the unruly environment and created new rules. Among the changes he implemented were regulating the caddies and prohibiting the sale of old golf balls on the course (Italian boys who were truant from school were a particular problem in both areas). Later in his career, Bendelow would go on to design hundreds of courses in the United States, including Medinah's three courses near Chicago.

The most well-known golfer at the turn of the century played Van Cortlandt Park in November 1900. On a seasonable morning in mid-November, Harry Vardon—at the time, three-time British Open champion, and the reigning U.S. Open champion—played two exhibition matches in the Bronx. The Saturday match was a newsworthy event that attracted a crowd of between 2,000 and 2,500 fans who were eager to see the Englishman—who wore a red sweater and knickerbockers—play. The greens were in terrible condition due to the time of year; the greenkeeper put sand on the putting surfaces before the matches, which proved to be a mistake. The sand clumped up, making putting a challenge. As the next day's *New York Times* coined the putting surfaces in a memorable phrase, they were "fearfully heavy." Vardon ended up shooting an eighty-one and an eighty-two, although he easily beat his competitors, who shot ninety-four and ninety-nine. The course organized a committee to keep the crowd orderly; their duties included holding up a long rope to keep the spectators at bay. The rowdy New

Yorkers were not easily contained, and although twenty of New York's finest were on hand to help, "the mob of urchins were allowed to roam at will over the links, yelling at every other stroke." It was the noisiest match Vardon had ever been in.

It was no accident that Clare Briggs played at Van Cortlandt Park, since it was a hangout for newspapermen and reporters. The writer H. B. Martin was one of the founders of the "New York Newspaper Golf Club" that played its golf over the links. Both the Newspaper and the Mosholu were clubs that allowed like-minded players to band together and form their own league or club, a common practice. These were social golfing associations rather than clubs with their own dedicated facilities. Neither required actual ownership of a course or clubhouse, simply the opportunity for members to play together.

The Newspaper Club's members included writers who would attain prominence in the field. Martin was an early ghostwriter for Walter Hagen, and the two sailed together on transatlantic ocean crossings. In addition to writing a golf column for the *New York Globe,* at various times during his career Martin also wrote for *The World* and *The American.* Other members of the Newspaper Club included *Herald Tribune* writer Grantland Rice and Bud Fisher, the creator of *Mutt and Jeff.* Heywood Broun, who founded the Newspaper Guild in 1933, was a member, as was Bill Hicks of the *Brooklyn Daily Eagle,* who was known for playing in his bare feet. Thomas Aloysius Dorgan was another member of the club; an illustrator for the *New York Journal,* he went on to make popular contributions to the English language. Not only did he coin the term "hot dog" for a wiener, but he also invented two superlatives still used today: "the cat's meow" and "for crying out loud."

In April 1914, Ralph played in a Gotham Golf Club event, and he retained a scorecard recording the day. Gotham was another association club that played over the Van Cortlandt course. There were many such clubs playing over the links in those early days; in addition to the original Mosholu Club, the Newspaper Club, and the Gotham, there was also a New York Golf Club and a Manhattan

Van Cortlandt Park, showing dirt teeing ground and sandbox near the tee. *(Photo courtesy of NYC Parks Department)*

Golf Club. A founding member of the Gotham, Ralph was among a group who pushed the city for changes to the course and its operation. The park was so popular that it was being overrun with non-golfers, so they asked the city for a minimum of two dozen signs to be posted around the course letting the unwary know it was for golfers only. The group also asked the city to provide sandboxes, brushes, towels, and water buckets to be placed on each tee box, similar to the standard practice followed at private courses. The towels were necessary so that players could wipe their hands after they piled up damp sand to build their tee.

The Gotham golfers were clamoring for sandboxes because wooden tee pegs were not yet popular. Players gathered sand from around the tee box and mounded it up to tee up their ball. With the considerable amount of play Van Cortlandt was getting, it was in need of boxes that could be used to hold sand so that the teeing grounds didn't become completely worn down from golfers gouging sand out of the playing surface.

Cutting in line was a continual problem at Van Cortlandt, as players ignored the warnings on the back of their scorecards. In an attempt to speed up play, the Gotham golfers requested that "duffers and beginners" be forced to use a nine-hole course nearby named the Mosholu Links. They also advocated for city employees to be used as starters on Sundays and holidays to help rein in the spirited crowds trying to play there.

Ralph returned to play Van Cortlandt many times over the years, including an appearance in a Red Cross War fundraiser with Mary Alice in 1917. Due to his collegiate "credentials" with the Amherst student newspaper, Ralph was admitted as a member of the New York Newspaper Club and kept records of playing in tournaments with them over the years, including in 1918, 1919, and 1920. This association would prove quite beneficial to him in future years. In the 1920s, a "Scottish-American Golf Club" also played over the Van Cortlandt Links. By that time, however, Ralph was playing at private clubs and not at public links, although, proud of his heritage, he was a member of the St. Andrew's Society of New York the entire time he lived in the city.

Over subsequent decades, many well-known figures—including Babe Ruth, Willie Mays, Jackie Robinson, Joe Louis (who at one time had a job as an ice deliveryman), The Three Stooges (who had a locker there), and Sidney Poitier—played Van Cortlandt. Pictures from Parks Department archives from the 1930s depict a crowded course lined with well-dressed golfers hitting off elevated tee boxes that look to be made of compacted sand. An ever-popular destination, Van Cortlandt was typically crowded, and most pictures show a plentiful number of golfers, often with eight people standing around the teeing ground, most carrying a handful of clubs in small bags. Although at various times over its history the course was not maintained well, when Ralph played the course it was in prime condition. He described it as being "well-groomed" in 1911. Despite being a public course, Van Cortlandt was a widely respected place to play golf in the early part of the twentieth century.

Early golf at Van Cortlandt was an occasion worthy of fine dress. *(Photo courtesy of USGA)*

CHAPTER 3

Bitten by the Golf Bug

THE AGE OF EXPLORATION WAS flourishing the year Ralph began his own golf journey. Two weeks after his first documented course, the lost city of Machu Picchu was discovered in Peru, and several months later Roald Amundsen led an expedition of men to the South Pole, the first in history to visit the polar ice cap. Some of the greatest golf courses ever to be built in North America were not yet in existence in 1911, including Pine Valley, Cypress Point, Merion, Augusta National, Banff Springs, Pebble Beach, Riviera, Seminole, and Ralph's future home course of Winged Foot.

Ralph's home city experienced a terrible tragedy in the year he picked up the game. Late in the afternoon on March 25th, a fire started at a ten-story factory in Greenwich Village that produced women's blouses. The fire was likely ignited by an unextinguished cigarette and spread rapidly because there were hundreds of pounds of flammable fabric scraps around. To prevent thefts by workers, the exit doors were locked, and when the fire started, the manager who held the key escaped without first opening the door. By the time the horse-drawn fire engines arrived at the building, it was engulfed in flames. The fire department's ladders only reached the sixth floor. With no other means of escape, many of the women who worked in the factory jumped to their deaths. In total, 146 people died in the tragedy, which led to countless improvements in fire safety, including standards on the availability of fire extinguishers, building codes that maintained proper means of egress, fire alarms, automatic sprinklers, and improved firefighting equipment. That same year, the city began to acquire its first motorized trucks to use in responding to fires, although the last horse-drawn equipment wasn't fully phased out until 1922.

It was not uncommon at the time for large-scale manufacturing to be located in New York City, especially for garment and textile makers, but also across a whole spectrum of industries. Ralph's own company operated the largest pencil factory in the world along the East River on Thirteenth and Fourteenth Streets, and his office was located there. On the days he was not traveling, it was an easy commute for him from Upper Manhattan to Eagle's offices, taking the Third Avenue elevated subway. A German immigrant, Daniel Berolzheimer, started the Eagle Pencil Company in 1856, with a factory in Yonkers, New York, and a pencil shop on John Street in Lower Manhattan. As the business grew, Eagle acquired a full city block on Avenue C between Thirteenth and Fourteenth Streets and purchased the city's first iron-framed building for use as its factory, in 1877. Factories along the East River were common, since they could be easily accessed by boat.

April brought another noteworthy fire to New York City, this time much less severe than the Triangle Shirtwaist Factory fire, but it did destroy a big part of the Polo Grounds. The stadium was quickly rebuilt as a more durable structure and by mid-season was ready to begin hosting baseball again. In May, the "apogee of Beaux-Arts architecture," the New York Public Library, opened on Fifth Avenue and Forty-Second Street.

In golfing news, Charles Blair Macdonald's National Golf Links of America formally opened in 1911. As the game continued to evolve, so did its scoring terminology. Originally, "bogey" represented the more common measure of a score and was used to denote error-free play. Ralph's scorecards show how prevalent the bogey measure was, and a space to write in a bogey score remained on scorecards until the late 1920s. Almost all of his scorecards of this period show a spot to write in both a bogey score and a par score. "Par" originally meant slightly better than bogey play. The word "par" came to golf through the financial markets, where par represents the normal price of a share.

The par gauge itself went through a series of revisions. At the turn of the century, the USGA's guidance related to par was as follows:

Par 3	Up to 200 yards
Par 3 ½	201 to 250 yards
Par 4	251 to 375 yards
Par 4 ½	376 to 450 yards
Par 5	451 to 500 yards
Par 5 ½	501 to 550 yards
Par 6	551 yards and longer

The USGA revised their earlier guidance in 1911, defining holes up to 225 yards as par threes, those between 226 and 425 as par fours, those between 426 and 600 as par fives, and those above 600 yards as par sixes. Apparently, not all courses followed their guidance, as indicated by some cards of the period, which still contained half pars. The logic behind not allowing half-pars is straightforward, since a golfer can only shoot a round number on any given hole.

Glenn Curtiss again made news early in 1912 by piloting the first flying boat in January. But the most shocking news of the year came in April, when the Titanic sank on its maiden voyage to New York. Three months later, Horn & Hardart opened their first Automat in the city. An early fast-food restaurant, they offered diners comfort food served through a wall of sleek coin-operated vending machines. The cafeteria-style luncheonettes were a big hit, offering sandwiches, pies, coffee, and scores of other food items for a nickel. New Yorkers immediately took to the self-service aspect of the operation, since the format eliminated the need to wait for a waiter or waitress. Harried city dwellers would just pop a nickel into the machine, open the glass door, and voilà, their food was ready to eat.

On October 5, 1912, the Yankees played their last game at Hilltop Park in Washington Heights, a fifteen-minute walk from the Kennedy apartment. The Yankees played for the next ten seasons at the Polo Grounds, which they leased from the Giants, before eventually moving across the river to the Bronx. Ralph diligently worked on his game over the coming year and played regularly on local public courses.

In August 1913, the Kennedys headed to the elevations of New Hampshire for a summer vacation. The mountains were a popular vacation spot in the early teens because they were easily accessible by train and because of the cool mountain air during the summer. Traveling in 1913 wasn't particularly fast; there were few real highways, and in any case the Kennedys didn't own a car. It took them almost a full day to transit to Northern New England. As August commenced, their late-night train lurched out of New York, belching smoke into the starlit skies, beginning their long rail journey. Arriving in Boston the following morning, they switched to the Boston & Maine Railroad, leaving the city's North Station at 7:50 a.m., which deposited them in Bethlehem, New Hampshire, at five o'clock. Following a quick change of trains to a branch line, they were in Bretton Woods by 5:52 p.m. In addition to carrying passengers, trains were also an important carrier for mail and parcels. American Express, still primarily a freight and parcel company, had the railroad's "Express" concession and was responsible for carrying light packages along the rails.

Ralph ventured up to the Mount Pleasant course at the Bretton Woods Golf Club and played on a gorgeous summer day, enjoying the crisp mountain air at the course's 1,600 feet of elevation. Since early courses were frequently located near railroads and telegraph lines paralleled the tracks, one of the local rules on his card indicated that a ball within twelve inches of a railroad track or telegraph pole could be lifted and dropped one club-length without penalty. Telegraphs were a widely used form of communication during the early part of Ralph's lifetime, and even as telephone usage rose, they remained in use throughout the 1920s and 1930s.

The golf bug bit Ralph hard during that lazy summer holiday, and he embraced the game with a zest that he never lost. As the *Joplin Globe* recounted years later, "The golfer started his queer hobby back in the White Mountains in the summer of 1913; there he played over ten different courses, having the club professional of each course attest to the score."

The Boston & Maine's White Mountains division served as the Kennedys' lifeline while they were on vacation and provided local service to a number of small towns, including Bethlehem Junction; Ralph took the train there to swing his clubs at the Maplewood Country Club, shooting a 94 on the 5,315-yard course. The course was also located next to telegraph lines, and a local rule allowed balls driven from the 13th, 14th, or 15th tees that struck poles or wires to be redriven without penalty. The course had other challenges of the period, as well; balls lying in horse hoofmarks could also be lifted without penalty. Although the current course is a Donald Ross design, Ralph's card indicates he played it when it was a design of Alex Findlay.

Mary Alice joined Ralph when he played the nine-hole Kearsarge Golf Club in North Conway, an hour from Maplewood. Both shot a 51 on the 3,039-yard course, also designed by Findlay. Their scorecard lists a place for bogey scores only and shows that the course began with a 353-yard "Moat" hole, playing to a bogey five. An unusual local rule on the first hole let the golfer know that if they hit their tee shot out of bounds, another ball could be placed on the teeing ground after brushing the surface with the back of their hand, with loss of distance only. Those omnipresent telegraph wires passed through Kearsarge also, and a ball driven into them from the first tee could be replaced without loss of a stroke.

As an emerging pastime, golf continued to grow but still had not been widely embraced by the masses. By 1913, there were only 350,000 golfers in America who played the roughly one thousand courses then in existence. This was about to change, as the events of the U.S. Open unfolded in Ralph's birth state of Massachusetts. Francis Ouimet shocked the golf world in September with his win at the Country Club over Ted Ray and Harry Vardon. The twenty-year-old amateur won with only ten clubs in his bag, and with a ten-year-old caddie. As noted on the card from Kearsarge, the rule at the time for hitting out of bounds called for a penalty of only one stroke. The rule was meaningful for Ouimet, since on his fifth hole on the last day of the tournament, he hit out of bounds and only incurred a one-stroke penalty. A two-stroke penalty would have caused him to miss the eventual playoff with Vardon and Ray (assuming all else played out as it did). The world closely followed the tournament at the Country Club because there was a press tent set up for the first time at a golf tournament, and ten telegraph lines were connected so that reporters could get their stories out.

The country continued to modernize in the early twentieth century and was looking westward. The early teens were still a time when there were company towns in rural America, and 90 percent of Americans still lived east of the Mississippi. Henry Ford instituted his assembly line concept the same year as Ouimet's upset victory. Ford could mass-produce a car in record time, and Americans began to buy and drive Model T's in record numbers. Another of Ford's innovations was the introduction of a five-day, forty-hour work week. Previously, the standard practice was to work either six full days or five and a half days. This change freed up people to pursue more leisure-time activities, including golf. In Ralph's home city, another Beaux-Arts masterpiece opened in 1913, the current Grand Central Station, on Park Avenue between Forty-Second and Forty-Fifth Streets.

Excited by his new passion, in October, Red traveled south and played the Suburban Golf Club of Baltimore County, a nine-hole layout that cost him a total of forty cents to play: twenty cents per nine holes. Suburban had a generous local rule indicating that a ball played from the ninth tee striking telegraph wires could be taken back to the tee and played again without penalty.

Ralph's friendship with Clare Briggs continued, and in November, they played together at the Durham Country Club in North Carolina, a 3,100-yard nine-hole course playing to a par of 35 ½. (Hole No. 5 was a 210-yard par 3 ½.) Ralph didn't have a particularly good day, shooting a seventy-one, or two times par. His score improved over the course of his round, although it was difficult for it not to, since he took a "vulture" on the opening par three, his nine strokes over par turning his face as red as his hair. Briggs was a more proficient golfer, shooting a fifty-three. Caddies continued to be a pesky problem during this period, as the card at Durham warned players not to buy balls from them, because doing so "encourages dishonesty," presumably from caddies not returning lost balls to players but holding onto them to sell to future duffers. North Carolina was the locale of several early visits for golf; Ralph also swung his hickories at the nine-hole Raleigh Country Club in April of the following year, a course predating its Donald Ross design.

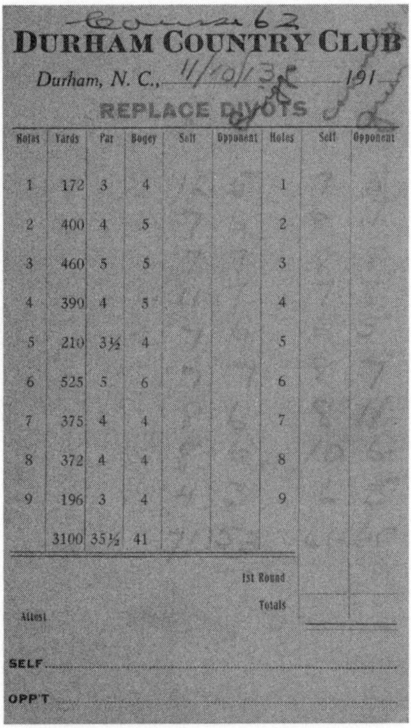
DURHAM COUNTRY CLUB

Durham, N. C., 191

REPLACE DIVOTS

Holes	Yards	Par	Bogey	Self	Opponent	Holes	Self	Opponent
1	172	3	4			1		
2	400	4	5			2		
3	460	5	5			3		
4	390	4	5			4		
5	210	3½	4			5		
6	525	5	6			6		
7	375	4	4			7		
8	372	4	4			8		
9	196	3	4			9		
	3100	35½	41					
						1st Round		
						Totals		

Attest

SELF

OPP'T

Ralph's 1913 scorecard from the Durham Country Club showing a ½ par hole and bogey scores. *(Photo courtesy of USGA)*

During this period, Briggs published a successful book of cartoons titled *Golf: The Book of a Thousand Chuckles.* Among the illustrations in the book is one showing a golfer who was stymied, a common practice at the time. The stymie rule was in effect during match play between two golfers. If one player's ball blocked his or her opponent's on the green, the ball blocking the path to the hole could not be moved if it was more than six inches from the other. If the two were within six inches, then it was permissible to move the ball. The majority of scorecards during this era had a "stymie measure" or "stymie gauge" on them, which was a marking on the card measuring six inches, taking the guesswork out of how far apart balls were. Playing golf with the stymie rule was a

Claire Briggs's illustration of a caddie from yesteryear selling a golf ball. *(Author's Collection)*

different game involving more strategy, including trying to intentionally put a ball in front of an opponent's. If a golfer's ball was "stymied," they had to try to putt around or over their opponent's ball.

Golf was still in its infant stages as Ralph was taking up the game, formally less than twenty years old in America. To give a sense of how nascent the game was, handicapping was a new and formal affair. The game was small enough to allow the USGA to print a list of handicap holders in their 1914 annual. Of the seventy-three total golfers listed, only two were scratch: Francis Ouimet and J. D. Travers. A. W. Tillinghast was listed as a five.

There was not yet a provision in the rules allowing a player to clean their ball on the green. Cleaning a ball disqualified a competitor in stroke play competition or resulted in the loss of a hole in match play unless there was a special rule in effect. There was also no limit on the number of clubs players could use. Although the rules set no upper limit, period pictures seem to indicate that most players tended to play with less rather than more, particularly since golf bags of the era were small and couldn't accommodate many clubs.

The Panama Canal opened in 1914, as did the first eleven holes at New Jersey's Pine Valley Golf Club near Camden, both of which would be included in the future plans of the traveling golfer. Automobiles were not the only technology gaining traction; telephone usage was also increasing rapidly. By 1914, there were 70,000 telephone operators nationally. The first cross-country call was completed the following year, with operator assistance, as it was not yet possible to direct-dial long distance.

Mary Alice and Ralph played together at the Pelham Bay Park Golf Links in the Bronx on August 1, 1914, a pleasant summer day with temperatures in the low seventies. It was significantly more pleasant in New York than in Europe, as Germany and Russia had just declared war on each other. Germany declared martial law the day before, and all the stock exchanges in New York had closed due to the developing situation and rapid escalation of tensions in Europe. Mary Alice shot a 139 on the 6,371-yard course, and Ralph shot a 113. Architects really tested early players of the game; the tenth hole at Pelham Bay was a 625-yard bogey-seven, par-six hole that melted down the Kennedys. Ralph took a twelve on the hole, beating his wife by one stroke. Pelham Bay still had issues similar to those confronting Van Cortlandt in its early days, since the scorecard included a local rule that permitted any ball landing in a rut made by greenkeepers' horses, wagons, or tools on the "fair green" to be dropped without penalty.

By now, Ralph and Mary Alice had moved to 225 Audubon Avenue, a multi-family apartment building on the East Side in Manhattan's Washington Heights neighborhood, near 176th Street. The middle-class neighborhood they lived in contained a cross-section of residents engaged in a wide range of occupations. Among their neighbors were a domestic servant, a bookkeeper, an engineer, a produce broker, and a salesman. Mary Alice listed her occupation in 1915 as "housework." Ralph's brother, by this time a doctor at Presbyterian Hospital, was still living with them, although over the coming years he spent little time with his relatives. Robert Kennedy served as a first lieutenant in the Medical Corps from 1917 through 1919, including a tour of duty in France, where he directed a field program on trauma.

Ralph played the well-regarded and "unusually hilly" Dunwoodie course in Yonkers in 1915. Dunwoodie opened as a 5,799-yard private course in 1906, and among its early members were Douglas Fairbanks Jr. and Mary Pickford. Before Ralph signed up to be a founding member of Winged Foot, he and Mary Alice were members of Dunwoodie (Ralph also served on their Board of Governors) and played there until 1924. The course was convenient from the city, located near the New York & Putnam Railroad, not far from the Van Cortlandt course. Mary Alice worked on her game and became a proficient golfer; over the coming years, she was the ladies club champion at Dunwoodie multiple times. Aside from an odd course here or there while on vacation, Ralph played almost all his golf in the late teens in the New York area.

Today, the Baltusrol Golf Club in Springfield, New Jersey, has two A. W. Tillinghast golf courses that opened for play in 1922. Ralph played Baltusrol several years before those courses were designed. He first teed it up on August 20, 1915, on a different design that predated the Tillinghast courses, one measuring 6,189 yards; the course hosted the U.S. Open the same year. The tenth hole at this time was a short par-four of 330 yards, and it featured an island green (the hole's name on the scorecard was appropriately "Island"), likely the first one built in the country. Royal Cortissoz, writing about the challenging hole in the *New-York Tribune*, described it as "an emerald disk entirely surrounded by a narrow belt of water. A duck of a hole, tantalizing and inspiring! One could have profitably spent a whole summer playing it in hopes of a three." Ralph didn't have his game together at Baltusrol and had one of those rueful days that cause golfers to question their love of the game. He laid some serious turf and shot a 136, including four tens and an eleven, the showery and windy conditions of the day not helping the cause.

The PGA of America was founded on January 17, 1916, in New York City. Rodman Wanamaker, a department store magnate, was the driving force behind the association. The group that formed the PGA met at the Taplow Club in the Martinique Hotel, on West Thirty-Second Street and Broadway. Commercially oriented from the start, the purpose of the PGA was to allow golf professionals to enhance their equipment sales by forming an association. Among those present at the PGA's founding was A. W. Tillinghast.

In May, Ralph played the Mosholu Links, an actual course and separate entity from the original Mosholu Golf Club that was formed by the original Riverdale group at Van Cortlandt. The Mosholu Links opened in Van Cortlandt Park in 1914 as a nine-hole course located close to the Van Cortlandt Park course. Thousands of yards of rock had to be removed to build Mosholu, although more remained to be blasted and excavated after the course opened, as it was expanded to an eighteen-hole course two years later. The course was initially built without bunkers, which was not uncommon at the time; sand traps would be added later after the architect got a feel for how the course was playing. The course layout was dictated by stone walls and woods from an old farm on the hilly property. The full-length course would eventually play 5,200 yards, and among its notable holes were the dogleg

Building the early links in Van Cortlandt without power machinery. *(Photo courtesy of USGA)*

right 13th, which played almost 400 yards and crossed a ravine, with swamps on both sides of the fairway.

Ralph and Mary Alice played Mosholu again after it was expanded to an eighteen-hole course with RAK and MAK written on the top of the scorecard, their scores 109 and 122, respectively. The 13th proved to be as difficult as it sounds, the Kennedys taking a nine and a ten on the hole. One year earlier, *Golf* described Mosholu as the quintessential New York course: "If America is the melting-pot of the nations of the world, Van Cortlandt Park is the melting-pot of the nations of New York. The scene is one to thrill the heart of every American. On the links may be seen golfers of every nationality from Briton to Japanese; men and women; the well-to-do and the poor."

On August 29th, Ralph made the short journey out to Long Island, where he strolled along the emerald fairways at the Devereux Emmet-Walter Travis-designed Garden City Golf Club, as his twenty-first unique course. A well-regarded course, Garden City had hosted the U.S. Open once and the U.S. Amateur three times prior to Ralph's visit. He was impressed with both the course and the food, and in particular liked the broiled live lobsters, deep-dish meat pies, and fresh-baked cherry tarts.

Ralph played the Wykagyl Country Club in September, a course his friend Clare Briggs lived near and in the "building of which he had taken a keen interest." That same month, and in the midst of the war, Ralph and Mary Alice played in a Red Cross tournament in which she won low net. Ralph returned to Baltusrol again in November, playing a redesigned course that had been lengthened to 6,212 yards. Lou Gehrig was attending grade school during this time period at Public School 132, less than ten blocks from the Kennedy apartment, on West 183rd Street. In 1917, Lou enrolled in Manhattan's Commerce High School.

During World War I, Ralph made his first of what would be many visits to the Peachtree State with the intention of playing golf. He played the Savannah Golf Club on December 9, 1917. It is appropriate that Ralph played Savannah early in his odyssey, since the historic club opened in 1794. Both Savannah and Augusta were important Southern cities early in the twentieth century. The Wright Brothers established a flight school in Augusta during this period, which was set up at Wilbur's urging for the Army Signal Corps. The school was used to train pilots for both the First and Second World Wars. Augusta's location on the Savannah River also made it a center for the ice trade; multiple warehouses were located along the river and were used to store ice as far back as the 1820s.

On August 6, 1918, Ralph played at Wykagyl again, in a New York Newspaper event, and shot a ninety-two, his game steadily improving by this time. In mid-September of the same year, Ralph agreed to organize his office workforce at Eagle with the expectation of a 100 percent subscription rate to a Liberty Loan drive. He was justifiably proud of his accomplishments raising money during the First World War and included service on the Liberty Loan Committees and on Red Cross fund drives in his summary biography prepared for Amherst years later.

Woodrow Wilson instituted the first draft in the country since the Civil War in response to the war in Europe, calling it the Selective Service Program. All men between the ages of twenty-one and forty-five were required to register in three waves. Ralph was thirty-two when the war started and dutifully registered on his first eligible day, September 12, 1918, at the 22nd Regiment Armory in Manhattan. The boxes he checked about himself on the draft form indicated that he was tall and had blue eyes and red hair. He was never called up for duty.

In his job as a pencil salesman, Ralph made regular visits to the South; his biannual visits helped to open up the Southern market for Eagle. One of the early courses he played, in 1918, was the Roebuck Golf & Automobile Club (course No. 86) near Birmingham, Alabama. Unusual for the time in the South, its greens had grass rather than the more typical sand.

Eleven days before the Treaty of Versailles was signed, ending the First World War in June 1919, Ralph and Mary Alice traveled up to Massachusetts to play the nine-hole golf course at Amherst

College (course No. 96). The Kennedys played several others courses in Western Massachusetts on their visit, including the Country Club of Springfield.

Ralph returned to western Massachusetts a month later to play in a group golf outing in Holyoke, Massachusetts, as guests of J. L. Wyckoff, president of White & Wyckoff Manufacturing Company. The New York Stationers Golf Outing included many of Ralph's colleagues in the industry, among them, Eberhard Faber, president of his eponymous pencil company. The local newspaper highlighted the tournament and included a picture of the participants. It was a dapper group smiling in the *Holyoke Daily Telegraph*, sitting on the large porch of the course's clubhouse. Each man who played is holding a golf club, wearing long pants and light-colored dress shirts, and the majority are sporting bow ties. Ralph is sitting in the front row wearing a necktie and eyeglasses; the latter is something he would wear his whole adult life. The newspaper noted the unusual: that most of the participants came to the tournament—played at the Mount Tom Golf Club—by automobile. Ralph returned to play in the outing for the next several years. In 1920, he is again pictured sitting with the well-dressed group, this time wearing a bow tie. He is beaming in the picture, having just won the Autocrat silver medal as the prize for runner-up. The following year, he is pictured donning a bow tie and a tam-o'-shanter, as well, something he was fond of wearing.

As his first decade of playing the game wound down, there was not much indication that Ralph would be more than a recreational golfer, having played roughly one hundred unique courses through 1919. This was about to change, as was the country in which he lived. As the war ended, Europe remained in tatters, and America was beginning to emerge as a world power; she was about to enter a period of economic supremacy. And, the red-haired golfing sensation was about to get a very big idea and would soon increase the amount of golf he played substantially.

CHAPTER 4

The Quest Begins

UNTIL NOW, RALPH PLAYED ALMOST all his golf while on vacation, as entertainment at home, or occasionally on his travels as an Eagle pencil salesman. This changed when he met Charles Leonard Fletcher one day at Van Cortlandt Park. A reporter for the *New York Sun* who played in the Newspaper Club, Fletcher told Ralph that he held the world record for the highest number of unique golf courses played. Fletcher had played 240 unique courses and retained the scorecards to prove it. Ralph went home, counted his cards, said he had a total of 176 (although current records show he was only up to one hundred unique ones at this time), and decided to try and top Fletcher.

Both Ralph and the news media repeatedly referred to Fletcher as an English music-hall actor who traveled on the Orpheum circuit. Fletcher said that he learned the game from Sandy Herd, the Scottish-born 1902 British Open champion, and he is reported to have emigrated to the United States in the 1920s.

Fletcher had many career changes over his lifetime and lived the life of a nomad, something he reflected back on without much nostalgia. He told the *Salt Lake Tribune*, "After all, I would have been better off if I had stuck to newspaper work, for I would have by now had a home, a standing in the community and might have amounted to something instead of being a rolling stone, spending all my time traveling around the country sleeping in strange hotels and leading a nomadic life."

A nomadic life he did indeed live; ships records over his lifetime show he traveled frequently between Southampton (England), Liverpool, and New York. He also traveled to Australia, Hawaii, and San Francisco by ocean liner. His passport application lists his occupation as being in the "motion picture business," and on other travel records his occupation is listed as "author" or "motion picture writer." Census records over the years show that he typically lived with large numbers of people. By 1930, he had moved to Los Angeles to pursue his interest in the movies, and the census lists him as a guest living with twelve others in one dwelling. His occupation by then was "golf teacher."

By the time Fletcher retired from the game, he played a total of 658 unique courses. To give insight into the man of many careers, he published a booklet in 1935, *How to Play Bad Golf*, a tongue-in-cheek tutorial explaining what not to do in golf. In the brochure, he claimed to have played 503 total courses (up until that time) and indicated that he "played in every country in the world excepting Russia and South America." Fletcher is listed in the brochure as an "Instructor-at-Golf" at A. G. Spalding & Brothers, a retailer of sports equipment in Los Angeles.

Although his claims sound impressive, several things about Fletcher's story don't add up. First and foremost, there is no record of him immigrating to the United States in the 1920s or at any other time. The fact that he applied for an American passport in 1918 and played golf in Van Cortlandt Park in 1919 also undercuts the accuracy of the newspaper stories about him. In fact, he was born in Brooklyn to parents who were from New York and Massachusetts. No doubt he traveled back and forth to England frequently and performed on the stage; perhaps he "acquired" an English accent while overseas and used it in his vaudeville routines in the United States. Or perhaps, when the newspapers were referring to him as an English music hall performer, they meant that he performed there at one time, rather than asserting he was born there. His claim of having played in *every* country except Russia and those in South America also seems hard to believe given his limited resources.

The truth of Fletcher's accomplishments is probably lost to history, but what is beyond dispute is that he was the motivation for Ralph to begin his long odyssey; and without question, Ralph surpassed Fletcher's record of unique courses played.

Ralph Kennedy could not have picked a better time to begin his quest—the stock market was about to boom, with the economy poised to flourish. He was also living in the most dynamic city in the country as the Jazz Age was beginning to emerge, with skyscrapers continuing to rise, and with new technology breakthroughs coming on a frequent basis. Unbeknownst to him, tournament golf was also about to enter arguably its most exciting decade, and the emerging golf courses that would be designed over the next dozen years would stand the test of time and be among the best ever built. It was an exciting time to be an avid golfer in New York.

In Washington, D. C., the country's elected officials were busy legislating in 1920. In January, the 18th Amendment was passed, prohibiting the sale and consumption of alcohol nationwide, although thirty-three states had already passed anti-drinking laws, including most of the South, where they feared drunkenness among blacks. Prohibition remained unpopular, with spotty enforcement in the Upper Midwest, California, and the Northeast, particularly in New York. On the positive side, on August 18th, women across the country could finally vote for the first time with the passage of the 19th Amendment. By 1920, the Kennedys had moved half a block away, to 217 Audubon Avenue. The couple continued to be renters, with the sturdy husband's occupation listed in the census as "Salesman Pencil Co." Ralph's mother-in-law, Alise M. Barber, was also living with them at this time; she was recorded as seventy-one and widowed. Their neighborhood was largely an Eastern European immigrant one; the majority of the residents in their building listed their descent as being of Russian, Polish, German, or Romanian heritage.

The early part of the new decade was a good one for music, new technology, golf, and Lou Gehrig. The Cotton Club opened in Harlem, about thirty blocks from the Kennedy apartment. Many of jazz's greatest performers played at the Cotton Club, including Louis Armstrong, Count Basie, and Duke Ellington, although the club was a white-only establishment. A radio station in Pittsburgh became the first to begin regular radio broadcasts in 1920, the same year that the Bell System employed 170,000 telephone operators, an increase of 100,000 in six years. In baseball news, 1920 brought victory to the Commerce High School team, with a win at the National High School Baseball Championship, played at Wrigley Field in Chicago. In shades of his greatness to come, Lou Gehrig contributed a grand slam to help win the game. On the same day, June 26th, Ralph was up in Holyoke, Massachusetts, playing in the annual Stationer's Golf Tournament. The rules of golf were evolving, and the basic penalty for hitting a ball out of bounds was now stroke and distance, although this could be modified by local rule.

That summer, the hearty New Yorker and his wife played one of the toniest clubs in the country, the Ardsley Club (as course No. 111). Formed in 1895 by the extraordinarily wealthy, their founding members were a who's who of the robber barons, including Jay Gould, Cornelius Vanderbilt II, J. P. Morgan, and both John D. and William Rockefeller. Located in Westchester County and originally known as the Ardsley Casino, their first clubhouse sat in a prominent location overlooking the Hudson River. Willie Dunn Jr., a Scottish émigré, designed the course, which was called the "finest and longest golf course in the world." A multi-faceted club, the Casino also sported grass tennis courts and stables. Their well-to-do members had many ways to get to the sprawling enclave: the New York Central Railroad ran along the Hudson River and stopped near the course, at the Ardsley-on-Hudson station; the clubhouse was fitted with a private dock to accommodate the yachts of the wealthy members; and the club also arranged its own special transportation, in the form of a horse-drawn stagecoach, the Tally-Ho!, which made a trip twice a week from lower Fifth Avenue up to the club. It was travel in the most stylish sense: Alfred G. Vanderbilt served as the coachman of the Tally-Ho! and wore a black ascot and gray felt top hat while doing so.

Ralph played a lot of local golf during the early twenties and regularly participated in New York Athletic Club (NYAC) events held at clubs around the metropolitan area. Among the caddies he had in his early golf days was a local Westchester boy, Eugenio Saraceni. Saraceni dropped out of school in the sixth grade to begin caddying at the Apawamis Club in Rye. The son of Sicilian immigrants who would later Americanize his name to Gene Sarazen, he would go on to win forty-eight professional tour events and become one of the greatest golfers of all time.

Another local course Ralph played in 1920 was the Englewood Golf Club, a well-regarded course in Northern New Jersey that hosted the U.S. Open in 1909. As the crow files, the course was located less than ten miles from his apartment, although he was separated from it by the Hudson River, with the dramatic Palisades headlands between him and Englewood. It was a brief, fifteen-minute walk from his apartment to the Dyckman Street ferry, which provided frequent service and ran boats across the river every ten minutes for a nickel fare. The ferry ran frequently because the New Jersey side of the Hudson was a popular spot for tourists who used the beach there, and it was a good place to sit and watch steamboats going up and down the Hudson. On warm and humid evenings, city residents took the ferry back and forth to cool off, catching breezes blowing down the river.

Englewood had several members of note, including Eugene Homans, whom Bobby Jones would play in the final round at the U.S. Amateur at Merion in years to come. Fellow Newspaper Club golfer Grantland Rice was also a member. A scratch golfer who took up the game at age thirty, Rice was good friends with Bobby Jones; he started covering Jones when Bobby was just fourteen years old. As avid a golfer as Ralph, Rice played whenever he could and traveled with both his typewriter and his golf clubs. A member of several clubs, Rice also belonged to the upper-crust Maidstone Club on Long

Island. During the winter, he traveled to Los Angeles with his wife, and they would stay at the Beverly Wilshire for the season and play at the Lakeside Golf Club of Hollywood, where he had his third membership. Among the golfers Rice played with at Lakeside were W. C. Fields and Oliver Hardy.

Rice could live such an elaborate lifestyle because he was an extremely well-regarded—and-paid—journalist in his day. His contract with the *Herald Tribune* in 1925 paid him $52,000 per year, the same amount Babe Ruth made playing for the Yankees. Rice attended Vanderbilt University and was a double major, studying both Latin and Greek. Besides his coverage of Bobby Jones, one of the most insightful items Rice wrote was about the royal and ancient game: "Golf is 20 percent mechanics and technique. The other 80 percent is philosophy, humor, tragedy, romance, melodrama, companionship, camaraderie, cussedness, and conversation." Rice served as the editor of *American Golfer* magazine for a number of years. A prolific writer, he was in print for a period of fifty-three years, producing sixty-seven million words, including twenty-two thousand columns and fourteen books.

Rice was rightly credited with his preternatural ability to create sports legends in the 1920s. Among those he covered extensively who rose to prominence were Babe Ruth, Red Grange, Bill Tilden, and Jack Dempsey. In his frequent travels, he covered a wide range of sports, in the process creating some enduring phrases. His description of the Fighting Irish's backfield in a 1924 game played at the Polo Grounds, as the "Four Horsemen of Notre Dame" (after the "Four Horsemen of the Apocalypse"), remains a part of sports lore to this day; his skillfully written article took the newspaper's lead and appeared on page one, column one, of the next day's *Herald Tribune.*

It was good to be Grantland Rice. In January and February while in residence at the Beverly Wilshire, he wrote in the morning and played Lakeside in the afternoon, sometimes with Bing Crosby and Humphrey Bogart. When spring training rolled around in March, he headed to Florida; as the baseball season started, he headed north. When not on the road, he spent the summer and fall shuttling between his apartment on Fifth Avenue and Maidstone in East Hampton. His biographer, Charles Fountain, credits Rice in no small part with helping golf rise in popularity. Fountain wrote that "His presence alone is enough to grant an event significance, for he is unquestionably the best-read and most admired sportswriter." His writings between Ouimet's 1913 U.S. Open win and Bobby's Grand Slam in 1930 helped to define the sport to many Americans. Fellow sportswriter Red Smith said about Rice, "Wherever Grantland Rice sits, that's the head of the table."

Republican Warren Harding succeeded Woodrow Wilson in 1921, and when Rice wrote a few nice words about the new president, he was invited to play golf with him one month after his inauguration. The prolific writer served as president of the New York Newspaper Golf Club at one time.

Lou Gehrig graduated from Commerce High on January 27, 1921, and in February he enrolled at Columbia University on a football scholarship. That fall he began college, where he pledged Ralph's legacy fraternity: Phi Delta Theta.

A 1921 Dunwoodie newsletter mentioned that Ralph liked to travel to play different courses and that he frequently took the train and played courses located near stations. He became adept at adapting his schedule and habits around train timetables. While traveling to play a new course, he liked to take a caddie if they were available. The enthusiastic, well-groomed golfer was pictured in the NYAC's newsletter as runner-up in their championship that year wearing plus fours, looking sharp and well coiffed as usual. An illustration of him also appeared in the local golf association's newsletter, *Metropolitan Golfer,* wearing his signature tam-o'-shanter and smoking a cigar.

Ralph played only a limited number of new courses for the year, all in the tri-state area. Among them was the private Grassy Sprain Golf Club, located in Yonkers, not far from his apartment in Manhattan. Ralph's scorecard from the course reminded the player to "fill up holes made in a bunker." The reminder was necessary because Ralph played his entire lifetime on golf courses without rakes in the bunkers, and it was each player's responsibility to smooth out any impressions they made with their feet. Another Westchester course he played during the year was the Green Meadow Country Club. The course was designed in 1917 by a local professional, Maurice McCarthy. Ralph mentioned in an interview that Bob Hope also was a member at Green Meadow before moving out to California. Hope had a home on Central Park West for most of the 1930s; a proficient golfer, he played to a handicap of four during his prime golfing years. Like Charles Fletcher, Hope also spent some time on the vaudeville circuit during the 1920s.

The golf year ended on a happy note for the Kennedys: "Woman Gets Hole in One," the headline in the *New York Sun* declared. "Playing in a club tournament last week, Mrs. R. A. Kennedy of Dunwoodie, made the thirteenth hole in one shot, using a mid-mashie [today's 3-iron]. The hole was playing 120 yards and the ball landed on the green, just short of the hole and then trickled in." Ralph was proud of his accomplished wife, but also jealous that he had not yet had one, despite his many tries.

The Kennedys most certainly noticed something different in New York City in the early part of the decade as their urban environment was adapting to the automobile. The first yellow-and-black-checkered cabs appeared, replacing the previous cars, which were French-made and painted in red and green panels. The new, large, iconic taxis, which came to symbolize New York, were produced in Kalamazoo, Michigan. Their drivers were required to wear a knitted cap, white shirt, jacket, and tie. The first permanent traffic signals also went up in New York in the early twenties, not coincidently, in response to the alarming number of pedestrian deaths caused by automobiles. Traffic during this time was also a nightmare, and it could take forty minutes to travel twenty blocks in Midtown Manhattan. Those original traffic signals were something straight out of Keystone Cops; made of wood and steel, they were operated manually by a policeman who stood above the traffic on the top of the stand.

Ralph visited the Country Club at Brookline in 1922, the same year Jess Sweetser won the U.S. Amateur there. En route to his victory, Sweetser beat Bobby Jones in a semifinal match, 8 & 7. Aside from

An early New York City traffic signal. *(Author's Collection)*

the fact that Bobby got beaten by such a wide margin, the round was memorable because of an attempted stymie Sweetser laid on Jones on the 6th hole. Bobby's ball was fifteen inches from the cup, and when Sweetser putted his ball, it stopped one inch from the hole, directly in Bobby's line. Jones took out his niblick and used it to jump the ball over Sweetser's, flying it directly into the hole. It was a technique Jones had mastered, and he demonstrated it years later, in the 1930s, in a series of instructional films made in Los Angeles.

Ralph returned to Baltimore in 1922 and played the Suburban Golf Club again; by this time, the course had been expanded to a 6,161-yard, eighteen-hole course. Although he originally played the course in 1913, Ralph's rule was that if a course was renovated, lengthened, or substantially changed, he could play it again and count it in his tally as another unique course. He would do this at a number of courses over the years, most notably at the Augusta Country Club, Baltusrol, St. Albans, and Knollwood. The scorecard at Suburban had changed from his initial visit; local rules no longer offered relief from hitting a telegraph wire, but instead offered relief from telephone wires. Over the course of the year, the number of telephones in New York City had reached one million, with a new one being added at a rate of one per minute. To keep up with demand, the New York Telephone Company had to hire 620 new operators in one year. It now had 101 central offices in the city.

Using his connections at the NYAC, Dunwoodie, and the Newspaper Club, Ralph secured invitations to a trio of historic private courses in Westchester County, beginning with the Saint Andrew's Golf Club in Yonkers, his first visit to a USGA founding member club. Fifteen minutes farther north, he played at the Century Country Club in Purchase, a course that would become a favorite of President Eisenhower in future years. Next, he visited the Knollwood Country Club, also located close by, and played their original Lawrence Van Etten course as his 131st. A. W. Tillinghast, Seth Raynor, and Charles Banks were brought in in succession to redesign and expand the course, and Ralph returned in 1928 to play it again as his 470th. Knollwood is notable because Augusta National co-founder Cliff Roberts was a member, and he met Bobby Jones there for the first time. Frequently playing courses located in Westchester County, in 1931 Ralph visited the Whippoorwill Club, which had recently been redesigned by Charles Banks. The architect was so proficient using the latest technology available to assist in building golf courses that he was given the nickname of "Steam Shovel" Banks.

Nineteen twenty-three was a year of growth and progress for both Gehrig and Kennedy. Ralph was now a Winged Footer and continued to practice and hone his golf skills locally, and Gehrig's talents as a ballplayer continued to emerge. Yankee Stadium opened on April 18th, and on that same afternoon, Gehrig pitched for Columbia against Williams College in Morningside Heights. He dropped out of Columbia before his junior year and on April 30th signed his first modest contract: $400 a month for the remainder of the season with a $1,500 sign-on bonus. On June 11, 1923, Gehrig walked the short distance from Morningside Heights to the Bronx, on his way to Yankee Stadium for a workout with the team. He played his first game on June 15th but was not a regular starter; he was used in a pinch-hitting role for the next year or so. Not particularly confident in his ability to make a living at baseball—and because his family needed the money—in the fall of 1923, he took a job as an office clerk at the New York Edison Company.

The early part of August brought warm and sticky temperatures to New York. Refrigerator sales began to increase dramatically during the middle of the decade as electric refrigerators were beginning to replace ice boxes. As a popular but not completely understood new appliance, Frigidaire had salesmen going door-to-door in 1923 to explain the benefits to potential customers. On average, refrigerators of this period were a high-maintenance proposition and required two service calls per year from a repairman.

Amherst College graduate Calvin Coolidge took over the presidency on the 3rd of August after Warren Harding died suddenly. Coolidge was not much interested in golf, playing only occasionally, and very poorly. Three days after the new president was sworn in, Ralph took the Long Island Railroad out of Pennsylvania Station to play the Lido Golf Club, a masterpiece designed by Charles Blair Macdonald and his protégé Seth Raynor. The golf course was built on reclaimed land that was dredged at considerable expense, and it gave the designers a great deal of freedom to shape holes. This approach facilitated the building of a lagoon, which formed the contours of a prototype "Channel" hole that demanded two forced carries over water. Never one for modesty, Macdonald thought it one of the best par-fours ever to have been created. When leading professional golfers of the era were polled in the late 1920s and asked what the greatest courses in the United States were, Lido ranked second, behind only Pine Valley. Winged Foot's professional, Claude Harmon, called it "the greatest golf course ever." Although Lido received accolades from many golfers in its time, Ralph never mentioned it among his favorites.

It would have been possible for Ralph to use steel shafts when he played another Raynor course that summer: the Greenwich Country Club in Connecticut. The USGA had recently allowed the use of steel-shafted clubs for the first time, although they were not widely adopted

An image of the famous Channel hole at the well-regarded Lido Golf Course on Long Island. *(Author's Collection)*

immediately, and Ralph stuck with his hickories. A crisp black-and-white photograph survives in one of Ralph's scrapbooks from his visit to Greenwich. The contented and youthful-looking forty-two-year-old is pictured sitting on a bench at the course with two friends, looking like a sophisticated Jazz Age player, wearing his snappy plus fours and smoking a pipe.

America's ascendance and power in the post-war era continued to rise, her rich natural resources driving expansion. The growth of the internal combustion engine and rising automobile usage were changing the world. Motorized equipment was impacting golf, as well, and was leading to improved course maintenance in the early twenties—at the expense of employing men and animals to keep up courses. Ford now produced a "car" which dragged a triplex cutter, and the company advertised that it could do the work of four horses and two men.

The Kennedys took the train back out to Long Island in the spring of 1924 to play at the popular Salisbury Golf Links, whose No. 1 course opened in 1917. Salisbury Links eventually featured five different courses, all designed by Devereux Emmet. The couple returned in August to play courses Nos. 2 and 3 (courses 184 and 185 in Ralph's odyssey).

Ralph kicked off 1925 with a long journey commencing in late January; departing from Pennsylvania Station, it was a ten-mile ride powered by an electric engine to the Manhattan Transfer. After switching engines, the steam-powered locomotive billowed white smoke into the cold air as it rhythmically rolled down the tracks, headed to the land of drawls and twangs. He was on his way to the more civilized pace of the South and would be away from home for more than a month, visiting the Lone Star State in the cooler winter months. He was combining his occupation as a traveling salesman with his new goal to play as many new golf courses as possible. Switching back and forth between trains and streetcars, he played at the state's premier private clubs while calling on customers hawking his famous No. 2 pencil. He visited the Donald Ross-designed River Oaks Country Club in Houston before heading northwest to Dallas, where he played a trio of private courses: the Dallas Country Club, the Cedar Crest Country Club, and the A. W. Tillinghast-designed Brook Hollow Golf Club.

His excursion continued as the iron horse trundled in a smooth cadence to Fort Worth on February 9th. Fort Worth's motto, "Where the West Begins," is apt, and it was not an unusual sight at the time in Cowtown for a member to ride on horseback to their golf course. While in town, Ralph played the Glen Garden Country Club as course No. 202, the pleasant Texas winter sun shining down on him. Glen Garden was originally built in 1912 as a nine-holer with prairie grass fairways and sand greens and was later expanded to eighteen holes. His scorecard admonished players to keep golf bags off the greens and recommended that only one caddie be permitted on each green. Reminding us that the heat in Texas could be stifling, particularly in the pre air-conditioning era, the card also contained a prominent advertisement for "Fly Screens," which allowed homeowners to catch cool breezes while keeping out bugs.

There is no notation on the card of who caddied for Ralph, although among the caddies at Glen Garden when Kennedy visited were a pair of thirteen-year-olds who would go on to become golf legends: Ben Hogan and Byron Nelson. Two years after Ralph's visit, Hogan played against Nelson for the caddie championship; Nelson beat him by one shot on the last hole of a nine-hole playoff with a stymie.

Ralph's long trip continued as February gave way to March, and in between hawking pencils to customers, he made time for golf. He had vacated the vast expanses of Texas in favor of soaring pine trees, visiting the Sandhills region of North Carolina. He played the Donald Ross-designed Southern Pines Country Club before moving to the larger Pinehurst Resort. Pinehurst's abundance of courses made it the perfect town for the way-faring golfer. He played the resort's courses in numerical order, tackling the No. 1 course first. A course of 5,919 yards, No. 1 was the first eighteen-hole course at the resort. Local rules at Pinehurst allowed players to clean their balls once they were on the sand greens, provided they got the consent of their opponent.

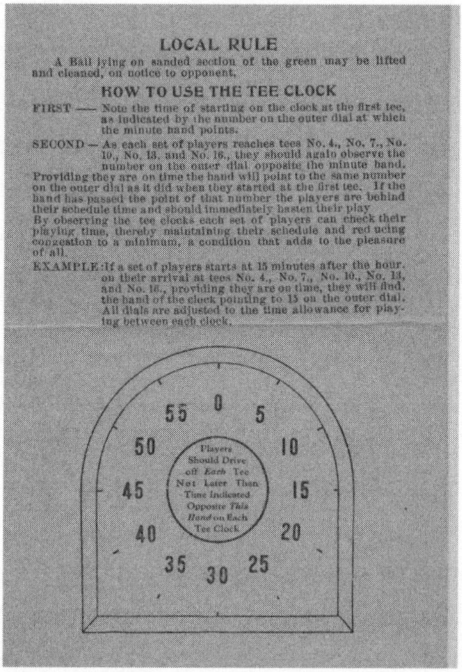

LOCAL RULE

A Ball lying on sanded section of the green may be lifted and cleaned, on notice to opponent.

HOW TO USE THE TEE CLOCK

FIRST — Note the time of starting on the clock at the first tee, as indicated by the number on the outer dial at which the minute hand points.

SECOND — As each set of players reaches tees No. 4., No. 7., No. 10., No. 13. and No. 16., they should again observe the number on the outer dial opposite the minute hand. Providing they are on time the hand will point to the same number on the outer dial as it did when they started at the first tee. If the hand has passed the point of that number the players are behind their schedule time and should immediately hasten their play

By observing the tee clocks each set of players can check their playing time, thereby maintaining their schedule and reducing congestion to a minimum, a condition that adds to the pleasure of all.

EXAMPLE: If a set of players starts at 15 minutes after the hour, on their arrival at tees No. 4., No. 7., No. 10., No. 13, and No. 16., providing they are on time, they will find the hand of the clock pointing to 15 on the outer dial. All dials are adjusted to the time allowance for playing between each clock.

The back of Ralph's Pinehurst card with instructions on how to play fast. *(Photo courtesy of USGA)*

Over the next three days, Ralph stayed in the quaint village and played the three Donald Ross courses in succession, beginning with the most well-known, No. 2. The New Yorker putted well on the relatively flat sand greens. It wouldn't be until 1934 that Ross raised them to an inverted style and grass started to replace the sand. The resort encouraged its guests to play fast, and rather than just asking them to do so, they devised an elaborate technique to help. They had a system in place with clocks set on several holes out on the course. Their scorecard contained a picture of a clock so that the player could tick off their starting time. Their lengthy instructions not only assumed that the reader was daft, but they were so precise and verbose that the reader had no choice but to simply give up upon reading them. When he finished off Pinehurst's No. 4 course, Ralph had now played on 210 different golf courses. Plumes of smoke filled the smoking car as Kennedy relaxed with a cigar to begin his long rail journey home. The accomplished salesman was sated from a successful trip as he turned into his sleeping berth for the overnight trip to Pennsylvania Station.

The Kennedy residence remained unchanged through 1925; the couple was still living on Audubon Avenue, although they were now alone since Mary Alice's mother had passed away earlier that year. The middle year of the decade was memorable in the worlds of baseball, golf, and publishing. Painting a picture of the era in colorful terms, on April 10th, F. Scott Fitzgerald's *The Great Gatsby* was published. Although Lou Gehrig played seldom during his early major league career, that was about to change. On June 1st, manager Miller Huggins put him in as a pinch hitter. The next day he replaced Wally Pipp at first base, beginning what would become the longest consecutive game streak in the major leagues.

The pencil salesman visited Macon, Georgia, on a return trip through the South in 1925 and played at the Log Cabin Club. Founded in 1913 as a nine-hole layout, the course was later expanded to eighteen holes and subsequently changed its name to the Idle Hour Country Club. To keep the club going through the Depression, they used a secret source of revenue to finance their operation: slot machines.

Continuing to build momentum, and with his course count ever expanding, the gallivanting traveler was always looking for new courses to add to his list. A frequent visitor to Kentucky, Ralph played at the Audubon Country Club in Louisville on the same trip, which offered a unique local rule: golfers could take relief should their ball end up lying in a crawfish hole.

Like an insect with his antennae up, Kennedy found a cluster of courses to play on his return journey from the South. The indomitable pencil salesman disembarked in Washington, D. C., and traveled the short distance from Union Station to play at the East Potomac Golf Course complex on a Friday night and Saturday morning. Situated on a man-made island just south of the Jefferson Memorial, the complex, when it first opened in 1921, operated as a segregated facility and only allowed blacks to play on Sundays. Located smack dab in the middle of the action, with the Washington Channel on one side and the Potomac on the other, the white spire of the Washington Monument is an omnipresent sight for golfers at East Potomac. The thoroughgoing golfer played six different nine-hole courses, lettered "A" through "F," as numbers 217–222 in his rapidly growing collection of new courses and cards.

His summer travels in Massachusetts took him to the Worcester Country Club in 1925, playing the course the same year it hosted the U.S. Open and two years before it hosted the first Ryder Cup. The Donald Ross-designed course opened in 1914, and the recently retired President Taft—an avid golfer—hit the first official tee shot on the course. Hitting off the first tee under pressure wasn't one of the Big Chief's strong suits, and he duck-hooked a couple of balls wildly off line before he was able to coax one into the fairway. During his August vacation, Ralph returned again to the state in which he was born and played the United Shoe Machinery Golf Course in Beverly, as course No. 230. The course, which played to a bogey of eighty, was the first of several courses Ralph played that were corporate-owned, as paternal companies were still common.

Five years into Kennedy's golf journey, he was amassing a respectable number of new courses played each year. Yet at forty-three years of age, and at a pace of roughly twenty-five courses per year over the past half-decade, his pace to date would not indicate an unassailable life total if he was seeking to play golf on more courses than any man ever had.

CHAPTER 5

The Media Discover Red Kennedy

Publicity was one of Ralph's strong suits, and he had a knack for getting his name in print. Although he and Mary Alice had already been mentioned in the New York newspapers by 1925, it was in connection with local tournaments, and not related to his ambitious goal. It was a *Muskogee* (Oklahoma) *Phoenix* article describing his traveling exploits published in February 1926 that was the first one pasted into his scrapbook: "Golfer Playing Here Has Played 260 Links in Eighteen States." As the tiny article noted, "R. A. Kennedy, a wandering golfer and salesman who started in 1911 to play as many golf courses as possible, made an eighty-eight at Meadowbrook yesterday and will leave for Tulsa today to play all five courses there." Prior to 1924, Ralph never played more than thirty new courses in a year; in both 1925 and 1926, he began his big push and doubled that annual total. The coming year included visits to Virginia and the oil patch of Oklahoma and Texas, as well as Tennessee and Georgia.

Methodically crossing off new courses, he returned to a frequently visited state, Kentucky, and played another course operating for the benefit of company employees: the Producer's Wood Preserving Company in Louisville. He played well and shot an eighty-one on the 6,044-yard course. He had been tinkering with his swing, working on perfecting his craft, and it was beginning to show. On the same trip, he played two nine-hole courses also in Louisville: the Standard Club and the Crescent Hill Golf Course. His visit to Louisville the following year included stops at the newly opened Big Spring Golf Club as well as the Green Fields Country Club, and his return visit to the Bluegrass State the year after that tacked on seven more courses.

Returning home from his Southern trip, the Winged Foot golfer won some bragging rights. His tempo pitch-perfect and his putting stroke fluid, he was now in a groove and finished first in the New York Newspaper Golf Club's tournament on June 6, 1926, held at the Oak Ridge Country Club in Tuckahoe, beating thirty-one other golfers with both low gross and low net.

The Kennedys returned to Long Island later that summer and played Salisbury's No. 4 course one month before it hosted the ninth PGA Championship, won by Walter Hagen. Whereas the No. 1 and 2 courses were open to the public, Nos. 3 and 4 were private courses reserved for members. The 1926 PGA saw fewer spectators than normal because two different airplanes planning to fly from New York to Paris crashed in Long Island, which diverted attention away from golf. Since aviation feats were all the rage, it was more exciting to go gawk at the wreckage rather than watch golfers smashing their drives.

The format of the PGA Championship was a testing twelve consecutive rounds in six days: a thirty-six-hole qualifier followed by five days of thirty-six-hole match play. The *Brooklyn Daily Eagle* was thrilled with Hagen's third consecutive PGA victory, gushing over his performance: "The deeply sunburned, debonair, dark-haired son of a Rochester carpenter proved that he stands above all others as a match play golfer." Using the rules of the time to his advantage, and in an effort to avoid being stymied by his competitor, Leo Diegel, Hagen putted out of a shallow sand trap to ensure that his ball ended up in a location where Diegel could not block him. The same day that Hagen secured his victory in the PGA, the Yankees secured the American League pennant and entered the World Series by beating the St. Louis Browns. Although they would lose four games to three, Gehrig achieved a notable highlight when he drove in the winning run in the first World Series game he played.

August 26, 1926, was a beautiful summer day with temperatures in the mid-seventies; the skies were as blue as a robin's egg, sunlight slanting out of the summer sky. RAK's scorecard shows he took advantage of the ideal conditions to roam the links of the original Deepdale Golf & Country Club in Lake Success, New York, another Charles Blair Macdonald course. Macdonald is considered among the founding fathers of American golf and was one of the driving forces behind the creation of the USGA. An obstinate, rambunctious, and domineering man, he commanded great respect based on his knowledge of golf course design. He attended the University of St. Andrews in Scotland and spent time in the British Isles studying the architecture of their best courses. His first design, the seminal National Golf Links of America, set the standard for excellence when it opened in 1911. Macdonald was brought in to Lake Success on Long Island when William K. Vanderbilt II decided to convert a 200-acre portion of his summer estate to a golf course. Seth Raynor, Macdonald's construction foreman, is credited with the co-design of Deepdale. The course contained many of the typical holes that Macdonald and Raynor favored, including prototype Biarritz, Cape, Alps, Short, and Punchbowl holes. Given the Vanderbilt pedigree, Deepdale was an exclusive course to which Ralph was lucky to secure an invitation, especially less than six months after it opened.

While on Long Island, Ralph played another course with Vanderbilt heritage located close to Deepdale, the Glen Oaks Club in Great Neck, whose initial clubhouse was the former mansion of William K. Vanderbilt II. The course was built at great expense the year before Ralph's visit, and the club was one of the first to put in irrigation to water the entire course, including tees and fairways as well as the greens. Another of Ralph's special visits of the year was to the Meadow Brook Club in Westbury, Long Island, a course designed by Devereux Emmet.

It was a year of forward progress related to the game's equipment, specifically golf clubs. The first set of numbered clubs was offered for sale, beginning the transition away from mashies and niblicks into the era of standardized iron clubs. A patent was also filed on April 15th for the "Adjustable Golf Club." The application was eventually approved and was issued several years later to Joseph A. Novak and Franklin C. Fisher, both of San Francisco. Novak is an interesting character in the history of the game. A native of Montana, he took his first job as a golf professional in Butte at the age of sixteen. Heading farther west, in 1918 he took a job as a professional in Spokane, Washington. A talented golfer, Novak played in the U.S. Open in 1922, 1924, and 1925. At the time, he was serving as the professional at the Berkeley Golf Club near San Francisco and resigned the day the patent was filed. He confirmed these details with a reporter via telegram, noting that he wanted to focus his efforts on perfecting his "Whole-in-one" club, as he then called it. Before leaving Berkeley, he demonstrated the club for members by going around the course with just a driver and his new contraption. His club was quite versatile and could be adjusted to various lofts, including a 1-iron, 2-iron, 3-iron, 4-iron, 5-iron, or a putter.

Philadelphia was the place to be on September 23, 1926, when Jack Dempsey and Gene Tunney squared off in an epic boxing battle. They jousted for ten rounds in a downpour in Municipal Stadium, and eventually Tunney beat the popular 6-foot-1 champion to claim the world heavyweight title. Pullman cars filled with dignitaries from all over the country were jamming into the city to watch the fight.

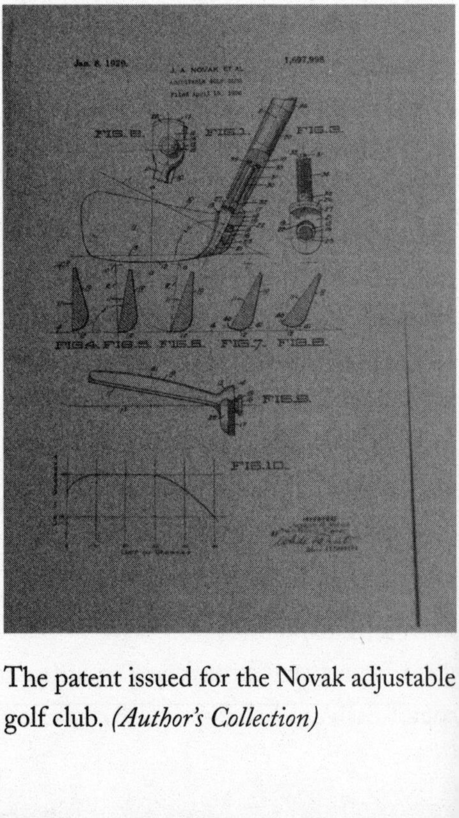

The patent issued for the Novak adjustable golf club. *(Author's Collection)*

The crowd of 120,757 was gigantic by any standard and drew so many spectators that both the Giants and Dodgers postponed their home games because thousands of their fans went south. The *Herald Tribune* sent Grantland Rice to cover the big match.

A little more than a month later, passengers in New York's Pennsylvania Station saw an eager, blue-eyed, strawberry-blond golfer carrying a small golf bag on his way to Philadelphia, where he changed trains for the short ride back across the Delaware River to Southern New Jersey. He was about to play at one of the most significant courses he ever played. Ralph was invited to Pine Valley on Halloween, but unfortunately the weather was not cooperative. Although seasonably mild with temperatures in the mid-fifties, the day brought showers and a two-club wind. As was designer George Crump's vision, Ralph used every club in his bag at Pine Valley, known as one of the most challenging and difficult courses from the day it opened, thanks to its unorthodox design. It was considered an accomplishment if a golfer could break 100 the first time they played Pine Valley, and although Ralph was a sixteen handicap, he did not. He shot a 106 and found the 7th hole—nicknamed Hell's Half Acre—to be particularly difficult, taking a nine on the long par-5. Like all holes at Pine Valley, the 7th has a forced carry off the tee, although the fairway is generous if a golfer hits a reasonably straight shot.

Pine Valley is very different stylistically from Ralph's home course of Winged Foot, where there are not forced carries off the tees, and he had a tough time making the required adjustments. Ralph once described himself as not being particularly long off the tee; thus, he would have found the second shot on number seven challenging, because it requires the golfer to carry their shot over a sandy waste area that is 100 yards long and dotted with clumps of native grasses and unraked sand. The hazard is long and wide, and Ralph didn't manage it well, hitting his spoon (today's 3-wood) less than perfect and wasting strokes in the sand. The well-traveled golfer had a good eye for golf courses and immediately fell in love with Pine Valley. From this point forward, when asked what his favorite golf course was, he almost always said it was course No. 301 in his numbering sequence, the sandy course in South Jersey that gave him conniptions.

Ralph finished off his golf travels for the year with a December visit to Augusta, where he played both of the Country Club of Augusta's courses: the Hill and the Lake. Regarding the 6,153-yard Hill Course, he wrote on his card, "this course has sand greens." The course he played pre-dated changes Donald Ross made the following year, when he converted the greens to grass, reworked the bunkers, and rerouted several holes. Playing the 6,074-yard Lake Course on the same day, Ralph wrote on his scorecard, "this course has grass greens." Seth Raynor had just converted that course's greens from sand. A consistent golfer regardless of the style of green, Ralph shot an eighty-seven on each. Caddie warnings continued on the scorecards, specifically, "Players should see that caddies do not walk in bunkers or deface putting greens." Players were also reminded that they "must not sole the club in hazards even when grass exists on cops [cops are straight, elevated, grass bunkers]."

The local newspaper, the *Augusta Chronicle,* picked up Ralph's trail and featured a short article about him on December 7, 1926, by which point he had played almost fifty new courses since his previous newspaper appearance on his Oklahoma trip. As the *Chronicle* article, entitled "Man Who Played 309 Courses is Visitor in City," explained, "R. A. Kennedy of the Winged Foot Golf Club and the Dunwoodie Golf Club is stopping in Augusta for a few days and while here played over the hill and lake courses at Augusta Country Club. Mr. Kennedy, who is forty-five-years-old, has played over more different courses than any other amateur in the country with one exception. He has played over 300 courses and hopes to play 500, after which he intends writing a book describing the various courses he has played on."

The coming year was one that history would remember for a significant aviation event. Not only was 1927 notable for Lindbergh's solo flight across the Atlantic (he took off from Roosevelt Field on Long Island, thirty miles from the Kennedy home), but it was also a year that media coverage accelerated for the blue-eyed duffer. On January 11th, the *New York Sun* noted that the "Winged Foot man has already played 310 courses during his sixteen years at the game."

The pencil salesman departed early for his semiannual Southern trip in 1927, getting on the rolling stock in January. The train pulling out of the Manhattan Transfer was belching smoke from its stack into the chilled winter air, while inside his warm berth, the brawny duffer was creating his own thick haze by puffing ceaselessly on his cigar. His 4,000-mile journey gives a good indication of his stamina; it was an itinerary that would leave most golfers in a state of exhaustion. This particular trip took him much farther south than he normally traveled, and he made a wide arc, taking the train down to the Gulf Coast, reaching Louisiana on the 23rd. He arrived in the Crescent City in an era when it was bustling, with a busy port, streetcars, and eclectic brass bands. A city with its own distinctive style, New Orleans was dotted with flickering gas lamps and quaint houses featuring carriage-ways leading to interior courtyards. Cotton was still a big business in the South, and warehouses lining the Mississippi were chock-full of the valuable commodity. He enjoyed the distinctive French Quarter with its elegant second-story galleries decorated with wrought-iron railings. Although Mary Alice was at home in freezing temperatures, it was cloudy and in the mid-sixties when he teed it up at the Metairie Country Club, a private Seth Raynor design opened several years earlier. America's diverse geographic regions allowed Ralph to experience widely disparate styles of golfing terrain. The Mississippi River Delta is characterized by low-lying, flat terrain punctuated with semitropical vegetation that is absent from courses in the Northern climates. Stately live oak trees draped with Spanish moss provided the backdrop for his golf in Louisiana's southern parishes at the Audubon Golf Club, the New Orleans Country Club, and the West End Country Club.

Kennedy continued west by train, playing a mix of nine-hole and eighteen-hole courses, half with sand greens and half with grass. His next stop was Texas, and just across the Louisiana border, he played at the Beaumont Country Club. Zigzagging his way through the Southwest, bypassing Houston, he continued on to San Antonio and played the Willow Springs Golf Course; then it was up to play Waco Municipal, before continuing on to Fort Worth to tee it up at the River Crest Country Club. Continuing east to Dallas, he finished off his Lone Star State golf playing at the Glen Haven and Crescent Golf Clubs. His train lurching out of Northern Texas, the massive journey for the inexhaustible salesman continued through Oklahoma, with a stop in Oklahoma City to play the Lincoln Park Golf Club, then it was up to the Tulsa Country Club (an A. W. Tillinghast design), through Fort Smith, Arkansas (the Municipal Golf Course), and down to Hot Springs, to play the Oaklawn Golf Club. The clicking and clacking of steel wheels turning on the rails continued up through Memphis as he played a trio of courses: the Chickasaw Golf Club, the Colonial Country Club, and the Overton Park Golf Course. His briefcase now bulging with scorecards, it was then back on the rails to play the Chattanooga Municipal Course before continuing to Winston-Salem's Forsyth Country Club and Durham's Hillandale Golf Course, before heading home.

Ralph's scorecard from his visit to the Metairie Country Club. *(Photo courtesy of USGA)*

Giving his well-worn travel guide a workout, he planned out his jaunts in advance. Since he was without a car, his regimen was to play at courses that were easy to get to by public transportation. Seven of the courses he played on this trip were accessible by streetcar or trolley. In a sign of how ubiquitous the form of transportation was, cities far and wide had them, including Oklahoma City, Tulsa, Memphis, Fort Worth, and Fort Smith.

Ralph's small market media coverage continued, this time in Arkansas. The *Fort Smith Times* headline of February 25th touted the "Champion Tourist Golfer." The article noted how he loved to travel and notch up new courses. Highlighting his fortitude, they explained that he had taken only two days sick because of illness in the sixteen years he had been pursuing his quest, both due to the flu. An article in the *San Antonio Express* relayed some of the secrets to his success, reporting that he "never had a bunion because he wears two pairs of socks." And that he "never wears a glove because they're sissy."

Back in New York, the Kennedys played their final Salisbury course on Long Island, No. 5, in the early spring. Ralph continued to play locally in Connecticut and New York during the summer months, including the new course at Yale University. He was befuddled by the putting surfaces of the Macdonald-Raynor design, telling the *New York Sun*, "The Yale Course greens are the biggest I've seen in my ramblings—some of them are 150 feet across. You can't use an ordinary putter from the edge of one of the greens. A jigger or cleek is needed to chip up to the pin."

As his profile was being raised, he even got publicity from his home clubs: the *Winged Foot*, the NYAC's newsletter, pictured the strong-jawed redhead wearing plus fours while holding an umbrella and smoking a pipe.

The summer brought a celebratory frenzy to New York when the city threw a ticker tape parade for the national hero Charles Lindbergh on June 13th. It was also a great year for the Yankees and Lou Gehrig. On June 23rd, Gehrig hit three home runs in one game for the first time in his career and finished the year with a .373 batting average. The Yankees easily won the World Series that fall, sweeping the Pittsburgh Pirates in four games. Six players from the 1927 team (as well as manager Miller Huggins) would eventually enter the Hall of Fame: Gehrig, Babe Ruth, Tony Lazzeri, Earle Combs, Herb Pennock, and Waite Hoyt. Gehrig and Ruth batted back-to-back and formed the backbone of the famed Murderers' Row lineup. They hit 107 home runs between them.

By 1927, golf had exploded in popularity across the nation. Publicity brought on by Francis Ouimet's win in 1913 spurred many people to join the game. The general economic boom of the Roaring Twenties also helped. There were now 2,925 courses listed in the *Golf Guide*, five times the number at the turn of the century. Growth of the game out West was accelerating; by now, New Mexico had seventeen courses, all nine-holers with sand greens. The length of courses and the types of greens built continued to be in transition. Nevada now had one golfing ground, a nine-hole course with grass greens, located in the higher elevation and cooler climate of Reno. Grasses that could withstand prolonged exposure to heat were not yet fully available, although grass greens were beginning to be used more frequently in warmer climates. As the game gained in popularity, so did eighteen-hole courses; and by now, half the courses in the Tar Heel State were nine-holes and half were eighteen-holes. Sand greens were not limited to courses below the Mason-Dixon Line. Fifteen percent of the courses in Oregon also had sand greens, and more than half its courses were nine-holes. Of the ninety-four courses in Texas, forty-three had sand greens, thirty-seven were grass, and fourteen were built with greens of cottonseed hulls.

The 610-page *Golf Guide* appropriately captured the zeitgeist of the time. The *Southern Golfer* advertised its monthly magazine in the *Guide*, which was now edited by H. B. Martin. Their advertisement contained an image of a Little Black Sambo-like caddie holding a small golf bag. He is illustrated wearing worn and patched overalls, and has a goofy smile on his face and only one tooth. Racial progress was slow, and not much had changed since the *Golf Guide* of 1899 depicted four little black boys, with the caption, "These youngsters develop into good caddies." Unfortunately, the 1920s were a popular time for the Ku Klux Klan; at one point, they had over four million members.

Ralph added course Nos. 348 and 349 in 1927, playing at the Teterboro Golf Club in Northern New Jersey twice on the same day, on both their East and West courses. The scorecards for Teterboro listed eighteen hole numbers but left the hole's distance and par blank, to be filled in by the player.

An image of New Jersey's lost Teterboro golf course. *(Author's Collection)*

With great fanfare, the 1.6-mile "Holland Vehicular Tunnel" opened in 1927, connecting Lower Manhattan to Jersey City. It was the first tunnel to solve the problem of mechanical ventilation, which was necessary because of exhaust fumes. The tunnel was celebrated because it was the first time that residents of Manhattan could reach the mainland traveling east without taking a ferry, the McAdoo tunnels, or a railroad. Over fifty thousand cars went through the new tubes beginning at 12:01 a.m. on November 17th, and they streamed through continually for twenty-four hours, as the curious went back and forth as a sightseeing excursion. Technology continued to progress in other industries, as well: the first transatlantic phone calls became commercially available in 1927 (at a rate of $25 per minute), and Pan American Airways was founded the same year.

Spurred on by Charles Fletcher's challenge, Ralph had played a total of four hundred courses by the end of 1927. He had gained over 100 courses on the year, passing his friend and nemesis. His pace was about to quicken as the decade of the twenties entered its final two years; he would remain at an elevated level and play over 100 courses per year for each of the next five. The majority of his conquests to date were in Tennessee, Georgia, and Kentucky in the South; New York and New Jersey in the Mid-Atlantic States; and Connecticut, New Hampshire, and Massachusetts in New England. The coming year would be a breakthrough one for Ralph, as the media coverage of his exploits continued to build.

Nineteen twenty-eight would be a momentous year in the golf world, but also in the world of medicine. Penicillin was discovered by a Scottish doctor, Sir Alexander Fleming, who was working in London. Ralph's kid brother was by now a surgeon at Columbia-Presbyterian Hospital, which had moved into a sprawling new complex occupying the old site of the Hilltop Park baseball stadium. In Pebble Beach, California, the Alister MacKenzie-designed Cypress Point Club opened for play. Many classic courses in the United States were established as Ralph's quest picked up steam, including Yeamans Hall near Charleston in 1925, Riviera in Los Angeles and Oak Hill in Rochester in 1926, and the Alister MacKenzie-designed Crystal Downs in Michigan in 1929. So many new and well-designed courses were built between 1919 and 1930 that it has been termed the Golden Age of golf course architecture.

March brought some unrest for Ralph's employer; there was trouble at the Eagle Pencil factory in Manhattan. A group of 100 men and women stormed the company factory on Fourteenth Street demanding work, asserting that they were starving. The factory employed 1,300 workers, but they were not looking for new employees. The mob hurled stones and other detritus at the building, and police reinforcements had to be called in to calm the situation. Three men and one woman were arrested.

Cover of a 1928 *The Elks Magazine* featuring Ralph Kennedy, on the lower right. *(Author's Collection)*

Ralph was featured on the cover of *The Elks Magazine* in April; a hand-drawn illustration of the handsome gentleman was based on a black and white photo he sent them, although this would be just a prelude to his appearing soon in a magazine with a far larger circulation. The cover of the magazine is baseball themed, showing exuberant fans celebrating. Ralph is wearing a red sweater that matches his hair color, and he has rosy cheeks. In his right hand, he is clutching, what else, but a full-length pencil. As you gaze at the cover, it is evident why his nickname was "Red."

The first of two big leaps in raising Ralph's profile nationally came later in the year, when on September 8th, readers of the *Saturday Evening Post* were greeted with a cover featuring the happy golfer on it. The *Post* was the most popular national magazine at the time with a circulation of 2.8 million readers. The color drawings of him are informative, because surviving pictures of Kennedy are in black and white; thus, the color illustrations give a more vivid picture. On the *Post* cover, he has on a busy sweater and a green tam-o'-shanter and is swatting a bee flying near his face. He is depicted with a cigar hanging out of his mouth, wearing baggy plus fours and Argyll socks, and is positioning himself to hit a golf ball with a hickory-shafted club. Both the *Elks* and *Post* covers were drawn by J. F. (John Francis) Kernan, a friend of Ralph's and an alumnus of the Newspaper Golf Club. Ralph's connections growing out of his affiliation with the club were beginning to pay life-long dividends.

Ralph's likeness on the cover of the *Saturday Evening Post. (Photo courtesy of Curtis Publishing)*

Ralph made his first visit to play golf in New England's largest state the week that his breakthrough *Post* issue was out, as reported in the local newspapers. Traveling with Mary Alice, Ralph rode the Maine Central Railroad, and they had their tickets punched quite a few times, although she sat out most of the golf rounds. He began by playing three Donald Ross courses: the Biddeford and Saco Country Club, the Portland Country Club, and the Penobscot Valley Country Club. Fully exploring the state with the jagged coastline, he then played another pair of courses: the Augusta Country Club and the Martindale Country Club. Shifting their mode of transportation to steamers, the pair began island-hopping so that they could play a couple of scenic links set in the mid-night blue waters of Casco Bay, including the Diamond Island Golf Club and the Great Chebeague Golf Club. With six par fours and three par threes, the latter course was one of the shortest he ever played at 1,980 yards, and he went around its nine holes in thirty-five strokes.

Ralph wasn't the only enthusiast playing a lot of golf. In October, the *Pittsburgh Press* mentioned another stage actor who had played a substantial amount of golf. "Frank Craven has a show *The Nineteenth Hole*, he plays more golf than anyone in America, he plays twice a day in the show. While in Philadelphia last week he played his 300th course." The *Press* likely didn't have a large fact-checking department, since it was a tall order to make a claim that no one in the country played more than Craven, given Kennedy's obsessive quest and Fletcher's course total.

The schedule of Ralph's 1928 business trip to Kentucky permitted time for him to visit the Louisville and Nashville Railroad's Golf Club. The course was built two years before for the enjoyment of railroad employees. His late November visit coincided with abysmal weather, and he played in intermittent snow showers with a chilly wind blowing all day. Nevertheless, the indestructible Kennedy is pictured in the newspaper the next day standing on the final green, looking none the worse for playing in poor weather, wearing his tam-o'-shanter, a sweater, and plus fours. Part of the reason he was happy was that he shot a seventy-five on the 5,300-yard course. Their scorecard offered stern and practical advice to obstinate golfers: "The rule of five minutes does not mean that you have the right to hold up the course for five minutes while you look for your ball."

The company's *L & N Magazine* featured a small article about Ralph after his visit. As he usually did, he offered high praise for the course, and in turn they spoke of him in grandiose, if not always accurate prose, "While his scores as a rule did not cause the re-write man to paw futilely for the perfect adjective, still he has quite a cage full of birdies, a modest aerie of eagles, and he frequently breaks seventy-five in his steady march to par."

A frequent visitor to Georgia, Ralph returned to both Atlanta and Augusta late in 1928. While in Augusta, he played the Donald Ross-designed Forrest Hills-Ricker Hotel course, located on a 1,000-acre estate at 800 feet of elevation. He also played Augusta Municipal, a nine-hole course of 3,000 yards, as his steady march of progress continued—it was Ralph's 538th course played. Augusta was an easy location for Ralph to visit because it had good train service. The Pennsylvania Railroad coordinated its schedules with both the Southern Railway and the Atlantic Coast Line Railroad. Rail travel was convenient and comfortable; trains were fitted with dining cars, parlor cars, lounge cars, and Pullman sleeper cars. An overnight train leaving Pennsylvania Station at four o'clock in the afternoon would trundle into Augusta the next day in time for lunch.

It was on his Georgia trips that Ralph got to know an influential Southern reporter—commonly known by his initials—who worked for the *Atlanta Journal*, a widely read newspaper whose motto was "Covers Dixie Like the Dew." Oscar Bane (O. B.) Keeler started to cover Ralph regularly in 1928, and this was probably the most significant event that would lead to an explosion of newspaper coverage for the traveling New Yorker. Newspapers were the primary information source for most Americans, so Ralph's travels were becoming known across the nation. Even readers in small and midsized cities typically had the choice of multiple newspapers each day. New Yorkers had a choice of over ten dailies that were printed in the morning and evening. Extra or special editions were also rushed out if important news had broken.

Keeler and Ralph were contemporaries, born twelve days apart. Not only did Ralph visit with the Southern gentleman regularly on his frequent visits, but he also exchanged letters with him for twenty years. They became such good friends that Keeler ended up closing his letters to Ralph with "Love and kisses." Although Keeler wrote for the *Atlanta Journal*, his column "O. O.'s by O. B." was syndicated nationally; thus, readers across the nation were now starting to follow Ralph's progress, including those in smaller markets reading newspapers such as the *Ames Daily Tribune* (Iowa), the *Corsicana Daily Sun* (Texas), the *Pampa Daily News* (Texas), and the *Kokomo Tribune* (Indiana).

Born in Marietta, Georgia, O. B. began covering Bobby Jones's career when the fourteen-year-old phenom won the Georgia Amateur. Not only did Keeler cover Jones's career, but he also became his protector and ended up handling a lot of Bobby's interactions with the media, in effect acting as his press agent. Jones and Keeler traveled over 150,000 miles together, primarily by train. O. B. co-authored Bobby's 1927 autobiography, *Down the Fairway* (Grantland Rice wrote the foreword), published while Jones was only twenty-five years old. When Bobby signed a contract with Warner Brothers after he retired to do a series of instructional films, Keeler went with him, bringing enough corn whisky to ensure they both remained well hydrated during Prohibition. Keeler chronicled every tournament shot Bobby ever played, and he was the only man to witness all of Jones's major championship victories. Keeler coined the term "Grand Slam" for Jones's feat in 1930, winning all four tournaments that were then considered the most important—the U.S. Open, British Open, U.S. Amateur, and British Amateur.

In his first feature interview with Keeler, Ralph explained that he was not as crazy as he seemed, since his sales job for a pencil company took him regularly to twenty-six states. Ever the modest man, he said, "I am not a crack golfer. I can play a round in the eighties as a rule on a regular course. I've never bettered 100 at Pine Valley, it is true, but I jumped on a couple of little 2,000-yard courses up in Maine not long ago, and beat them to death—a sixty-four and a sixty-six. The two hardest courses I've tried are my home club, Winged Foot, and the new Yale Memorial Course."

The *New York Evening Post* weighed in on Ralph in November, impressed with his accomplishments and accompanying the article with a nice picture of him wearing his tam-o'-shanter, a big cigar dangling out of his mouth. As the year came to a close, the *Herald Tribune* picked up coverage and termed Kennedy "The World's Champion." Through the end of the year, his cumulative course count showed that he played courses in twenty-six states, primarily in the Northeast where he lived; New England, where he vacationed; and the South, where he traveled for business frequently.

Early February 1929 brought unusually mild weather to New York, and Ralph once again boarded a long-distance southbound train, smoke billowing out of its funnel as it labored down the tracks. The salesman was once again on his way to Kentucky and booked plush accommodations, staying at the Brown Hotel in Louisville. Among the courses he enjoyed on his winter trip was the hotel's eighteen-hole Lilliputian course. Not much documentation remains of the course, which was built by "E. A. Shaw (Patents Pending)," according to their scorecard. The card also shows that the course played to a par of forty-two and included twelve holes that had a par of two. The average guidance time given to play for a twosome was a breezy twenty minutes. Players were told to carry only their putters, since the niblicks needed to make the full shots would be found on all pitch shot holes. Ralph considered it a real golf course and numbered it at the top of his scorecard as such. Perhaps it was an indoor course with grass (or a par-2 course), since the scorecard did remind players to replace their divots.

The history of business and golf were intertwined from the game's beginning in America. Not only were wealthy individuals sponsoring new courses, but corporate entities were doing so, as well. Various Standard Oil companies were established in different geographic regions over time, and when the gargantuan company was forced to break up in 1911, Standard Oil of Kentucky—known as Kyso—won the right to the oil operations in Kentucky, Georgia, Florida, Mississippi, and Alabama. During his visit to Kentucky, Ralph played his third company-owned course: the Standard Oil Company of Kentucky course, located in Louisville.

By April, Lou Gehrig was on his way to his 600th consecutive game, and Ralph had played 550 courses. New York's local golf association, the Metropolitan Golf Association (MGA), published their twice-a-year handicap revisions in the newspapers, and by midsummer Ralph was carrying a better-than-average thirteen.

At the height of the stock market boom in 1929, Ralph visited the summer playground of the moneyed class and played six rounds of golf in the Hamptons. He had the chance to sink putts at the nine-hole Bridgehampton Golf Club, the nine-hole Amagansett Golf Club, and the Riverhead Country Club, an eighteen-hole course built in 1921. With good fortune shining on him, he also played the Holy Trinity of East End courses that golfers dream of playing just once in their

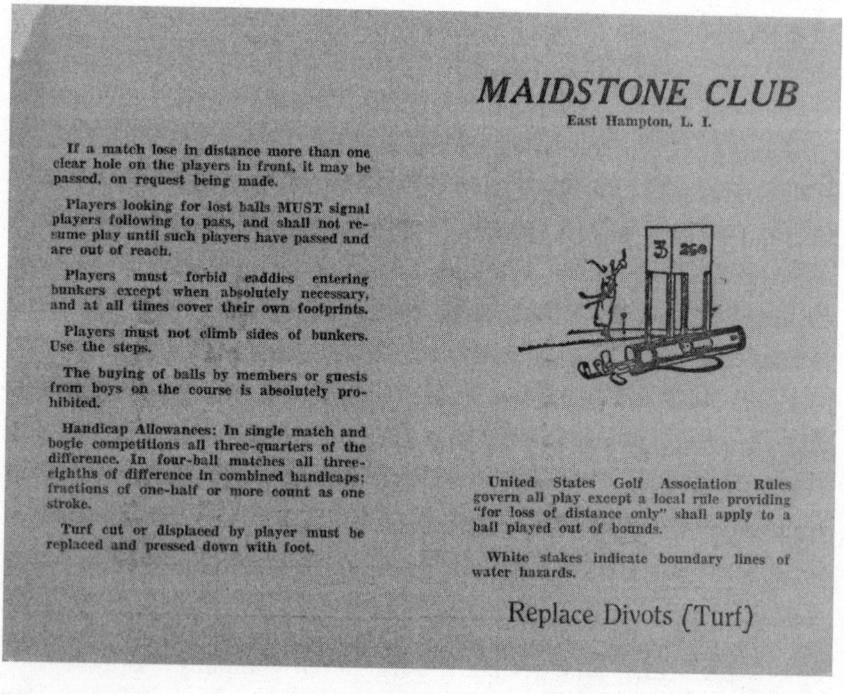
If a match lose in distance more than one clear hole on the players in front, it may be passed, on request being made.

Players looking for lost balls MUST signal players following to pass, and shall not resume play until such players have passed and are out of reach.

Players must forbid caddies entering bunkers except when absolutely necessary, and at all times cover their own footprints.

Players must not climb sides of bunkers. Use the steps.

The buying of balls by members or guests from boys on the course is absolutely prohibited.

Handicap Allowances: In single match and bogie competitions all three-quarters of the difference. In four-ball matches all three-eighths of difference in combined handicaps; fractions of one-half or more count as one stroke.

Turf cut or displaced by player must be replaced and pressed down with foot.

MAIDSTONE CLUB

East Hampton, L. I.

United States Golf Association Rules govern all play except a local rule providing "for loss of distance only" shall apply to a ball played out of bounds.

White stakes indicate boundary lines of water hazards.

Replace Divots (Turf)

The front of the scorecard from Ralph's visit to the Maidstone Club in East Hampton. *(Photo courtesy of USGA)*

lifetime, let alone all three during the same week: Shinnecock Hills, the Maidstone Club, and the National Golf Links of America. The weather matched the brilliance of the course when he golfed at the Willie Park Jr.-designed West Course at Maidstone in East Hampton on July 17th: it was a pleasant seventy-six degrees with fine sunlight pouring down on him, the gentle ocean breezes making club selection tricky. Maidstone is situated directly on the Atlantic, built along a ridge of sand dunes, and the quaint picture on the front of the course's scorecard shows a hand-drawn image of an old-fashioned sand tee box.

Although the first patent in the United States for a tee was issued in 1896, it was for a rubber tee with a slightly concave top, and the idea did not immediately catch on. Dr. George Grant, an early black graduate of Harvard and a dentist, was issued a patent in 1899 for a tee that had a wooden base. His motivation wasn't commercial—he didn't like to get his hands dirty with moist sand—so he didn't develop the idea beyond the patent. The first one-piece tee was patented in 1924, and it was the first to enjoy commercial success. Invented by Dr. William Lowell (also a dentist), it was marketed as the "Reddy Tee" and painted red on the top. Even as tees began to replace sand, courses did not immediately eliminate the old-style sand boxes, as evidenced by the Maidstone card. The Maidstone card also highlights the fact that illegal golf ball sales were a continued problem, stating, "the buying of balls by members or guests from boys on the course is absolutely prohibited."

Maidstone has always been a special place to play golf and has always maintained an affluent membership. Pan American World Airways founder Juan Trippe was an early member; one method he used to get to the course was to pilot his own flying boat from New York City to East Hampton. Unfortunately, Ralph was not able to enjoy the signature drink of Maidstone—a Southside—after his round, since he played during Prohibition.

Three days later, Ralph played again at a club that was a founding member of the USGA, Shinnecock Hills, entering the oldest golf clubhouse in the United States, one built in 1892. The McKim, Mead, &

White-designed shingle-style clubhouse sits at the top of a bluff overlooking the Great Peconic Bay, with a view of the wooden National Golf Links of America windmill in the distance. Among the founders of Shinnecock Hills was William Kissam Vanderbilt, grandson of "Commodore" Vanderbilt, one of the wealthiest men in the country. The Vanderbilts knew how to build impressive houses and owned large mansions in Newport, New York City, and on Long Island; consequently, it is no surprise that the clubhouse the founders commissioned was one of the finest of its day.

The Shinnecock Hills course that Ralph played was one in transition. Their original eighteen-hole layout was revised four times before the current course—designed by William Flynn and Howard Toomey—was completed in 1931. Toomey and Flynn began to make changes to Shinnecock in 1927 when Highway 27 bisected their original course. Ralph played in the midst of the changes being implemented; thus, the myriad of challenges that greet the present-day golfer are a different set, and in a different configuration, than those he encountered. The 1929 course played to a par of seventy and was 6,108 yards long. It began with a par-4 hole named Westward Ho and had a fourth hole named Eastward Ho. The 3rd hole he played was a "Short" prototype, and the 6th a "Biarritz." The exceedingly difficult Redan hole was the 14th on the routing he played, a hole that Charles Blair Macdonald and Seth Raynor designed in 1916, which was not changed during the redesign.

The following day Ralph finished the Triple Crown of Long Island golf by playing the National Golf Links of America in Southampton. The course was less than twenty years old and was highly regarded from the day it opened to universal accolades. Securing access to private clubs typically wasn't difficult for the natural salesman; he regularly played at some of the best clubs the country had and tapped into his extensive web of contacts, and he was also able to leverage the professional at Winged Foot to help. Ralph commented that he had a tough time gaining access to the course, saying, "Probably no course anywhere is more exclusive." He felt it was easier to get into the

White House than it was to get invited to play at the Southampton club and observed that prospective candidates for membership had to wait a decade to be admitted, and that "Golfers from other clubs get no automatic playing privileges at the National." Several years later, Ralph highlighted the fact that "Women apply in vain. As guests they are allowed to play, but must give way to male foursomes. Men who fail to replace divots face a two-week suspension of playing privileges." The National's autocratic founder, Charles Blair Macdonald, was very much at the helm of the club when Ralph played it, and, at the time, the membership rolls included Andrew Mellon, Marshall Field, E. F. Hutton, and Condé Nast.

Light was pouring in from the panoramic wall of windows as the sated golfer had lunch overlooking the National's glorious 18th green, the sparkling waters of the Great Peconic Bay shimmering in the distance. The special lunch at the National is something a golfer

The dining room of the National Golf Links of America in Southampton, New York. *(Author's Collection)*

remembers for as long as they have a memory of the club. Ralph savored his meal there: Long Island lobster served with fishcakes, crab cakes, beef and kidney pie, shepherd's pie, and macaroni and cheese, eaten in a majestic green-colored dining room.

After completing the world-class trio of golf courses, Ralph's preferences were clear. Surprising for a man with such good taste, he wasn't overly impressed with the National: "My criticism of National Golf Links may sound odd, but as I played it the course seemed to have too many great holes. There was, that day at least, no relief, no contrast. I enjoyed Maidstone and Shinnecock Hills, both nearby considerably more."

As the decade was winding down, the nation's total wealth had more than doubled since 1920. New golf courses opened at a rapid rate during the decade, and by 1929 there were just shy of 6,000 nationally. The goal-oriented Kennedy had doubled the number of courses played in three short years, finishing with 645 courses as the decade came to a close with a bang when the stock market crashed on October 29th. Although most Americans would have a tough time over the coming decade as the country entered the Great Depression, Ralph would keep plugging along on his journey.

Before following Ralph on his continuing travels, a brief pause is in order to take a detailed look at the golf club of which he was a founding member.

CHAPTER 6

The Winged Foot Golf Club

THE WINGED FOOT GOLF CLUB was organized in 1921 by members of the New York Athletic Club. Ralph was one of 200 NYAC devotees who founded the golf club, whose logo—like the NYAC's—is based on the Roman god Mercury's winged sandals. Kennedy was urged to be a charter member of the new golf club in a brochure sent to NYAC members: "Do it now. If you walk once around these links we'll have you on our list. Memberships are now selling at $1,350—soon they will be at the final stage, $1,600. We are going to play our golf this year on our wonderful Winged Foot links, will you be with us?" To put the price of joining in perspective, a nice car—a Studebaker Light Six Touring Sedan—sold for about the same amount of money as the cost of joining.

Winged Foot Golf Club's distinctive logo. *(Author's Collection)*

To build their club, Winged Foot obtained 280 acres of land and selected A. W. Tillinghast as the designer for their two championship-caliber courses. Tillinghast had recently completed Baltusrol's courses, and his mandate from Winged Foot was to "Give us a man-sized course." Located in the golf-rich county of Westchester, the club selected ideal terrain for interesting golf, the land having been traversed at least four times over the millennia by ice sheets, which left a distinctive imprint. The ice sheets, part of a geological formation termed the Manhattan Prong, deposited large boulders and left rocky outcroppings in its wake in Manhattan, the Bronx, and Westchester. The courses at Winged Foot were built by 200 workmen using sixty teams of horses and nineteen tractors; and they had a challenge, which involved draining several swamps, cutting down thousands of trees, and blasting several tons of rock.

Among the early ideas considered when the course was under construction was the installation of a radio system throughout the grounds. A transmitter was to be placed on the top of the clubhouse and receiving stations at each tee box so that golfers could be paged while out on the course if needed. The greens committee endorsed the idea to broadcast a reminder at repeated intervals, reminding golfers to "replace divots." Thankfully, the idea was never implemented.

Man-sized courses Tillinghast did indeed build, courses worthy of the learned and athletic membership. The club's opening day brochure described the fairways as generous, since they were more than fifty-five yards wide on average and in some places expanded to sixty-five yards across. Upon its completion, Tillinghast remarked about Winged Foot, "The holes are like men, all rather similar from foot to neck, but with greens showing the same varying characters as human faces."

The courses at Winged Foot have always been accorded respect by the golf world. Featuring tree-lined fairways, their relatively small greens are taxing: the putting surfaces average 5,168 square feet, about three-fourths the size of typical greens. Almost all the greens slope from back to front, putting a premium on a player's ability to place the ball where they intend. On opening day, the East course had a total length of 6,631 yards; the West course played a fraction longer, at 6,697 yards. As was the custom, each of the holes was given a name, typically with a humorous bent to them. The first hole on the East course is named "Reveille," and the final one "Taps." The West course includes a par-3 7th hole named "Babe-in-the-Woods," along with a 17th named "Well-Well." The keys to low scoring at Winged Foot when the course opened: driving the ball long and straight, approaching the greens from the correct angle, keeping your ball below the hole, and putting well.

Serendipitously, the club had its unofficial launch on Saturday June 16, 1923, Ralph's forty-first birthday, although he wasn't among the members teeing it up. Official opening day was September 8, 1923, when members of the New York Athletic Club took on members of the Boston Athletic Club in singles and foursomes matches. The NYAC members played well and beat their counterparts from up north in both matches. Ralph did not play on official opening day, either, but first sent his tee shots bounding down the new fairways of both the East and West courses on September 16, 1923, as course Nos. 163 and

The Winged Foot clubhouse shortly after it opened, in 1929. *(Author's Collection, from Wendehack)*

164, respectively, in his card sequence, shooting a ninety-seven and a ninety-eight. Ralph and Mary Alice both became regular golfers at Winged Foot, playing often over the next several decades.

Winged Foot's iconic clubhouse was designed by architect Clifford Charles Wendehack in the English scholastic-style, using stones taken from the site, and was completed in 1925. The large, rambling clubhouse, one of the finest in the nation, has a generous-sized locker room, a warm and inviting grill room with an oversized fireplace, and several large and well-lit dining rooms and lounges. Already an active and popular member by 1925, Ralph was pictured in Winged Foot's *Putt Putt* magazine, looking the confident golfer that he was, his closely cropped hair parted on the side.

August 3, 1928, was a clear day; but, as is common in New York's summertime, it was hot with heavy air and high humidity. The sticky conditions didn't bother Ralph Kennedy one bit. The founding member got his first hole-in-one ever on the East Course's par-3 3rd hole named "Cave." Since Ralph wasn't particularly long off the tee, he hit a mashie (today's 5-iron) to the 140-yard hole. His ace took a big monkey off his back since Mrs. Kennedy had gotten one seven years before.

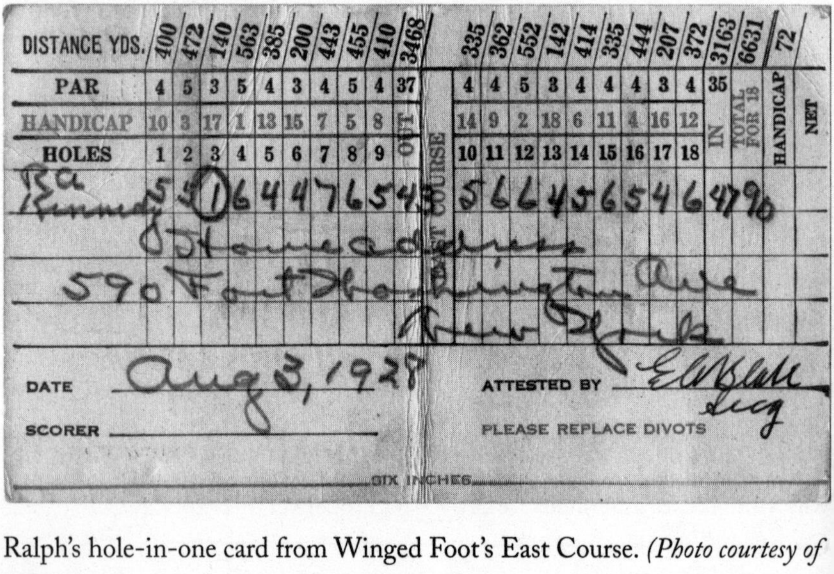

DISTANCE YDS.	400	472	140	563	385	200	443	455	410	3468	335	362	552	142	414	335	444	207	372	3163	6631	72	
PAR	4	5	3	5	4	3	4	5	4	37	4	4	5	3	4	4	4	3	4	35			
HANDICAP	10	3	17	1	13	15	7	5	8		14	9	2	18	6	11	4	16	12				
HOLES	1	2	3	4	5	6	7	8	9	OUT	10	11	12	13	14	15	16	17	18	IN	TOTAL FOR 18	HANDICAP	NET
R.A. Kennedy	5	5	1	6	4	4	7	6	5	43	5	6	6	4	5	6	5	4	6	47	90		

EAST COURSE

Home address

590 Fort Washington Ave

New York

DATE Aug 3, 1928

SCORER

ATTESTED BY

PLEASE REPLACE DIVOTS

SIX INCHES

Ralph's hole-in-one card from Winged Foot's East Course. *(Photo courtesy of USGA)*

Ralph was a passionate golfer and played the club's storied courses in all four seasons. He was among a group of about sixty golfers who would go out regardless of conditions in the winter. The enthusiasts scraped snow off the grass and painted their golf balls red so they could find them. The club even printed a seasonal scorecard for their "Snowbirds" course.

As a measure of how quickly Winged Foot was regarded as a world-class club, USGA secretary Prescott S. Bush awarded the 1929 U.S. Open to the West Course a mere six years after it opened. Five months before the championship, the president of Winged Foot, Nibs Nobles, sent a letter to Ralph, addressed to "Red," asking him to be a scorer for the U.S. Open. A knowledgeable and obviously well-traveled golfer, Ralph served on the greens committee at Winged Foot in the late 1920s and early 1930s, and was on the committee when the Open was held there. Times were good when his home club hosted the national championship during the height of the Roaring Twenties; the Crash of '29 was still four months away. The punchbowl was still out, the party was in full tilt, and people had swagger; markets were rising and women dressed fashionably in flapper garb; it was the apex of the Jazz Age. The frenzied market was such an important part of the era that Nobles had a Stock Exchange Board installed on the clubhouse's veranda so that spectators at the Open could keep up with the market while enjoying the golf.

The buzz going into the tournament was about the West course's "bottle-necked" greens and slim fairways. The *Brooklyn Daily Eagle* noted how "The greens follow a set pattern. They are actually shaped like a bottle with the small end turned toward the fairway. The rear is built up so that there is always a slope against which the player can shoot." The contestants in the 1929 U.S. Open included Gene Sarazen, Walter Hagen, Horton Smith, and Joe Kirkwood. The latter was setting quite a record of his own, playing a substantial number of unique courses, one that potentially rivaled Ralph's. The general consensus was that the course favored the long hitters such as Tommy Armour, Craig Wood, "Wild Bill" Mehlhorn, and Macdonald Smith. Some competitors, who had completed practice rounds, were complaining about the course's "mean" or "dirty" steep-banked bunkers. Although the 1930 U.S. Open at Interlachen in Minnesota the following year was the first to feature a play-by-play radio broadcast of the tournament, the 1929 U.S. Open was the first to feature radio reports from the course, which were transmitted nationally.

Several members of the Newspaper Club covered the tournament in person, including Grantland Rice for the *Herald Tribune.* Ralph's friend O. B. Keeler accompanied Bobby Jones up from Georgia to cover the tournament for the *Atlanta Journal.* His lucky stars fully aligned, Ralph was introduced to the legendary golfer at the Open by Keeler.

Tillinghast gave his insights about the course in the program issued for the tournament: "The key to low scoring over Winged Foot is the consistent play of hard-hit, accurate seconds to the greens, and incidentally the constant driving out far enough to get home under control. The strain of Winged Foot is mental rather than physical, for the absence of hills makes play not arduous. The terrain is pleasantly undulating." He described the myriad of challenges on the par-3 10th hole, beginning with swampland to the right of the fairway. "Either a high drifting iron, probably a two or a spoon, or a slight pull in to the green is necessary here, for trouble is all around: rough and waste land in front and on the right; woods on the left. A green with unusually steep slope."

Tillinghast also described the challenge at the finishing hole: "Missing this green with the second will likely run the score to one more than par, for getting back dead is not easy." The program also contained an article written by Grantland Rice giving hints on how to be a spectator: "Notice how closely Bobby Jones keeps his feet together on all short shots, especially the short pitch, chip shots, and putting. This helps him ward off tension."

Bobby was the favorite going into the tournament, having already won eight major tournaments by age twenty-seven. He arrived eight days before the first round to warm up, and his assessment after a practice round was thus: "If a man doesn't have to play a lot of diagonal shots at those bottle-necked greens his task shouldn't be too hard." Wearing his normal attire of a long-sleeved dress shirt with a tie, Bobby played his first round Thursday at 10:45 a.m. Good weather conditions and a light wind greeted the golfers on their first day, June 27th. Jones got off to a poor start, taking double bogeys on the first and third holes. He quickly improved his chances of staying in contention by gaining multiple strokes on the field over a short stretch, recording a score of three on five consecutive holes to begin the back nine. He finished the day in first place, one stroke ahead of Gene Sarazen and Al Espinosa.

Hopefully, the founding member brought an umbrella, rain slicker, and a change of clothes for his duties as a scorer on the second day, because he would need them. The winds were blowing in the morning, and then a soaking rain began to drench the course in the afternoon. A damp, nasty, and chilly wind, more reminiscent of a British Open than a U.S. Open, was blowing by the time Jones teed off at 2:00 p.m. Putting was the greatest challenge for most competitors because of the soggy conditions, making the greens difficult to navigate. Bobby Jones and Tommy Armour somehow managed their way through the sheets of rain better than the others and were among the notable outstanding putters on the day. There was so much water on the greens that on several holes Jones opted not to use his Calamity Jane putter, instead choosing to putt with his midiron because he felt it would initially get the ball airborne and help to navigate the puddles more effectively. Jones described the second round as one "when every hole was in running water." At the conclusion of the day's play, Jones dropped back into second place, tied with Denny Shute and one stroke behind Sarazen and Espinosa.

The public eagerly anticipated the final thirty-six holes of the thirty-third U.S. Open, to be played on Saturday, and it was shaping up to be a closely contested tournament, with the leaders so tightly bunched after the first two rounds of play. New York City Mayor Jimmy Walker was among the spectators for the Open, as were New York Yankees stars Babe Ruth and Waite Hoyt. Most men wore formal straw hats to the event to keep the sun off their faces; women donned hats with wide brims, or those in the flapper style for the same reason. The fashionable and well-dressed crowds at Winged Foot used hand-held periscopes that were distributed on the course so that spectators could see the action despite the throngs, who paid three dollars each to watch the golf. A. W. Tillinghast was also among the spectators watching the world's best golfers try to defeat his great course. When one fan said to Tillinghast that a "fellow" just took three shots in one of his traps, he shot back, "Well, maybe the trouble isn't with the trap."

Saturday brought improved weather, but it was still windy and Bobby played well during the morning round, carding a seventy-one and taking the sole lead, besting Sarazen and Espinosa by more than three strokes. Jones played consistently over the first seven holes of his final round in the afternoon, but trouble began when he hit a spectator with his tee shot on the eighth hole (note: the spectator was fine). His mashie approach shot missed the green and went into a bunker. His caddie handed him a niblick, which was the standard club then used to hit a sand shot. Bobby wrote in his autobiography two years before that there were two kinds of golf: tournament golf and non-tournament golf, and he always felt that tournament golf took a lot out of a golfer. He was feeling the strain when he hit his niblick less than perfect, and Winged Foot penalized him severely. His wobbly ball landed on the putting surface and then rolled into a bunker on the opposite side of the green. He entered the opposite bunker and did the same thing again, hitting a poor sand shot, and the ball went back into the bunker out of which he had just played. Once the ball was finally on the green, he handed the club back to his caddie, but not before holding it in front of his face and mumbling something to it—presumably not a sweet thought.

Even after recording a seven on the hole, Jones still held the lead, although coming down the stretch nerves continued to haunt him and he played poorly the remainder of the afternoon. He continued to leak oil on the back nine, losing another stroke on the 13th hole, and took another seven on the par-4 15th.

When he missed a short putt at the 16th, he had lost a six-shot lead and needed two fours simply to tie. Managing a par four on the 17th,

Bobby Jones putting at the 1929 U.S. Open at Winged Foot. *(Photo courtesy of USGA)*

he had to par the final hole in regulation in order to make it into a playoff with Espinosa. He missed the last green with his second shot, and as Tillinghast outlined in the program, it is difficult to make par when doing so. After chipping onto the putting surface, he had one final stroke to make. If he didn't sink the putt, he would finish second. Both Keeler and Rice were at the final green to watch the young Georgian navigate his way into the hole. Although both of the great reporters were present, the pressure was too much for them, even as spectators. "I couldn't look," said Keeler after the round. Rice also didn't have the nerve to watch. The explosive crowd reaction when the ball trickled into the hole told them all they needed to know. Both called Jones's curving twelve-foot par putt their greatest thrill in a quarter of a century following the game.

The playoff was set for the following day, Sunday, and was delayed as both Jones and Espinosa went to church in the nearby town of Rye and were late getting to the course. The playoff was anticlimactic. Jones blew Espinosa out by twenty-three strokes and carded an impressive thirty-three on the final nine holes. The *New York Times* said Jones was unbeatable and called him a "human machine on the links." The toll that the tournament took on him is visible in pictures taken during the trophy presentation. Jones barely ate during tournaments—in the 1925 U.S. Open, he lost twelve pounds in three days. He typically fasted during competitive rounds—for breakfast he had one piece of bacon, a small chop, and a cup of black coffee; and for lunch he had a slice of dry toast and a cup of tea—because he thought he played better when he ate light. It is a skinny, although, as usual, well-dressed and exhausted Jones who is pictured accepting the trophy from USGA president Findlay Douglas. After the tournament, Jones took the train home with O. B. Keeler for some needed rest. Keeler commented years later that he felt that Bobby won the U.S. Open over those early five holes in his first round when he carded nothing but threes.

The scribes working the typewriters were not particularly kind to the Mexican-American Espinosa after his defeat. In addition to calling him "chubb," one reporter wrote that "Espinosa isn't temperamentally a champion. The likeable son of sunny Spain just hasn't in his blood the acquisitiveness of the Conquistadores who trod the Americas pillaging, pirating, and continually fighting for the glory of Spain and the love of the thing."

Contributing to Bobby's victory was the fact that he generally avoided many of the difficult Tillinghast traps on the course, although his win was not without controversy. On the final regulation round, he was able to lift his ball from an unseeded area when he hit it off line on the 13th hole (named "White Mule"). Some reporters thought he was given special treatment because of his star status. Previous players who had hit to the same spot simply hit the ball out. Jones did not. He asked for a ruling, which he was entitled to, and was told by an official that he could take relief.

Winged Foot proved a true championship test for the 1929 U.S. Open. Tillinghast told *American Golfer* about his design philosophy for the course: "Winged Foot offers an unusual number of holes where, under normal conditions the brassie [fairway wood] is called into play for the second shots. There was a reason for this, for when the Winged Foot courses were created, it was impressed upon me that the course for the most part would be played by athletes, men of strength, for most of them as members of the New York Athletic Club have been prominent in various branches of sports. It was to measure up to real 'he' standards. Certainly I consider Winged Foot one of my best creations."

It was undeniably a different era in terms of social norms. A newspaperman for the *Brooklyn Daily Eagle*, commenting on Jones's victory and his continued momentum, spoke with someone at Bobby's home club and referred to him as the "Shinny, ebon-visaged Walter Kennon, darky locker room boy at the East Lake Club down in Atlanta." He was the same reporter who disparaged Espinosa—Ralph Trost—and he also called Winged Foot unfair because it called for "super-perfect" shots. He noted that even though Jones scored three eagles and

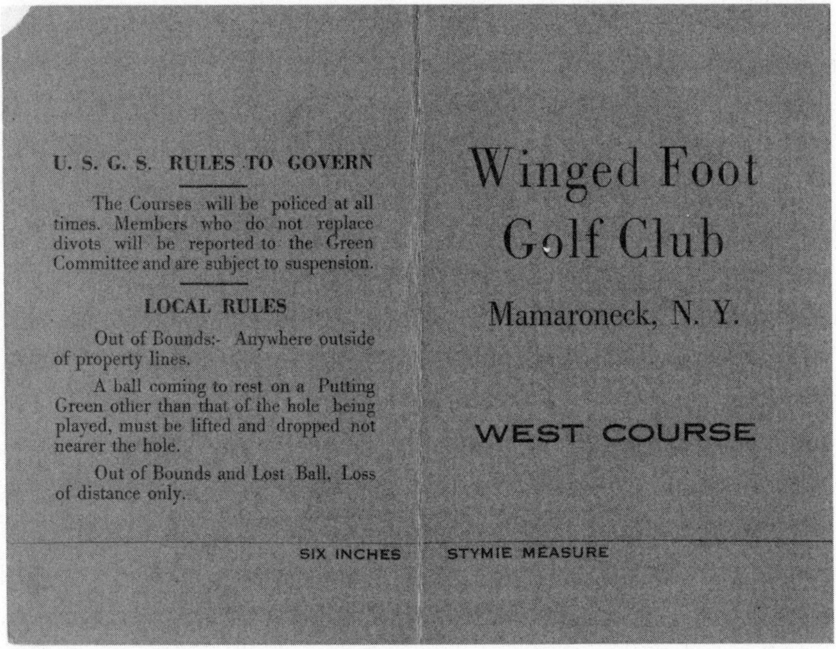

Ralph's first scorecard from the West Course, showing a stymie measure along the bottom. *(Photo courtesy of USGA)*

seventeen birdies, he still finished six strokes over par using his hickory-shafted clubs: "Machiavelli couldn't have done a more subtle job than the architect who created the Winged Foot greens. Those 'kidney traps' stuck into the sides of the greens were treacherous." As the Open came to a close, Red was a happy man. He had indisputably had an auspicious start to his time at Winged Foot: playing more than his fair share of golf, scoring his first ace, meeting Bobby Jones, and witnessing a memorable major championship.

The Kennedys continued to enjoy Winged Foot and played there often. Ralph's best score at the club was an eighty-three, which he shot on the East Course in 1932. Several years after the Open, the *Herald Tribune* ran a picture of four Art Deco era-dressed golfers wearing their flapper hats, with the caption "Four Women Golfers." Among them was Mary Alice, who was competing in a ladies' pajama tournament played at Winged Foot.

The Great Depression that began shortly after the 1929 U.S. Open took its toll on many clubs. Between 1932 and 1952, through a combination of tough economic times, war, and the ever-expanding need for land to build housing, more than 600 clubs nationally went out of business. Winged Foot's membership decreased from a high of 589 members in 1929 down to a scant 201 in 1933, the Kennedys remaining among them. Membership rebounded only to be hit again, like all clubs, during the Second World War. The *Herald Tribune* noted in June 1942 that membership had dropped from 564 to 480, and that the course had to cut down on maintenance due to gas rationing, implementing measures such as the use of scythes to cut the grass instead of lawnmowers. To conserve gas, members took the train instead of driving to the course.

The Kennedys were fortunate to be served by accomplished professionals at Winged Foot, including two Masters champions. Craig Wood represented the club when he won the 1941 Masters, serving as professional from 1939 through 1945. Claude Harmon also won at Augusta National while serving as the professional, succeeding Wood in 1945, winning the Masters in 1948, and continuing as professional until 1978. Tommy Armour was also a member of the club for almost two decades.

In addition to the 1929 U.S. Open, Winged Foot continued to host USGA events over the years. Ralph and Mary Alice also attended the 1940 U.S. Amateur held on the West Course. The weather was brilliant for the mid-September tournament finale, and their fellow member Dick Chapman earned championship honors. In the final match, Chapman walloped Pine Valley's Duff McCullough, 11 & 9, closing him out on the ninth green, the largest margin of victory in the Amateur since Charles Blair MacDonald's victory at Newport in 1895. The 1949 Walker Cup was contested on the West Course, and Ralph told the newspapers he was looking forward to it, and to seeing old friends from around the country who were competing.

Winged Foot provided the perfect milieu for Ralph as a lover of the game. The club's credo from 1923 was in sync with Ralph's personality: "If you have not known life in the open, and the companionship of men, you have not lived." Ralph remained ever faithful to Winged Foot and told the USGA *Journal* at the end of his playing career that he still loved his home course: "I don't know any course less taxing for the man of advancing age, there are no hills to climb. Yet, nobody ever murders our par." He also said, proudly, "Winged Foot doesn't take its hat off to anybody."

CHAPTER 7

El Gran Jugador de Golf

Although the Great Depression would take a heavy toll on most Americans (and many golf clubs), being a successful salesman for a large pencil company helped insulate Ralph from hardship. After all, as a consumer staple, there was always a need for pencils, and it proved to be a depression-proof business. The Crash of '29 was caused by a variety of factors, including market speculators using too much margin debt. It was not only the wealthy who were engaging in stock trading, but ordinary Americans were obsessed with the market, and they began speculating in large numbers. Market speculators used their candlestick-type phones in 1929; the profit seekers would bark their instructions into the fixed base of their phones while holding up the receiver to their ear. A record number of Americans were using their phones to call their brokers, whose offices were connected by "wire" (telegraph or telephone) back to their home office. "Wire house" branches opened across the country in the twenties—Charlie Merrill opened his first office in 1914—as more Americas joined in "the market." The era is perfectly encapsulated in the comments attributed to Joseph Kennedy—father of the future president—when he is said to have sold all his investments after getting a stock tip from a shoe shine boy in 1928.

By the time of the market meltdown on Black Tuesday, air travel had yet to grow into a large and viable industry. Although aviators continued to perform various endurance feats, during 1929 there were only 165,000 air passengers transported in the United States. As the new decade began, Harland Sanders started his first restaurant, the Sanders Court and Café, as part of a Standard Oil of Kentucky gas station in Corbin, Kentucky.

The new year brought Ralph some early bad news, when on the third day, his friend and early playing partner Clare Briggs passed away at the age of fifty-four. Grantland Rice and Rube Goldberg were among the many attending his funeral in New York. The accolades Briggs received were many, including one from the publisher of the *Herald Tribune,* who said he was "undoubtedly one of the greatest comic artists that American journalism ever produced." Former president, then chief justice, William Howard Taft even weighed in on Briggs's death, saying, "I've very much enjoyed his cartoons and am very sorry to hear of his death."

Despite the tough economic conditions and death of his friend, Ralph had one of his most productive years on the golf course in 1930. He knocked off more than one hundred courses and played a large number of them in New York, including many Upstate; he also played over fifteen in Massachusetts, with a concentration in the central and western parts of the state. Additionally, he traveled west and south on the country's byways, looking for golf in less traveled nooks, visiting Texas, Missouri, Indiana, Ohio, and Virginia, in addition to continuing his periodic visits to Kentucky, Georgia, and Tennessee. He also visited Florida, a state he did not visit often, and played a cluster of courses in the Tampa area. He told the *Evening Independent* that he was impressed with the Lakewood Estates Country Club in St. Petersburg, where he relayed with amazement, "the greens and fairways are kept clipped by the pasturage of a flock of goats."

One of his more eclectic accomplishments for the year was setting a record by playing golf in four different counties on the same day. He chose Arkansas as the venue and followed the meandering path of the Arkansas River southward on February 13th, playing the Clarksville Country Club, the Russellville Country Club, the Morrilton Country

Club, and the Conway Country Club, all nine-hole courses. His plans were thrown into disarray when his train was thirty minutes late on the last leg to Conway. As he tells the tale, "Determined to finish anyway, I rounded up a pro and six caddies and set out. The first six holes I played in twilight, the next two at dusk, the last—a 545-yard par-5 punisher—in almost total darkness. I would hit the ball, and a cry would go up from my far-flung caddies: 'Anybody hear it?' Miraculously enough, I was on the green in four and, by the light of a match held over the cup, holed out in five. Trying the same hole by daylight the next morning, I took a seven!" Calling on his liberal arts studies at Amherst, the *cum laude* graduate described his feat in poetic terms: "Only Gustave Doré or Edgar Allan Poe could have done justice to that night setting, but somehow I holed the putt, steering it home for the beacon light."

The 1930 census showed that the Kennedys had moved to 590 Fort Washington Avenue, a six-story multi-family apartment building that was built ten years earlier. Ralph and Mary Alice were living alone, and they would live at the address for the remainder of their lives. Their neighborhood remained one with a high proportion of immigrants, including many Russians, but also a large number of Irish. Their neighbors' varied occupations included several salesmen, a contractor, a jobber, a stenographer, an attorney, and an advertising man. Consumer technology was evolving during this era, as was the census. No longer asking if the resident was a Civil War survivor, the census taker now asked each household whether they had a radio set in the home. The answer for the Kennedys was yes.

It was an exciting summer for those following the rapid developments in aviation. May 31st brought the arrival of the Graf Zeppelin from South America, broadcast live on the radio from the hanger at the Lakehurst naval air station. The transmission began at 6:55 p.m. and went until 8:15 p.m., the announcer thrilling listeners with a blow-by-blow of the docking. A naval observer on board the dirigible predicted that within three years, there would be regularly scheduled passenger and mail service across the Atlantic in the lighter-than-air machines because it was such an efficient form of travel. Dirigible technology was improving and had become more reliable. On early flights, airships were damaged by weather; however, by 1930, navigation had progressed and dirigibles could better maneuver around storms. At the time, it was unclear which form of air travel would dominate in the future: airships, flying boats, or "heavier-than-air" planes. Speculation was that airplanes would be useful for short routes, flying five hundred miles at a time from one city to another. Blimps were thought to have an advantage for long-distance trips.

In June, Kennedy visited the City of Brotherly Love, and among the courses he played were the Lu Lu Temple Country Club and the Philadelphia Cricket Club's Flourtown Course. He took the subway to Lower Manhattan on July 2nd to see a ticker tape parade in honor of Bobby Jones. Jones was being feted not for his Winged Foot victory the year before, but instead, for winning the British Open and British Amateur championships in 1930. It was the second time Jones was honored with a ticker tape parade; the first was in 1926 after he won

Bobby Jones (center, with hat off) walking with dignitaries up Broadway in a 1926 ticker tape parade in his honor. *(Photo courtesy of Corbis)*

the British Open. Only the naval aviator Richard E. Byrd has been honored with more ticker tape parades than Jones, being showered in paper three times.

Ralph took one of the most significant trips of all his travels in the late summer, one that he enjoyed telling stories about for the rest of his life. The *Los Angeles Times* carried a small article in their August 6th edition, announcing that the itinerant golfer had set sail on the *Santa Inez* to play golf in South America, toting two trunks of golfing equipment. Ralph's goal at the beginning of 1930 was as grand as it would ever be; he told the *Times* that his ambition was to play every important course in the world, filling in the odd idle days by playing the "unimportant ones." They appeared to get most details about him right, although they did call him a "wealthy retired businessman," and he was neither wealthy nor retired.

Accompanied by his brother Robert, the pair started their journey traveling to Brooklyn. Their ship launched from the Hamilton Avenue pier bound for Valparaiso, Chile. The diesel-powered vessel they boarded had four decks and was operated by the Grace Line. Already a city of seven million, New York was the busiest harbor in the country, and the comings and goings of ships—sometimes including a list of prominent passengers onboard—was reported in a full page in the newspaper every day. Their ship had accommodations for seventy first-class and forty intermediate-class passengers; it had proper beds rather than berths and no inside state rooms. Its amenities included a swimming pool, social hall, lounge, smoking room, café, and, most important for Ralph, a space to practice golf.

After passing through the Canal Zone, the ship's itinerary featured various South American Pacific Coast cities. The scheduled ports of call were Cristobal, Canal Zone; Guayaquil, Ecuador; Callao (Lima's port), Mollendo, and Iquique, Peru; and Valparaiso, Chile. Six leisurely days after departing New York, the Kennedys had arrived in Panama, and on August 11th Ralph was itching to play golf. His most dramatic request for a tee time was from on board his ship. A ship-to-shore "Radiogram" message was sent from the *Santa Inez* at 9:52 a.m.: "Can

The Gatun Golf Course in Panama, adjacent to the Canal. *(Photo courtesy of University of Florida)*

Mr. Kennedy play golf in Gatun at 2:30 this afternoon?" Although a record only survives of the outbound message, we know from card No. 756 that Ralph was indeed able to get up a game that afternoon.

American Golfer described the Gatun Golf Club in 1916, jokingly calling it "The most expensive golf course in the world" because of the cost of constructing the canal. Built on dredged land and located between the Gatun Locks and the spillway near the Atlantic end of the canal, it was a verdant course kept in good condition by a herd of four hundred sheep. With a tropical climate, Panama gets one hundred inches of rain a year, ideal growing conditions for Bermuda grass, which thrives there. President Warren G. Harding, an avid golfer who played there a decade before Ralph visited, was among the early golfers to enjoy Gatun. A fairly rudimentary course, by 1922 *American Golfer* described its 2,778 yards as golf of the "poor man variety."

Ralph played an expanded version of 5,787 yards, accompanied by the professional, George Dewar. The Gatun Golf Course gave new definition to the term "water hazard," since the spillways and locks surrounding the course played as out of bounds. Although the first hole was only 351 yards long, it was eclectic, because it was 300 feet wide and situated between the seventy-foot-high canal locks as hazards on

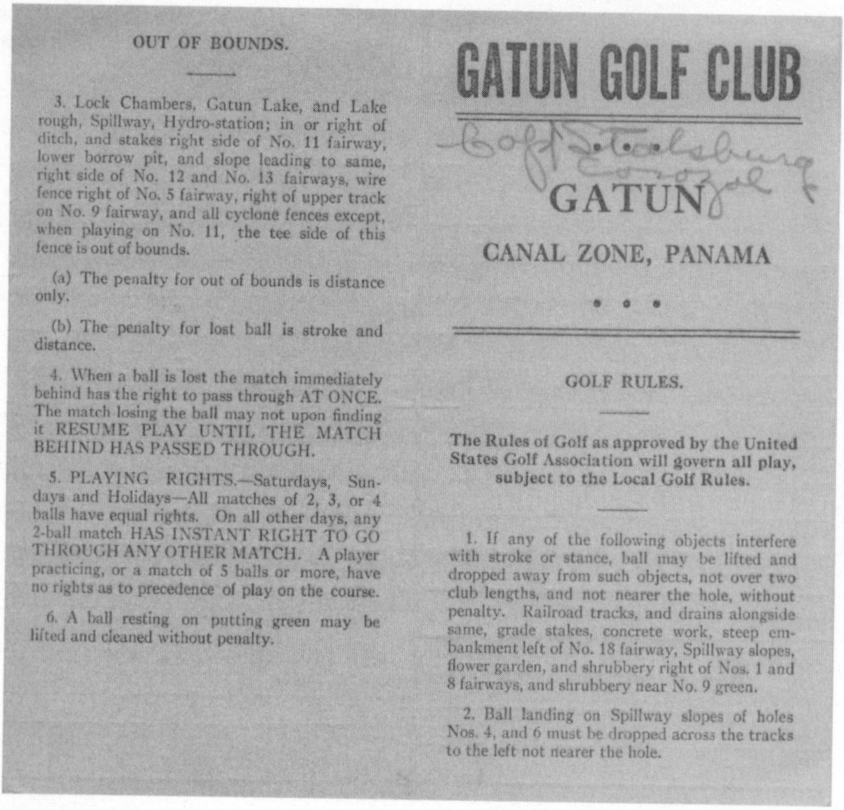

OUT OF BOUNDS.

3. Lock Chambers, Gatun Lake, and Lake rough, Spillway, Hydro-station; in or right of ditch, and stakes right side of No. 11 fairway, lower borrow pit, and slope leading to same, right side of No. 12 and No. 13 fairways, wire fence right of No. 5 fairway, right of upper track on No. 9 fairway, and all cyclone fences except, when playing on No. 11, the tee side of this fence is out of bounds.

(a) The penalty for out of bounds is distance only.

(b) The penalty for lost ball is stroke and distance.

4. When a ball is lost the match immediately behind has the right to pass through AT ONCE. The match losing the ball may not upon finding it RESUME PLAY UNTIL THE MATCH BEHIND HAS PASSED THROUGH.

5. PLAYING RIGHTS.—Saturdays, Sundays and Holidays—All matches of 2, 3, or 4 balls have equal rights. On all other days, any 2-ball match HAS INSTANT RIGHT TO GO THROUGH ANY OTHER MATCH. A player practicing, or a match of 5 balls or more, have no rights as to precedence of play on the course.

6. A ball resting on putting green may be lifted and cleaned without penalty.

GATUN GOLF CLUB

GATUN

CANAL ZONE, PANAMA

• • •

GOLF RULES.

The Rules of Golf as approved by the United States Golf Association will govern all play, subject to the Local Golf Rules.

1. If any of the following objects interfere with stroke or stance, ball may be lifted and dropped away from such objects, not over two club lengths, and not nearer the hole, without penalty. Railroad tracks, and drains alongside same, grade stakes, concrete work, steep embankment left of No. 18 fairway, Spillway slopes, flower garden, and shrubbery right of Nos. 1 and 8 fairways, and shrubbery near No. 9 green.

2. Ball landing on Spillway slopes of holes Nos. 4, and 6 must be dropped across the tracks to the left not nearer the hole.

Ralph's card from the lost golf club in the Canal Zone. *(Photo courtesy of USGA)*

one side and a steep slope on the other. When the course was built it wasn't fully excavated, so beneath the lush grass golfers sometimes hit buried rocks. Ralph's card explains the myriad of hazards outlined by the local rules that give relief from a host of man-made obstructions, including spillways and lock chambers.

Kennedy opined on the course's innumerable tropical charms: "Raymond Ditmars would feel at home on the Gatun links. The curator of reptiles would be so interested in the tiny green lizards that teem on the fairways that he mightn't keep his eye on the ball. Talk about quick movers, those bijou saurians can dart from here to there faster than the human hand can grab 'em. A local concession allows you to remove all lizards in the line of your putt, but try to do it!"

The following day, Ralph played the Radio Golf Club located in Balboa, near the Pacific outlet of the canal. Not much is known of the 2,122-yard nine-hole course, although it did not appear to be particularly challenging, its longest par four playing a compact 319 yards. There is no record of Ralph playing the Panama Country Club in the Far Hills archives since the Radio course was course No. 757, and his next sequentially numbered card was in Ecuador, although he spoke about the club at length with *Golf Illustrated* in 1934, using extraordinary language to describe the virtues of the location: "The Panama Country Club offers an equally enchanting glimpse of the Pacific Ocean limned against a background of palm stippled rolling hills. A thatched-roof hacienda . . . serves as the 19th hole hire, an outdoor replica of Sloppy Joe's Havana bar. Here is an El Dorado for those who like a dash of atmosphere with their drinking."

The brothers' next port of call, on August 15th, was eight hundred miles south in Guayaquil, the primary port of Ecuador. Although a Pacific Coast city, it sits at the same longitude as Toronto, given the shapes of the continental land masses. Located directly below the equator, the city was known for its alligator hunts, and as one of the primary places where Panama hats were made. The journey from the ocean into the city was an exciting one along the Guayas River, bordered by deep jungle on both sides. With an equatorial climate, Guayaquil receives an average annual rainfall total of thirty-six inches, all of it concentrated between January and May. The intense weather creates a situation where there are either torrential rains or, alternatively, desert-like conditions.

The nine-hole course at Guayaquil represented a unique philosophy in architectural design. Golfers often describe how a course can be played repeatedly and will never play the same way twice because of shifting winds, weather conditions, different tee boxes, and pin positions. The course at Guayaquil was an actual manifestation of the idea. As Ralph told the *New Yorker*, "The course I played in Guayaquil, Ecuador is under water six months of the year. When it's not, it's run through with six-inch-wide cracks. It has to be laid out again every year. The greens are made of cement, and when the ball hits one of them it bounces sixty to eighty feet. I had a terrible score." He gave O. B. Keeler entertaining accounts of his time there: "The fairways are baked and cracked mud. The 'greens' are of the same texture. You have to pick the ball up cleanly, as if playing off brick pavement. It took me a couple of holes to get the knack—I started with a seven and a six, but after that I managed fairly well and finished with an eighty-seven, defeating Saunders, the club champion, 5 & 4. He did a ninety-two. They regarded me as an expert after that. The club has 100 members, all enthusiastic."

The local rules on the card validate Ralph's exotic description of the course. Rule number five allowed the golfer to place their ball wherever they chose within one club length (not nearer the hole), while in the *fairway*. Rule number eight allowed balls on the putting greens to be lifted, and the ground to be smoothed before putting.

The headline in the local newspaper the day after Ralph's round, using roughly the same size font that newspapers in the United States would use when the Japanese bombed Pearl Harbor some years later, was "EL HOMBRE DE LAS MIL CANCHAS ESTUVO AQUI," letting readers know that the Man of a Thousand Links was in town playing their rudimentary course. He is pictured with two dozen or so of the enthusiastic members he mentioned, all dressed in white, wearing bow ties and Panama hats. Ralph, as usual, is beaming. They called him a player of merit, with good style and knowledge, describing his calculated moves and said that his game was near perfection. "El Gran Jugador de Golf," or the Great Player of Golf, as they referred to him, had just finished one of his most interesting courses. Ralph loved adventurous golf stories and recounted his tale in Guayaquil for the rest of his life when he spoke to reporters or at schools, Rotary meetings, or as an after-dinner speaker.

Like Magellan riding the high seas in search of new discoveries, the Kennedys next journeyed to Talara, Peru, another port city on the Pacific Coast. After dropping anchor in the hook-shaped, sheltered bay, the brothers were brought ashore by a smaller boat. Talara's boom came when oil was discovered in the late nineteenth century. Refineries began to locate there in the 1890s, and by the 1920s multi-national oil companies, including Standard Oil, were operating the Negritos field at Talara. Although there are no records of the course "architect," since foreign oil companies operated in the area, it isn't too much to speculate that homesick expatriates laid out a course. The course at Talara (course No. 759) was also unique, and quite different from his experience in Ecuador; it was situated in a stark desert environment, built on black sand with no grass at all.

To say the course had no grass is not an exaggeration. Surviving period pictures of the course show a bleak and desolate environment; in the distance, behind the golf course, are bare mountains, and beyond them, oil tanks. The scenic beauty of Pebble Beach it was not. The opposite of his Ecuadorian adventure, Talara has near-drought conditions almost all the time, receiving less than two inches of rainfall a year. The course presented a host of challenges for the vacationing golfer with sands blowing and shifting and penal holes. On one par three, the golfer had to hit their shot to a green one hundred and fifty yards away and a strenuous seventy-five feet above the tee box. Ralph

The bleak landscape of the Talara course in Peru. *(Robert S. Platt Collection, University of Wisconsin, Milwaukee)*

told *Golf Illustrated*'s George Trevor, "When a shot hits the fairway at Talara, the ball digs in for the duration and lies there like a dinosaur's egg in the Gobi Desert, cradled in a miniature crater." He played the nine-hole course with Tommy Thompson, presumably a member who worked in the oil industry locally. Transportation to and from Talara was by automobiles that had been modified to run on railroad tracks.

Endlessly entertained by his visit to Peru, Ralph told his friend Trevor, "Some Peruvian got the bright idea of sinking concrete foundations for the greens on the order of the cement gun platforms on which the German Big Berthas [World War I howitzers] rested. Visitors are told to use a high pitch to the sand greens. Sometimes the ball will bounce seventy-five feet and shoot off into the desert. Do the natives get a laugh!"

The next course he played was Negritos, located seven miles south, occupying the westernmost point of the continent. Kennedy's expectations of an exotic vacation were being met at every turn; transport to the course was in a truck that transited through a tunnel carved through the mountains. A crude and sandy nine-hole course, there is no scorecard of Negritos in the USGA collection because it was so basic a layout that it existed without a clubhouse and printed cards. He was thrilled by the uniqueness of it; as he told the *New Yorker*, "In Talara and Negritos you play on the desert. When your ball hits, it sinks into the sand. You're allowed to dig for it and place it where you can hit it." He elaborated farther on the environs to *Golf Illustrated*: "Typical Sahara Desert scenery—not a tree or a blade of grass within a hundred miles—the whole damn thing just one vast sand trap."

The Kennedys' antipodean adventure continued seven hundred miles farther south. Their boat docked in Callao harbor, and the dyad "motored" to Lima thirty miles away. The hearty and fit NYAC member played next at the Country Club of Lima located in the city's San Isidro neighborhood, as course No. 761, on August 22nd. The eighteen-hole course was built in 1924, and its elaborate clubhouse, in 1927. The holes on their unusual scorecard were numbered in Roman numerals.

Ralph, at this point forty-eight years old, was smitten with the entire experience at Lima and reflected back on it several years later, working himself into a lather: "The vivid flamingoes that saunter . . . across the Lima, Peru Country Club links furnish an eye-dazzling spectacle. Seen en masse those flocks of salmon-pink, tapering-necked birds remind you of a Joseph Urban theatre backdrop. You rub your eyes and blame it on that double Daiquiri cocktail you've just inhaled at the sumptuous bar." He continued to lay it on: "That Lima clubhouse is the last word in opulent magnificence. We supposedly lavish Yanks are mere pikers compared to the Peruvians when it comes to sinking money in a golfing pleasure-dome. Even Kubla Khan would blink his eyes if he could see that two and a half million-dollar Lima edifice built of Pyrrian marble imported from Italy. The nearest approach to the Lima Country Club in America is the palatial Mountain Brook structure at Birmingham, Alabama. This remodeled pre-war mansion, redolent of the Deep South of swords and roses, is remarkable for its priceless murals."

It seems, however, that Kennedy's frugal Scottish blood didn't exactly approve of such lavish spending: "To my mind such elaborate embellishments smack of the tail wagging the dog. A simpler setting best reflects the essentially democratic nature of golf." It's too bad that Ralph never took the time to write a book about his adventures, because with language like he used to describe the Country Club of Lima, he had an engaging and colorful style.

For their return journey, the Kennedys boarded a different Grace Line vessel, the *Santa Elisa,* which departed Valparaiso, Chile, on August 18th and picked them up in Callao several days later. Ralph said that he played in Colombia, Bolivia, and Chile, although there are no records documenting which courses he played in Far Hills, and his sequence of cards doesn't account for any such courses. Curiously, at the time, Colombia only had one course, located in Bogota; and land-locked Bolivia had one course, as well, named Oruro, a city far from the coast. Since records show they returned on the *Santa Elisa,* based on the ship's route it appears they never made it to Chile.

His next numbered card, course No. 762, dated August 27th, was back up the coast in Ecuador, this time in the port city of Ancon, another small camp-town near the sea, not far from Guayaquil. Ancon was settled in the early 1900s by British engineers working in the petroleum business. Ralph played the Ancon course with the same J. F. Saunders he played with at Guayaquil, beating him again, this time by six strokes. The Ancon card, like the card at Teterboro several years earlier, shows only hole numbers. It was the player's responsibility to write in the length of the hole and its bogey as they played what was presumably a course that changed frequently. Ralph's next course is unaccounted for; there is no card No. 763 among his cache of South American cards. Perhaps the missing card was either in Colombia or Bolivia, or maybe the Panama Country Club he waxed so eloquently about.

The *Santa Elisa* continued its eastbound passage returning through the Panama Canal, splashing through the turquoise waters of the Caribbean north to New York, but not without a quick stop in the tropical paradise of Havana. Havana is guarded by the imposing Castillo San Salvador de la Punta, a fortress protecting the narrow entrance to its harbor. Inside the sparkling blue waters is the Malecón, a four-mile-long rampart, behind which sits a beautiful esplanade and roadway. Ralph and Robert were excited to visit Old Havana with its narrow, winding streets, exploring it when it was an expanding and energetic city filled with gleaming new buildings and bright prospects. The city's prosperity was fueled by the sugar trade; its broad avenues were chock-full of well-dressed citizens promenading up and down the wide thoroughfares—the Prado being the most prominent—and under grand allées of trees. The country had just completed building a splendid Capitol Building, one larger than the U.S. Capitol, and it was the centerpiece of the city. Cuba was a popular destination during Prohibition because visitors could drink to their heart's content, and there were scores of casinos and luxury hotels. The cigar-smoking Kennedy reveled being in Cuba and enjoyed the plump and supple freshly rolled stogies close to the source.

Known as the "Paris of the Caribbean," Havana was a cosmopolitan city. Despite being in a tropical climate, its men dressed formally, wearing dress shirts, ties, and straw hats, and its women stylish, long dresses. The city had a modern university, a new palace for its president, and fine parks. Prosperity was everywhere in 1930 Havana. In addition to a well-regarded golf course, the nearby Vedado Tennis Club was popular with wealthy Americans because it was easily accessible by Pan Am Clippers that flew into Havana harbor from Key West.

Located eight miles from the city center, the Country Club of Havana was built in 1912 by Donald Ross through a small valley near the Almendares River. The area the course was built in had a multitude of challenges including out of bounds over a wall on the 5th hole and off the 14th fairway, beyond an old lime kiln. A demanding course dotted with palm trees, it had plenty of water, since the river snaked through the routing frequently. On four holes, the scorecard contained rules outlining what to do if an errant ball went into the river. Ralph's completed scorecard has the usual RAK written in as the scorer on September 5, 1930, as course No. 764. Playing in his usual plus fours,

The Country Club of Havana pictured in a period postcard. *(Author's Collection)*

he shot an eighty. Ralph rated the course among his favorites, as he did their sprawling clubhouse.

When the brothers sailed back into New York Harbor at the conclusion of their month-long trip, they were greeted by the completed site of the extraordinary Art Deco Chrysler Building, which had recently opened at Forty-Second Street and Lexington Avenue. The tallest building in the world when it opened, the gleaming skyscraper was clad in stainless steel, and its distinctive tapered crown was a sight to behold. The 185-foot spire was secretly raised at the building's completion so that it would rise above the pyramidal top of the seventy-two-story, copper-clad Bank of the Manhattan Building (40 Wall Street), which was completed the month before and held the tallest building distinction for only one month.

Shortly after the conclusion of Ralph's South American adventure, Bobby Jones completed the Grand Slam, on September 27th. During his last major tournament, the U.S. Amateur, played at the Merion Cricket Club, it was Bobby Jones against Englewood's Eugene Homans in the final match, played over thirty-six holes. Jones got off to a quick start and won four holes on Homans; it was only by laying Jones a stymie on the seventh hole that Homans was able to win just one hole on the front nine of their competition.

After returning home, Ralph traveled north to play once again in Massachusetts, at the Whitinsville Golf Club, another course built for the benefit of company employees, this time for the Whitin Machine Works. When the course was designed and built by Donald Ross in 1925, Whitin was the largest manufacturer of textile machinery in the world.

Ralph's far-reaching nautical journey had motivated him to up his tempo as the historic year was winding down. He didn't let the change of seasons deter him from some cool weather golf in Connecticut. Walking among the barren trees, Ralph could hear a rhythmic honking sound above, which was drowning out the sound of fallen leaves crackling under his shoes. Flocks of Canadian geese above were in full migration down the Atlantic flyway as another golf sprint was unfolding. The former collegiate miler kept up his typical torrid schedule, playing nine courses in all corners of the state in a short time, as he was now a man on a mission. He played at the Salmon Brook Country Club in Granby, the Shennecossett Country Club in New London, the Shuttle Meadow Club in New Britain, the Pequabuck Golf Club in Terryville, and the New Haven Country Club.

The *Hartford Courant* ran the following headline on November 2nd: "Ralph Kennedy Expects to Play 1000 Golf Courses." Explaining the method to the madness, "His business carries him into twenty-four states each year and golf course architects are constantly building new tests for him. He has played his 776th course and expects to round out an even 800 before the year closes. One hundred next year and another 100 in 1932 and his goal will have been reached. He has not planned

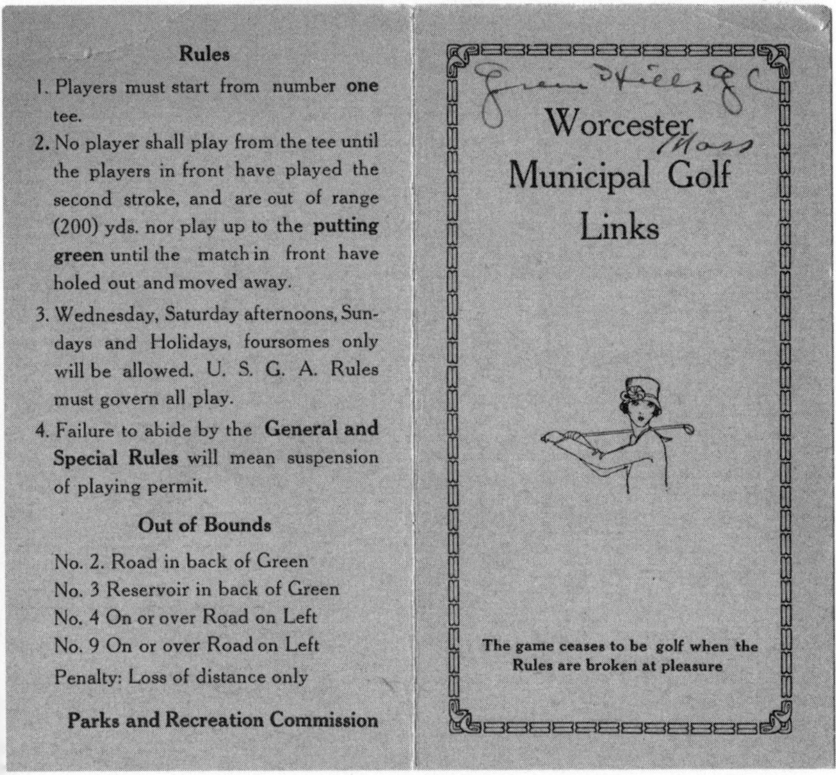

Rules

1. Players must start from number **one** tee.
2. No player shall play from the tee until the players in front have played the second stroke, and are out of range (200) yds. nor play up to the **putting green** until the match in front have holed out and moved away.
3. Wednesday, Saturday afternoons, Sundays and Holidays, foursomes only will be allowed. U. S. G. A. Rules must govern all play.
4. Failure to abide by the **General and Special Rules** will mean suspension of playing permit.

Out of Bounds

No. 2. Road in back of Green
No. 3 Reservoir in back of Green
No. 4 On or over Road on Left
No. 9 On or over Road on Left
Penalty: Loss of distance only

Parks and Recreation Commission

Worcester Municipal Golf Links

The game ceases to be golf when the Rules are broken at pleasure

The card from Ralph's 1929 visit to the Worcester Municipal Golf Links in Massachusetts, highlighting a female golfer in period clothing. *(Photo courtesy of USGA)* beyond two years ahead." As ambitious as ever, the goals he relayed to the newspaper meant that he expected to play two dozen additional courses in the final two cold weather months of the year.

Lou Gehrig was making history that year, as well. At the start of the 1930 season, Joe Sewell, a Cleveland Indian, held the active-player consecutive game streak; however, in May he became ill and didn't play, ending his streak at 1,103 games. Gehrig now had the longest streak among active players with 744 games and counting. During a game against the Indians that year, Gehrig was limping, and the speculation was that he might not play, spoiling his consecutive game streak. Nevertheless, he did start, but in the top of the seventh he took a seat on the bench and stayed there for the remainder of the game. Despite these physical ailments, the Yankees' first baseman had one of the best seasons a major leaguer ever would, batting .379, with 41 home runs and 174 runs batted in. The year turned out to be one of maximum achievement for Lou Gehrig, Bobby Jones, and Ralph Kennedy.

CHAPTER 8

Golf Nomad King

ALTHOUGH RALPH TOLD THE *HARTFORD Courant* in late 1930 that he wasn't planning ahead, he was certainly hitting full stride. The coming year, 1931, was Ralph's most productive. The Depression was hitting Americans hard, although many politicians were out of touch with the daily hardships people were experiencing. Calvin Coolidge, taking a laissez-faire approach, said that government could not guarantee prosperity, but rather it could only play a role to foster healthy trade. It was so bad in New York City that police reserves were used to maintain order when throngs of job seekers showed up to register at the Emergency Unemployment Relief Registration Agency. At one point, three-quarters of a million of the city's residents were seeking work. Long lines at soup kitchens were a regular sight in the city, as were demoralized adults foraging for food.

New York's imposing skyline continued to evolve with distinctive new architecture in the early thirties when the RCA Victor Building opened on Lexington Avenue and Fifty-First Street. The eight-sided, fifty-floor Art Deco masterpiece captured the excitement that radio communications of the era embodied; it was crowned with open tracery, copper finials, and gold outlining, designed to suggest radio waves atop the building.

Mary Alice accompanied Ralph on his first trip of 1931 through Arkansas, Illinois, Kentucky, Missouri, Texas, and Oklahoma. The

Depression would ravage Oklahoma a few years after their visit as the Dust Bowl added insult to economic injury. On February 24th, Ralph and Mary Alice played thirty-six holes at the Kennedy Indoor Golf Course in Tulsa. It appears they played the course more as a novelty given the name, since he did not count it in his numbering sequence.

Ralph and Mary Alice spent the night of the 25th in Miami, Oklahoma, a small town (1930 population of 8,064) with good accommodations. Miami (pronounced My-am-muh, named after a Native American tribe) punched above its weight during this era; it had a large and dramatic Louis XV theater on its Main Street, part of Route 66. Built in 1929, the ornate Coleman Theatre was designed in the Spanish Revival style and was fitted with extensive stained glass, mahogany wood interiors, bronze railings, and silk damask panels. The reason such a grandiose theater was built in Miami was that it was a prosperous town at the turn of the twentieth century. Lead and zinc mines were discovered in what became known as the tri-state mining area in 1906, and it created a boom; local millionaire George Coleman built the theater to showcase the town. (Coleman was also a proficient single-digit amateur golfer who would go on to become a member of Cypress Point, Seminole, and Augusta National. He was responsible for the famous game played at Cypress Point featured in Mark Frost's best-selling book *The Match*.)

Ralph got an early wake-up call and rose with a lot of energy on the 26th, and he would need it. He had luck on his side: the weather brought a fine Ozark day, one especially suited to golf, particularly in February. The itinerant golfer would spend the day up and down the Route 66 corridor playing golf in small-town America and would achieve one of his proudest feats on the mild Thursday: completing four courses in four different states in one day. His feat was made more challenging because he did not play in the summer, when there would have been more daylight.

His marathon began at a rudimentary nine-hole, 3,096-yard course with sand greens, the Rockdale Country Club, which opened in 1918. His next stop, which he got to in a "fast motor car," was across the border in Baxter Springs, Kansas, another town whose main drag was part of Route 66. In a sign of the ubiquity of trolleys in the early 1930s, the town of only 4,500 residents had one, and Ralph could have reached the course using it if he were not in such a hurry. Opened in 1924, the nine-hole Baxter Springs measured 3,001 yards and also had sand greens.

Hightailing it out of Kansas, Ralph's third stop—and state—on the day was sixteen miles away in the relatively big city of Joplin, Missouri, which had a population of 33,454. He played the Schifferdecker Golf Course, the only one of the four that had eighteen holes, and the sole course of the day with grass greens. He only played nine holes, cruising the links with alacrity in thirty-five minutes, accompanied by a caddie. His final conquest took him deeper into the Ozark Mountains, across the border into Arkansas, where he played the Bella Vista Golf Course, a nine-holer with sand greens. It took him longer than he wanted to get to Bella Vista, which was fifty-seven miles away. His driver tried a short cut which didn't work out, and it turned into a seventy-six-mile journey. Making matters worse, their bouncy ride was in low gear due to the poor, unpaved roads. He finished Bella Vista after the sun had set, playing the last several holes in the dark, caddies posted along the final holes to make sure he could locate his ball quickly. From sunup until sundown, he traveled over one hundred miles and played a total of thirty-six holes.

Much like the early days at Van Cortlandt, caddies apparently remained a national problem. The Bella Vista course was a family-owned business run by the Linebarger Brothers. The brothers built the course as part of a real estate development they had underway, and the trio ran a tight ship. Although a local service station advertisement on the back of the card promised "Service with a smile," the motto of the front of the card laid out the brothers' more autocratic attitude: "What We Say It Is, It Is." Caddies, who earned thirty-five cents for carrying a single bag, were admonished on a whole page of the card with "Rules and Duties: balls found by the caddies must be given to the players; caddies must not offer balls for sale; do not talk to the other caddies or players except when necessary; caddies must not go to the green unless requested by the player; watch the ball." Bella Vista was Ralph's 844th unique course.

The local newspapers were impressed by Ralph's feat; the *Joplin Globe* reported his accomplishment five days later: "Ralph A. Kennedy, a nomad of the golf links, achieved an ambition which had been in the back of his mind for eighteen years. The wanderer of the fairways, whose hobby holds a high place in the list of unique performances—possibly the strangest of all in the realm of golf—played four courses in as many states in one day." They noted that the small leather bag he carried was light; it contained three woods and eight irons, all hickory-shafted. His ambitions were much less in 1931 than they would be in the future. He told the newspaper that he hoped to eventually get to one thousand courses before he "calls it quits." He also said he liked the new larger ball and felt that it was easier to hit out of the rough.

The Joplin newspaper contained an extensive listing of the radio broadcasts planned for the day, as well as a large selection of used cars, including a Chrysler sedan for $350 and a Ford sedan for $100. A more prominent portion of the newspaper was occupied by local dealers who listed their offering prices for corn and livestock. The same day it reported the news of Ralph's exploits, the front page noted that there were four different bank robberies around the country in Nebraska, Louisiana, Wisconsin, and Ohio. There were seventeen "bandits" among the four robberies, who used a variety of techniques to commit their crimes, including walking in with machine guns and holding up the entire bank, then tying up and gagging people.

Stirred by both the Great Depression and Prohibition, it was a period when bandits were idolized, highlighted by "Pretty Boy" Floyd, "Baby Face" Nelson, and "Public Enemy Number One," the Chicago bootlegger Al Capone. Ralph and Mary Alice visited Joplin two years before Bonnie and Clyde would spend several weeks there, their visit ending in a dramatic shootout with the police where they ended up killing two officers. The taxis the Kennedys took on their trip through the region were of similar vintage to the old-style sedans that the notorious

A stylish couple in 1930 heading off for a golfing excursion. *(Photo courtesy of Corbis)*

couple drove, with side running boards, whitewall tires, externally mounted headlights, and a flat windscreen. Daily newspapers from coast to coast covered the stories of gangsters with regularity; Bonnie and Clyde were such a sensation that "Extra" editions of newspapers reporting their death sold half a million copies in Dallas alone.

The Chrysler Building did not remain the tallest in the world for long as Ralph and Mary Alice caught sight of a new tower reaching for the sky as their train approached New York on their trip home. Another Art Deco masterpiece, the limestone-clad Empire State Building, opened on May 1, 1931. In keeping with the exciting opening used for both the Woolworth and Chrysler buildings, the same format was followed, although this time the lights on the first night were lit by President Hoover pushing a button in Washington, D. C. At one hundred and two stories, the building remained the world's tallest for almost forty years. Mail chutes were a common feature in Manhattan buildings, and those in the Empire State were special. Office workers could put postcards and letters into the glass chutes, which dropped the mail into the basement, where they were collected for delivery. The building's height presented a unique challenge, so they installed dampers on the sixty-fifth and twenty-eighth floors to slow the mail so that it wouldn't get seared as it flew down the skyscraper at high speeds. On October 1st, another Art Deco wonder opened across town, the forty-seven-story Waldorf Astoria Hotel.

In 1931, number four on the Yankees was given the moniker that would stick with him when Will Wedge of the *Sun* wrote, "Gehrig certainly is one of the Yanks' prize locomotives—a veritable Iron Horse to pull the team along over the grades and certainly he has an important run on the main line; he is steaming along with the throttle open wide after the 1,307-game mark set by Deacon Scott."

MGA handicaps published at midyear show the lowest belonged to Englewood member Eugene Homans, listed with a handicap of one, as was Jess Sweetser, the former Amateur champion. Ralph's handicap had spiked to seventeen, as he had a difficult time adjusting to the new ball, which was larger and more difficult to control in the wind. In 1931, the USGA changed the standard size of the ball, making it both lighter and larger; as a result, the MGA adjusted their handicap limits and increased the maximum allowable from twenty-five to thirty. Mrs. Kennedy, playing in a women's MGA event at Winged Foot that summer, carried a lower handicap than her stocky husband, an impressive fourteen. Granny Rice weighed in on the new ball, saying he thought the larger size would make it easier for the masses to get it airborne, but also felt that its weight would accentuate any mistakes such as slicing, particularly in the wind. The new ball was nicknamed the "balloon" and was so unpopular that the following year, the USGA changed the standards again, sticking with the same larger size, but permitting a heavier weight so that it was not as impacted by Mother Nature.

Establishing golf handicaps for individual players has evolved over the years. In New York during this period, handicaps were established twice a year. The *New York Times*, as well as other newspapers, published a list of individual player handicaps. Handicaps were established by a regional golf association's committee, who in turn relied on individual committees at each club; they used the three best scores of the season in determining a player's handicap.

In addition to his February four-courses-in-four-states trick, other highlights of the playing year included a mad dash to play nine courses in three days in the Poconos. Kennedy also played many courses in New Jersey, Connecticut, Massachusetts, and New York. One of his visits to New Jersey proved a dramatic day. He hit his tee shot into the hole in one stroke, although it was not an ace. While playing the A. W. Tillinghast-designed Somerset Hills Country Club, he lost his first ball on the 2nd hole, one patterned after the Redan hole at North Berwick. When he reteed his shot, the ball went into the hole for an unorthodox par.

Kennedy took his usual Southern trip to Georgia, Tennessee, and Kentucky in May. In Tennessee, he played the Alicea Park Golf Course in Memphis, the Cleveland Golf & Country Club, the Graymere Country Club, and the Oakhurst Golf & Country Club. He also visited the Bourbon Country Club in Paris, Kentucky, a nine-hole course whose card was sponsored by a tobacco company: "Smoke Chesterfields, they satisfy." Smoking rates were rising at the rate of a hockey stick curve during the period, and many tournament golfers of the time were heavy smokers, including Bobby Jones and Walter Hagen.

O. B. Keeler mentioned one of Ralph's challengers again in his continuing periodic coverage: "About once a year Mr. Ralph Kennedy of Winged Foot comes in to see me—a brief stop on the longest trail that golf has ever known. At any rate it touches more different golf courses." Keeler wrote that Kennedy was still planning on stopping his chase at 1,000 courses. Quoting Ralph, "Then I'll call it a day. There's no point that I can see in piling on courses. I'll play a new course whenever I happen to be about it and feel like playing. But I won't go gunning for them, after the thousand." The challenger never really mounted a serious challenge to Ralph, who was now playing so much golf that he had to rent a bigger safe deposit box to store his cards, and he complained that it now cost him fifteen dollars a year to store them (over $200 in today's dollars).

His August trip to the Meadow Brook Golf Club in Hope Valley, Rhode Island, was exciting, as Ralph would just about get another hole-in-one. As he was playing the 9th hole, a par-3 of 170 yards, he sent a high 4-wood soaring over the trees. When he walked up to the sand green with his playing partners, they found the ball wedged in the hole, but not all the way below the rim of the cup. His fellow golfers told him it was a hole-in-one, and he told them it was not, that it would be recorded as a bogey. His reasoning was that because it was lodged between the flag and the outside of the cup, it was an unplayable lie; he had to remove the ball from the hole with a two-stroke penalty, place it on the lip, and then tap it in for a four. He later confirmed that he had done this correctly with the USGA.

Meanwhile in New York, Lou Gehrig's 1931 playing tear continued: on September 1st, he hit his third grand slam in four days and his sixth home run in as many days. On the 20th of the month, Gehrig had four runs batted in, which brought his total to 175, a new record. When the season ended on September 27th the Iron Horse had played every game of the season, the sixth year in a row he did so, and finished with 184 runs batted in. Ralph had an equally impressive year: he played 160 additional golf courses, or almost one every other day. The modest pencil salesman tried to convince *American Magazine* that he wasn't crazy. "I'm just a business man with a hobby," he told them. Although he claimed to play most of his golf on weekends, it would be pretty difficult to achieve the level of play he was without sneaking in just a few rounds on weekdays. The *Dallas Morning News* captured the essence of his journey in their headline, "World's Most Widely Traveled Golfer has made Freak Record."

On November 4, 1931, next to an article about Ralph hitting a milestone of 971 different courses played, O. B. Keeler wrote a second article titled "Work to Start on Bobby Jones' Perfect Course." He described how construction was about to begin on a golf course for millionaires. The course was going to be built on the former nursery owned by the Berckmans brothers in Augusta. The plan was to remove the valuable plants and shrubbery and have them replanted on the sides of the fairways. "This is the course Bobby Jones has dreamed about which he intends to make as nearly perfect as humanly possible. The course, situated in as nearly perfect topographical location as is imaginable was designed by MacKenzie and Bob."

Ralph returned to the nation's capital early in 1932 and went back to play one final nine-hole course at the East Potomac complex, their "G" course, as No. 986. Crossing the segregation barrier, he also played at their "colored only" course that had sand greens, the West Potomac Golf Course, as No. 987 (challenging, the course was not, playing 1,407 yards, with only two par fours). The East Potomac courses were the setting for a record-breaking golf attempt in July 1923, one that Ralph would have admired. Two golfers tried to break a record for most golf holes played in one day: 257, set the year before in Cleveland. William McGuire and Eddie Tipton teed off at dawn and began their marathon day. When the sun went down, they fell short of the record, having completed an exhausting twenty-four rounds on the nine-hole courses, for a total of 216 holes. McGuire took 1,084 strokes and wore a pedometer that showed he walked sixty-nine miles on the day. The newspaper did not report how many socks the two golfers wore, nor whether they developed bunions as a result of their attempt.

To round out his visit to the D. C. area, Ralph played at the golf club frequented by presidents, Burning Tree, on February 5th. It was course No. 990.

By 1932, Horn & Hardart Automats were thriving in the Gotham City. They had grown to forty-two locations, and it still cost only a nickel to buy a slice of coconut cream pie, a Salisbury steak, or a cup of coffee served from a dolphin-headed spout. On July 2nd, Franklin Roosevelt gave his acceptance speech at the Democratic National Convention in Chicago, setting out a new course for the country: "I pledge you, I pledge myself to a *new deal* for the American people." The patrician Roosevelt was about to take over the presidency from Herbert Hoover, who, like Coolidge, had taken a passive approach to the economy since the crash, and the new president had quite a challenge ahead of him.

The stymie continued to be in effect during the early thirties, although there was debate about whether it was a good rule or not. O. B. Keeler interviewed Bobby Jones about the stymie, which he was in favor of: "It may be because I can play the darned thing fairly well. But I think it belongs. There is only one stymie which cannot be played—the opponent's ball on the lip, and your ball as much as a yard away, so that to chip over the intervening ball your shot must go beyond the hole. It's a part of the match. The competitor who is playing best up to the green—who is inside with his approach—is the one who lays the stymie, nine times out of ten. He putts after the other fellow, you see. And so he gets a sort of reward for his previous good play." Jones also talked about the best way to swing the club to "loft a stymie," and his 1927 autobiography included a picture of him doing so. Keeler was not a fan of the stymie, his primary argument being that it compels a competitor to negotiate a hazard that was not on the course when the match started. He quoted Ellsworth Giles, who made a compelling case against it: "laying a stymie is the undeserved reward of missing a putt. If you hole the putt, you do not lay the stymie."

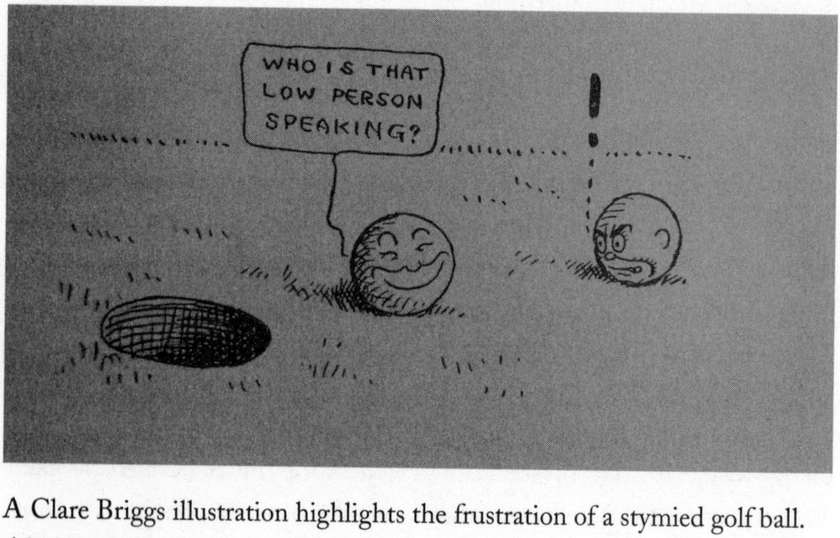

A Clare Briggs illustration highlights the frustration of a stymied golf ball. *(Author's Collection)*

The first Titleist golf ball appeared in 1932, made by a rubber company based in Acushnet, Massachusetts. The genesis of the new ball was a missed putt by company founder and MIT graduate Phillip Young. As golfers have from time immemorial, Young was sure that missing the putt wasn't his fault. He had a friend who was a dentist X-ray the ball and noticed that the core was off center. The breakthrough came when he created a machine that could wind rubber string around a rubber core, which led to a more consistent ball. In addition to making a consistent and quality product, the company also marketed Titleist from the beginning as a high-end ball. Achushnet's other effective strategy was to only sell Titleists through golf professionals instead of through retailers.

June 16th was Ralph's fiftieth birthday. Congress was in the middle of debating whether to repeal Prohibition, and Lou Gehrig was responsible for the Yankees' first run batted in of the day, as the Yankees beat the Chicago White Sox. Less than two weeks earlier, he had again hit four home runs in one game. It was not a particularly good day for golf, with humid and sticky weather punctuated by showers and thunderstorms. Nevertheless, Ralph took the train out to Long Island to celebrate by playing a special golf course located on the South Shore, in Great River. He tried to pick important courses when he was approaching a milestone in his journey, and he was about to play his 1,000th course. To give some sense of how respected it was at the time, he chose the Timber Point Club, a course designed by Charles H. Alison of the firm Colt & Alison. Alison designed some of the best golf courses in the world, so Ralph did his homework.

The private course occupied a fantastic piece of land on a promontory sticking out into the ocean, and it also had a place for members to relax on the beach, and its own yacht anchorage. The *Brooklyn Daily Eagle* described the club as an "exclusive organization," which was spot on, since it was limited to one hundred wealthy members at the time. The course rarely had more than a handful of foursomes on it, so Ralph was fortunate to secure an invitation for his special milestone. Although regarded as one of the best courses in the country, by the time Ralph played it, the club was under stress due to the Depression. Paradoxically, because the club had such well-heeled members, it was hit harder than other clubs. Because its members belonged to more than one club, and, for most, Timber Point was a second or third club, during times of financial hardship they dropped their membership and kept it at their home club.

The *Eagle*'s golf columnist, Ralph Trost, talked of the course in gushing terms: "There aren't many links like it. None that I have ever seen. It has the length without being overwhelmingly long, the strength without being unfair and, more than anything else, it has character. One cannot play Timber Point and then forget the course. Its stamp is indelible." A long course for its day at 6,825 yards, almost every hole on the course was noteworthy. A particularly well-regarded hole was the "Gibraltar," Timber Point's 15th, which many professionals called the greatest long par three they had seen. An uphill 200-yard hole, it played directly into the wind and used the Great South Bay as its backdrop. Its elevated green was completely encircled in deep sand traps. Giving an indication of the difficulty, the climb out of them was so steep that the scorecard reminded players to use the wooden steps provided, and to not attempt to climb up the sand. Playing from the tips, Ralph shot a hard-earned ninety-three on the difficult course, including a bogey on the Gibraltar hole.

The *New York World-Telegram* celebrated his milestone in an article titled, "Ralph Kennedy, the Man of a Thousand Golf Courses," calling him the "Golf Nomad King." The piece included a picture of the sturdy redhead holding up a club and his scorecard. Grantland Rice covered Ralph's big accomplishment in his widely syndicated Sportlight column: "Ralph Kennedy can at least lay claim to one form of championship in golf. He played his thousandth course this week and if this isn't a world's record it ought to be. The list includes 183 courses in New York, 108 in New Jersey, 104 in Massachusetts and 61 in Georgia, with most of the others scattered over 31 states. He figures he has played more than 5,000 rounds. Think of all the alibis the average golfer could cook up with that many openings." Although Ralph previously told Keeler that he would stop his pursuit when he reached one thousand, he had a lot more golf in him and was only a third of the way through his long journey.

Ralph used a *Fraser's International Golf Year Book* to map out which courses he wanted to play, and he was already at work thinking about his next goal. First issued in 1923, *Fraser's* listed courses around the globe, and Ralph used it in conjunction with railroad timetables. Between the two, they provided almost all the information the crazed golfer needed to map out his itineraries. *Fraser's* was chock-full of useful information, giving a summary description of large cities, listing all the courses, local hotels, and other pertinent information (although it did not include phone numbers). Fittingly, among the other advertisements in the thick *Fraser's* was one for Eagle golf pencils. The guide

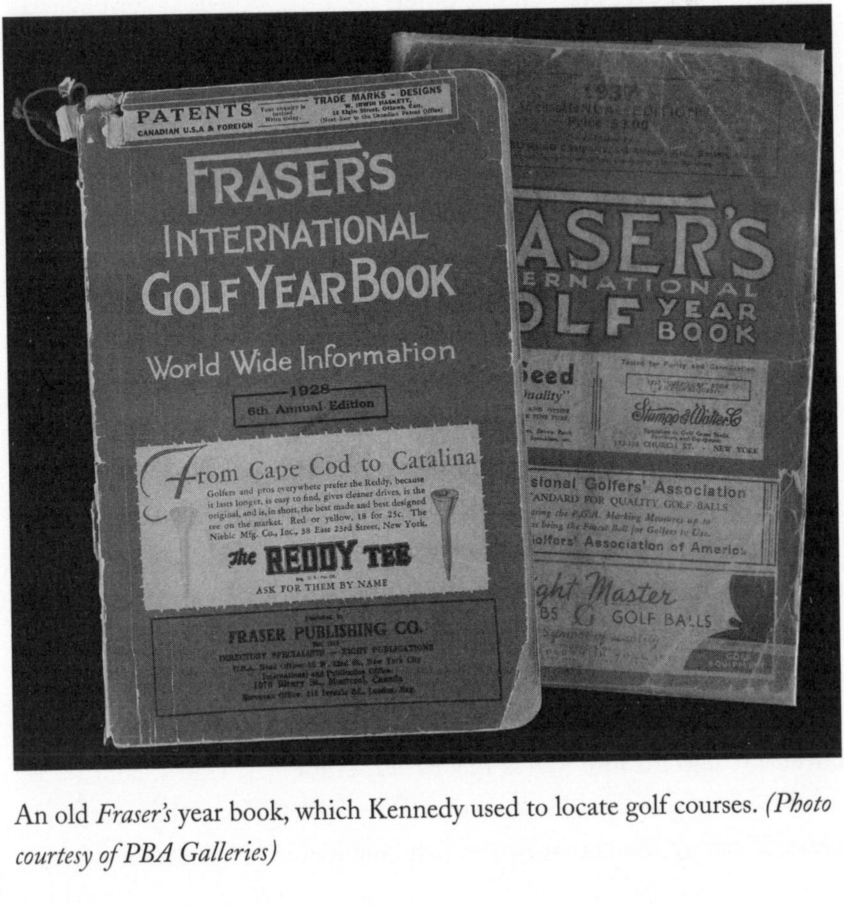

An old *Fraser's* year book, which Kennedy used to locate golf courses. *(Photo courtesy of PBA Galleries)*

suggested that touring golfers bring along a membership card from their home club before starting a trip, noting that it could be useful if they wanted to play other courses. If Winged Foot gave out such cards, Ralph's would have been gold-embossed and laminated given his high visibility. He once mentioned that people tried to impersonate him to attempt to gain access to courses and that he sometimes had to prove he was the *real* Ralph Kennedy.

After hitting the millennial mark, the tireless golfer traveled Upstate and played in the Adirondack Mountains, visiting the Sagamore Resort in Bolton Landing. He was invited to Sagamore by Dr. William G. Beckers, who was one of the founders of the club and the man who brought Donald Ross in to design the course. Afterwards, Ralph told the *New York Times*, "I class Sagamore within a group of the six best I have ever played. The others are Pine Valley, Yale Memorial, the Country Club at Havana, Timber Point, and Winged Foot. From a golfing point of view there are not trick holes and a good shot is never penalized." The beauty of its setting he found inspiring: "I found it plays just as hard as Pine Valley with perhaps this one difference—the New Jersey layout is more liberally trapped. But there is plenty of sand at Sagamore."

He elaborated, "Sagamore is a golfer's golf club. What I mean is it has a real spirit and atmosphere. The clubhouse is not pretentious, but perhaps that's why, like so many others I have visited, it is cozy and comfortable. The people I've met here are 'regular folks.'" He continued, "Golf is more than a game. It is the greatest preserver of health I know. It is a game in which you meet the finest kind of people. It is at once a mental relaxation and a physical stimulation. And—if you want to learn a man's character—just play a round of golf with him." New York's newspaper of record continued to explain that, at a testimonial dinner that Beckers arranged, Kennedy was quite the celebrity and raconteur and regaled the guests with stories of his South American adventure and his four-states-in-one-day stunt.

Ralph was invited back to play Pine Valley many times over the years, although the course's par-5 7th hole was in his head. His highest score on the course was a 118, and the day he shot it he took a fifteen on No. 7. On one of his return visits, he was dared by a friend that he still could not break 100. Their $100 bet, with odds of ten to one, came down to the final hole, a challenging par-4 finishing hole with a pond in front of an elevated and well-bunkered green. The sturdy Kennedy came to the 18th tee needing a par to break 100. Unsure that he could hit his second shot far enough to clear the pond, he laid up, electing to pitch onto the large and undulating green. Long putting was the favorite part of Ralph's game, which was good, because he left himself a tester to try to win the big bet. His forty-foot putt had a lot of break in it, but he hit it perfectly and it rattled into the bottom of the cup for a four. If his friend paid off the bet, the happy salesman went home far richer than when the day began, since $1,000 represented about 25 percent of an average worker's annual wages.

Interviewed again by O. B. Keeler, Kennedy described why he liked golf so much: "Some of the finest men I ever knew were fellows on the golf course." In the article, his Southern friend called him a member of the "dodo club," since he had made a hole-in-one. Tipped off to his travels by Keeler, journalists around the nation continued to track Ralph's progress far and wide. The *Evansville Courier and Journal* announced that "the noted vagabond of golf links to play here today," on his way through Indiana, picking up another eight courses. In October, Frank King drew a six-panel cartoon highlighting Ralph, as part of his syndicated *Gasoline Alley* series. The color cartoon featured an adult talking with a child about weird collections: "Some people collect bugs, others hotel soaps or bottles; but the strangest I've heard of was a man who collects golf courses," referring specifically to one thousand courses collected.

In October, Grantland Rice announced that Lou Gehrig was taking golf lessons from an otherwise unidentified "Instructor Hughes." This was the first time the lefty took up the game seriously, since previously he believed that golf would hurt his baseball swing. Rice thought Gehrig would be a natural because he knew how to use his hands and wrists. Rice had previously written that Gehrig wasn't much interested in golf, and while Lou would accompany the famed writer, Babe Ruth, and Sammy Byrd—a Yankee outfielder and talented golfer who finished among the top five in the Masters twice—when they played on the road, he would walk along with them and not play. Instructor Hughes, it turns out, was George Hughes, the professional at the Green Meadow Country Club in Harrison, New York, who was also Babe Ruth's instructor.

Lou Gehrig holding his golf swing at Green Meadow. *(Photo courtesy of USGA)*

Gehrig took up golf after the Yankees swept the World Series against the Chicago Cubs in 1932, and he warmed to the game quickly. During the off season, he started to exhibit Kennedy-esque symptoms, spending the winter in Southern Pines, North Carolina, where he played thirty-six, and sometimes fifty-four holes a day. Not surprisingly, he was good at golf and was shooting low scores by spring training. Hughes commented about Gehrig's ability: "Lou had gone around a nine-hole golf course once in his life when he came to see me and I gave him six lessons on the mashie-niblick, after which he made the course in 109. By the end of the season he was turning in eighty at Green Meadow and had that wrist roll down to perfection." In another interesting intertwining of people, Hughes served as the caddie-master when Gene Sarazen carried bags at Apawamis.

A major advancement in golf club design occurred in 1932 with the development of the sand wedge. The highest lofted club most golfers used through the early part of the twentieth century was the niblick (the equivalent of today's wedge or 9-iron), although some players used a jigger, as well, a low-lofted iron used for bump and run shots similar to a utility chipping club. Gene Sarazen developed the sand wedge, getting his inspiration while flying with Howard Hughes. After seeing the flaps of the wings come down on Hughes's plane, he thought about how to create the equivalent on a golf club, and his idea was to put a flange on the club. His new wedge also used punch marks, instead of grooves, on the club face. He used the club for the first time in the 1932 British Open at the Prince's Golf Club in Sandwich, England. There had been previous attempts to create clubs that extracted the ball from sand over the years, some successful and some not. Walter Hagen had previously tried a club with a concave face, which was deemed illegal.

Some of the courses Ralph played along the way weren't exactly great challenges. The Little Falls Country Club—in a town by the same name in New Jersey—that he played in July (course No. 1,010) was a nine-hole course of 1,535 yards. Ralph shot one under par for a total of thirty, with a scorecard as pretty as any professional's would look if he were tearing up the course: 3–3–4–4–3–3–3–4–3. The negligible course's holes were also named. The short par-3 5th hole played an almost comical distance of sixty-five yards and was aptly titled "Tom Thumb." The most challenging hole on the course was the 245-yard par 4 named "Over the Hill." Little Falls was just a warm-up to a month-long trip, as Ralph crossed the mighty Mississippi in August to golf in the Midwest, playing a smattering of courses as he passed through Indiana, Iowa, and Illinois, on his way to golf in the Far West. It was Ralph's first foray into the expansive area.

Visiting the Rocky Mountains for the first time, the gloveless golfer played the Casper Country Club, situated in a dramatic valley at the base of Casper Mountain, which rises a mile and a half into the sky. From there, he continued on to play a rudimentary golf course in Riverton, Wyoming. Sitting at 4,956 feet of elevation in the Wind River Valley, the land the course was built on was previously the habitat of the Northern Arapahoe and Eastern Shoshone Native American tribes. The tiny town was carved out of the Wind River Indian Reservation in 1906 as part of a treaty with the federal government, and it has a classic Western history; in 1838 it served as the location of a "mountain man rendezvous," a legendary gathering of trappers engaged in the fur trade. Riverton was about as far away from New York in both spirit and geography as Ralph could get. Both its physical manifestation and its Western frontier mentality were the antithesis of the metropolis in which Ralph lived. The freewheeling town's history was one of homesteading, ranching, and mining, and its 1,600 residents were a very different cohort than the inhabitants of the Kennedy apartment building. Many of the town's inhabitants were employed as farmers and ranchers, or worked in the coal mining or oil field businesses. A large number were employed at a plant that manufactured railroad ties. Rounding out the lot were an employee of Western Union, a blacksmith, a prospector, and a cowboy hand.

How and why a city of this size in the wilderness had a golf course is unknown. *Fraser's* referenced Riverton in its 1932 edition as a newly built course. Ralph referred to the nine-hole links with greens made of sand as a "goat course" and said it was overrun by jack rabbits and horned toads. He told *Golf Illustrated* two years after playing it, "A trigger-finger itch will bother the shot-gun addict who plays the Riverton, Wyoming, course. Gophers, rabbits, and prairie dogs gambol across the bleak tundras where sage brush and bear grass form the only vegetation. A chasm carry on that desolate layout haunts my dreams. You play across a devil's cauldron gulch 150 feet deep that looks as though it had been gouged out by a falling meteor. 'Tumbling on the brink of an abscess' as Irvin Cobb would say." There is no card for the course in Far Hills, suggesting it was a basic course indeed, laid out by locals who enjoyed hitting little white balls around for recreation. Ralph said that he played with the president of the local bank and that "The club has thirty members and the dues are $10 a year." It is safe to assume that Riverton did not have a clubhouse on the order of Shinnecock Hills or the National Golf Links of America.

Continuing his travels north, Ralph teed it up at the Meadow Lark Golf Club in Great Falls, Montana. Kennedy was accompanied on this part of the trip by Alfred Berolzheimer, the president of the Eagle Pencil Company. Berolzheimer accompanied Ralph to see the sights and occasionally played golf on the thirty-four-day trip. Alfred had a ranch out West so he could be closer to a key product for pencil production: cedar trees. Producing a pencil requires about twenty-five different materials sourced from all over the world. The best wood for making pencils is cedar, which Eagle obtained from forests in both California and Virginia. They imported graphite from Mexico, Ceylon, and Madagascar; gum from Persia; wax from Brazil; oil from sperm whales in the South Pacific; and a special clay mined in Germany. The stipulation on the trip was that Berolzheimer and Kennedy would travel as friends and not as boss and employee. The boss had an important asset for the trip—a car—and he agreed to stop each day at 4 p.m. so that Ralph could get some golf in.

They continued farther north, playing at the Glacier Park Golf Club in northern Montana, a short distance from the border with Alberta. Canada had experienced a dramatic growth in golf, as had America; it now had six hundred courses spread over its nine provinces, an increase of more than 300 percent since the end of the First World War. Traveling up the foothills of the Canadian Rockies to Calgary, Kennedy played the Calgary St. Andrew's Golf Club. The pair continued their trek west, visiting two world-class golf courses where the ball soared farther in the high-altitude air. Located at an elevation of 4,600 feet and situated within a National Park, Banff Springs is blessed with some of the most dramatic scenery in North America. Built along the Bow River in the Canadian Rockies, the golf course has stirring vistas of snow-capped mountains in all directions. Ralph described the first tee at Banff as "looking up a narrow valley squeezed between ramparts of the Canadian Rockies." Banff's most famous hole, named Devil's Cauldron (the 8th when he played it), is a jaw-dropping downhill par-3 in an amphitheater setting that plays over a small glacial lake with the commanding Rockies rising behind the hole.

Banff Springs was Ralph's first taste of a Stanley Thompson golf course. Thompson was the premier Canadian golf course designer of his era, and he was a colorful figure, described as having a roast-beef complexion. He wore a fedora and a three-piece suit with a watch chain

THE RULES OF PLAY
Are the rules and etiquette of golf as approved by The Royal and Ancient Golf Club of St. Andrews except where modified by The Royal Canadian Golf Association and local rules.

LOCAL RULES
A ball driven into or short of the Spray River from the Tee at the First Hole, or into or short of the Cauldron from the Tee at the Eighth Hole may be re-teed and played from the Tee, with Loss of Distance only.

A ball driven into the Lagoon or Bow River from the Tee at the Twelfth Hole may be re-teed and played from the Tee at a penalty of One Stroke.

A ball driven into any other water hazard on the course may be dropped on the Fairway at the nearest point to where it entered the water hazard at a penalty of One Stroke.

PLEASE REPLACE DIVOTS
Observe the Etiquette of Golf

STROKES ALLOWED
Single matches ¾ the difference between the handicaps.
Foursome matches ⅜ the difference between combined handicaps.
Fractions of ½ or over, count as one.

Ralph's scorecard from his memorable visit to Banff Springs, Canada. *(Photo courtesy of USGA)*

hanging down, and he had a penchant for drinking whiskey and eating big steaks. He smoked up to a dozen cigars a day. Thompson's specialty was building courses through areas that were thick with "rock and forest," and Banff Springs had both in abundance. He used dynamite to blow out portions of the rock while building the course. Traveling in style, Ralph and Berolzheimer stayed at the majestic Banff Springs Hotel, built in the Scottish Baronial style by the Canadian Pacific Railway, which also commissioned the building of the course in 1927. The bespectacled New Yorker noted, "Cross winds hurtling down at Banff must be felt to be believed. To keep down the cost of lost balls a little . . . Banff's superintendent has trained a terrier to retrieve shots sliced into the brush."

Kennedy next played at the equally well-regarded Thompson design at Jasper Park, 185 miles farther north, a course commissioned by a competing railroad, the Canadian National. Since it was built 5,000 feet above sea level, Thompson gave a great deal of thought to the design, maximizing the aesthetics of the location. He artistically routed the course so that the sight lines on most holes aligned with distant mountain peaks—some of which rise to 11,000 feet—and it was love at first sight when Ralph played the rugged course, which was also carved out of a thick forest. Although motorized equipment was emerging to help construct golf courses, because of the rugged terrain, Thompson used fifty teams of horses and hundreds of men between 1924 and 1926 to build Jasper Park. Ralph related, "On eleven of the eighteen holes at Jasper Park, majestic mountain peaks are the markers for your line of play." He came upon a bear at the course and asked the pro he was playing with what to do. He was advised that as they walked to the ball, the bear would run away, which is indeed what happened. Ralph was not alone in his admiration of the course; Alister MacKenzie gave Jasper Park the highest praise possible when he said in 1928, "I consider this to be the best course I have ever seen."

The demanding par-3 8th hole, Banff Springs, Alberta. *(Photo courtesy of USGA)*

Berolzheimer and the barnstorming golfer continued back east into Edmonton, where Ralph played the Edmonton Municipal Golf Links and then the Mayfair Golf and Country Club, a course Thompson redesigned and rerouted. America wasn't alone in possessing company-owned golf courses, and while in Edmonton, Ralph played another Thompson design, the Prince Rupert Golf Course, which was built for the Hudson's Bay Company in 1929. Heading into Saskatchewan, Ralph played at the Riverside Country Club and the Saskatoon Golf & Country Club on the 17th of August. Their visit to the vast Canadian province was brief, since by the 18th they had traveled five hundred miles to Manitoba to play at the Bourkevale Park Public Course and the St. Charles Country Club. The last Thompson-designed course Ralph played on the trip was the Niakwa Country Club in Winnipeg, situated on a plot of land that the Seine River runs through. Ben Hogan was among the golfers who would play at Niakwa in future years, winning a tour event there in 1946. Saying good-bye to the boss, the spirited Kennedy then picked up the train and traveled east to play the Royal Ottawa Golf Club on August 20th. If he still remembered any French from his Amherst days, he used it the following day at the Laval-sur-le-Lac Golf Club near Montreal, whose membership was made up largely of French-speaking Canadians.

Ralph took the train back down through Upstate New York and Albany before returning to his Manhattan apartment after a journey of more than six thousand miles. He mentioned to the newspapers on his return that he was happy to quench his thirst at the bar after his rounds and noted that it was "all very legal," since Canada did not enact Prohibition legislation. Ralph was reentering a country whose economy continued to be ravaged as the year came to a close. Although New Yorkers were celebrating the opening of Radio City Music Hall in late December, unemployment reached twelve million, up from four million just two years before.

As Ralph got back into his routine at home, on the other side of the planet, the new day dawned early in Tasmania, the springtime sun rising at half past four in the far reaches of the Southern Hemisphere this time of year. Aussie newspaper readers sipping their morning tea found among their usual updates of sheep, spuds, and studs the news that Ralph Kennedy, now a worldwide sensation, had played his 1,000th course. It had taken a full five months for word of his accomplishment to travel the 10,000 miles from New York to Launceston.

In many ways the antithesis of the average citizen, and riding high on the crest of his big achievements over the last two years, the husky, cigar-smoking Ralph Kennedy was a Man in Full sixty-six years before Tom Wolfe coined the term. As impressive as his run was to date, it was about to get significantly better, as some of his most awe-inspiring achievements were about to unfold.

CHAPTER 9
Down Magnolia Lane

Married for twenty-five years and doing far better than most, the Kennedys were in a position to afford a beach getaway to celebrate their anniversary. To escape the biting cold temperatures and perpetual gray that can envelop wintertime New York, in early 1933 the couple took a short vacation and set out across the Atlantic for the turquoise waters of Bermuda. Their voyage was aboard the Munson Line's *S. S. Pan America*, which offered the luxury of private bathrooms; their departure was noted in four New York newspapers.

Shortly after their ship docked in Bermuda, Ralph went on one of his golf binges, knocking off eight courses in a row like they were dominoes lined up waiting to fall. His torrid pace included collecting five new scorecards over a two-day stretch, from courses with thickly matted and spongy Bermuda grass. In a mere thirteen hours, he played the Castle Harbour Hotel & Golf Course, the Devonshire Country Club (9 holes), the Frascati Golf Club (9 holes), the Mid Ocean Club, and the St. George's Hotel Golf Links. Pursuing the game with less ardor than her antsy husband, Mary Alice's only round was at the Mid Ocean Club. An island newspaper, the *Gazette and Colonist*, was impressed with Ralph's stamina and noted how wind and rain didn't seem to slow him down. After his big flourish, he finished off at a relatively leisurely pace (for him), playing the Belmont Manor Golf

The hilly and scenic Castle Harbour course in Bermuda, in the 1930s. *(Author's Collection)*

Course, the Elbow Beach Hotel Club, and the Riddell's Bay Golf Club from sunrise to sunset.

He enjoyed the C. B. Macdonald Mid Ocean Club the best, saying it had "Perhaps the most striking marine vista I've enjoyed, from the 15th tee where the cliffs tumble precipitously into the green-blue Atlantic and the semi-tropic sun glints brightly on the white coral clubhouse above a secluded cove." The hilly Castle Harbour course also left a strong impression on Ralph: "It is the most eccentric. You really should have one leg shorter than the other to walk around it comfortably, and there are inclined railways and elevators to help you reach or descend to various levels, at that."

As their week-long break wound down, the prow of their ship splashed through the frigid waters of the Atlantic, passing into New York Harbor through the Verrazano Narrows to dock in Brooklyn. Upon their return, their trip was commented on by both the *Herald Tribune* and the *Daily Mirror.* The scissors and glue got a healthy workout back in the Washington Heights apartment; the Kennedys were quite enamored with the fact that it was legal to drink in Bermuda, and along with the newspaper clippings that mentioned them, they posted an abundance of labels from bottles of beer, rum, scotch, and whiskey into a scrapbook.

Nineteen thirty-three was the worst of times for Ralph's fellow Americans, but the best of times for the contact man at a large pencil company. The Depression was hitting the country hard as the year progressed, with the downcast standing on bread lines each day. Fully one half of all mortgages across the vast country were delinquent. The 6,346 banks that failed during the Hoover administration resulted in eight million depositors losing their money. In an attempt to stabilize the floundering economy, on March 6th, President Roosevelt—who was in office for less than forty-eight hours—shut down the banking system for an unprecedented four days. Citizens got by the best they could without banks; hotels and restaurants began to extend credit, salesmen on the road had to barter goods to get basic necessities, and it was difficult to get change from large bills. Unemployment would reach its highest level during the depths of the Depression, with one in four seeking work when the economy scraped bottom.

The *New Yorker* featured Ralph in its *Talk of the Town* section after he returned from Bermuda under the headline of "Record Man": "This not being a daily magazine, we can't keep up with Ralph Kennedy, but last we heard he had played golf on 1,085 courses. He's been at it twenty-three years and he figures that it has cost him in transportation and other expenses about $25,000." They noted that after he first played in Van Cortlandt Park, "He instantly got that wild look in his eyes that golfers can get, and has been running around the country and the world ever since. His wife hears from him all the time when he is away golfing, because he mails all his cards home, signed by the club pro at each links. She puts them in a safe-deposit vault for him. Mr. Kennedy never gets mad and throws his club away or breaks them against trees. He says you can learn a lot about a man's character by playing a round of golf with him. He is calm and steady in the pinches."

Mid-April brought typically showery and wet conditions to the Great Metropolis, including a soggy Easter. As springtime emerged, it wasn't unusual for the traveling salesman to depart the city that assaults the senses to do a swing through the mannerly South. So it was that on Saturday, April 22nd, Ralph Anderson Kennedy, member of Winged Foot and the New York Athletic Club, salesman extraordinaire for the Eagle Pencil Company, and globetrotting golfer, wrote the usual RAK at the top of his card, although it was a scorecard that few golfers are ever able to write their name on. He was playing his 1,093th unique course at the Augusta National Golf Club. Augusta National opened for play in January, just a few short months earlier. By now, Ralph was a golfer of renown, and his movements to the course were telegraphed by newspapers throughout the South. Three days before he played, Keeler mentioned that Kennedy was on his way to Augusta, and the day before his visit, the *Savannah Morning News* declared, "Leaves today for Augusta where he hopes to play the new Bobby Jones golf course. Mr. Kennedy has walked over the new Augusta course but has not been there since it was finished."

From the beginning, Bobby Jones envisioned Augusta as a national membership club, and one of the early golfers he asked to join was Grantland Rice—who eagerly accepted. Rice was a member of Augusta's organization committee and helped to recruit new members. The initiation fee was $350, plus tax, and annual dues were $60 per year. Both Jones and Cliff Roberts wanted to model Augusta's membership after the Royal and Ancient Golf Club of St. Andrews, which also had a low initiation fee and low annual dues. Ralph told the *Savannah Morning News* the year before that, "When I came down I was in hopes of playing the national course at Augusta but when I telephoned Bobby Jones he told me that it wouldn't be ready until June. When I was talking with Mr. Jones I seized the opportunity to ask him if the course will be too hard for the average player." Jones replied, "Well, just wait until you play it yourself, then tell me what you think about it." Kennedy speculated, "I am inclined to believe that it will be tough on the seventy shooter and not especially hard on players who score around 100." Now, he was about to find out firsthand how it played.

Kennedy was thrilled driving down Magnolia Lane and had a great sense of anticipation before playing the new course. Augusta has a timeless quality to it, and his walk through the old plantation property and clubhouse was stimulating. The clubhouse he toured was in its original state; it did not yet contain the Crow's Nest in the cupola. Ralph typically didn't write course notes on his scorecard, but he did on his Augusta National card. The card shows that the club's regular course played exactly 6,300 yards, and the championship tees measured precisely 6,700. Although not long off the tee, he played from the tips, by himself. He went around the MacKenzie-Jones design at the perfect time, with temperatures in the upper sixties and only some high clouds in the sky, the dazzling flowering shrubs blooming throughout the course.

He hit a nice tee shot down the dramatically downhill first hole, one that played 420 yards from tee to green. When Ralph played the course, the two nines were in their original configuration, which is

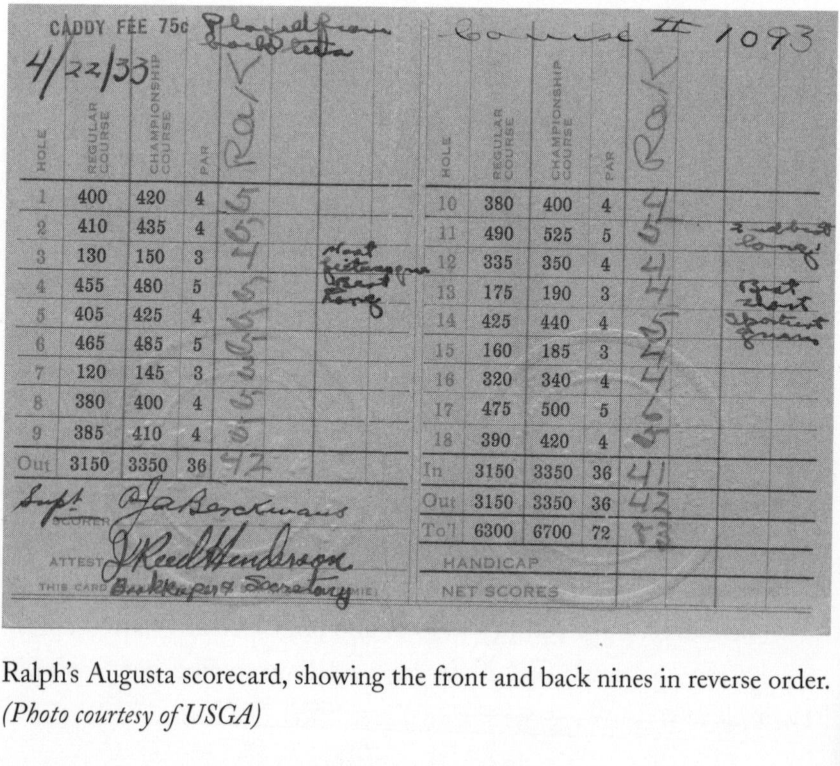
CADDY FEE 75c Played from back tees
4/22/33
Course # 1093

HOLE	REGULAR COURSE	CHAMPIONSHIP COURSE	PAR	RAK
1	400	420	4	5
2	410	435	4	5
3	130	150	3	4
4	455	480	5	5
5	405	425	4	5
6	465	485	5	6
7	120	145	3	3
8	380	400	4	5
9	385	410	4	4
Out	3150	3350	36	42

HOLE	REGULAR COURSE	CHAMPIONSHIP COURSE	PAR	RAK
10	380	400	4	4
11	490	525	5	5
12	335	350	4	4
13	175	190	3	4
14	425	440	4	5
15	160	185	3	4
16	320	340	4	4
17	475	500	5	6
18	390	420	4	5
In	3150	3350	36	41
Out	3150	3350	36	42
To'l	6300	6700	72	83
HANDICAP				
NET SCORES				

SCORER Supt. [signature]
ATTEST [signature] Bookkeeper & Secretary
THIS CARD

Ralph's Augusta scorecard, showing the front and back nines in reverse order. *(Photo courtesy of USGA)*

reversed from today's order. His first hole was not yet lined with cabins on the left, and the green was situated at the base of the hill, below and to the right of where it sits today. He started with a pair of bogeys on the demanding opening holes. On his scorecard next to hole No. 3 (today's par-3 12th), he wrote "Most picturesque." He was not able to walk over the Hogan Bridge to get to the third green because it did not yet exist.

He was impressed with what would eventually become the last hole of Amen Corner. Regarding the dogleg left hole with the meandering Rae's Creek running through it, he wrote, "Best Long," referencing his fourth hole (today's par-5 13th). Ralph's tee shot on the fourth had to carry long enough to get over Rae's Creek, which at the time cut across the fairway roughly 150 yards off the tee. Because the pine trees had not yet grown tall, once on the fourth green he could see clear to the top of the property, with a view of the antebellum clubhouse sitting on the high point of the old nursery grounds.

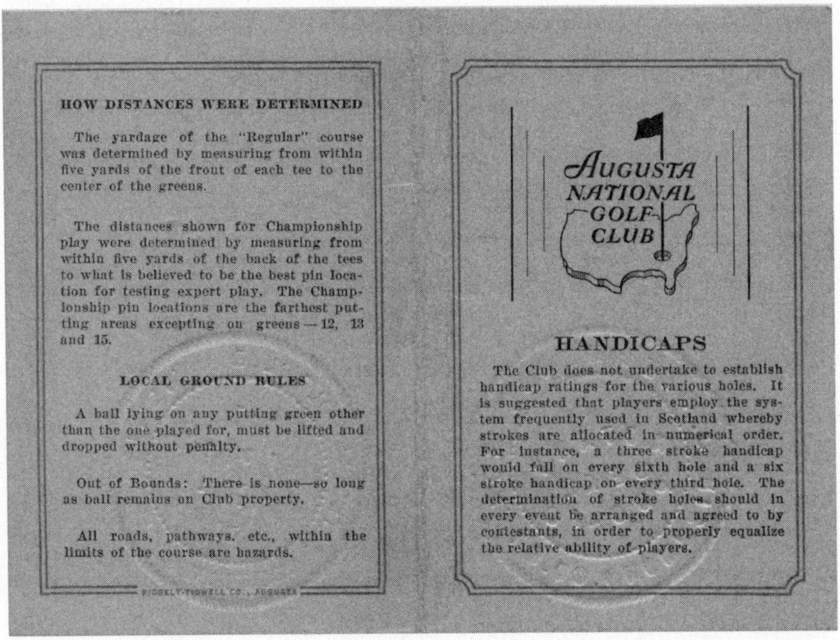

HOW DISTANCES WERE DETERMINED

The yardage of the "Regular" course was determined by measuring from within five yards of the front of each tee to the center of the greens.

The distances shown for Championship play were determined by measuring from within five yards of the back of the tees to what is believed to be the best pin location for testing expert play. The Championship pin locations are the farthest putting areas excepting on greens — 12, 13 and 15.

LOCAL GROUND RULES

A ball lying on any putting green other than the one played for, must be lifted and dropped without penalty.

Out of Bounds: There is none—so long as ball remains on Club property.

All roads, pathways, etc., within the limits of the course are hazards.

AUGUSTA NATIONAL GOLF CLUB

HANDICAPS

The Club does not undertake to establish handicap ratings for the various holes. It is suggested that players employ the system frequently used in Scotland whereby strokes are allocated in numerical order. For instance, a three stroke handicap would fall on every sixth hole and a six stroke handicap on every third hole. The determination of stroke holes should in every event be arranged and agreed to by contestants, in order to properly equalize the relative ability of players.

The front of Ralph's Augusta National scorecard. *(Photo courtesy of USGA)*

He shot a forty-two on the front, parring the par-5 fourth and sixth holes; at the time, the sixth (today's 15th) had no greenside bunkers. He also safely navigated the pond on the current sixteenth hole, taking a par three on what was his seventh hole.

On the back nine, he liked the sweeping downhill No. 11 (today's par-5 2nd), noting that it was the "2nd best long." He also liked the downhill par-3 No. 13, then named "Palm," before it was subsequently changed to "Flowering Crab Apple." He wrote that the demanding 190-yard hole was the "Best short." Although the large bunker that protects the front of the green was present, when he was fortunate to be walking on the new course, it was shaped more like a boomerang. On No. 14, "Magnolia" (today's par-4 5th), he noted that it had the "Sportiest green," referring to the two-tiered green with large undulations. This should not be surprising, since the inspiration for the hole was the Road Hole at St. Andrews Old Course, a hole with one of the most difficult-to-navigate greens in the world. He shot a forty-one coming in, writing in a par for the first three holes on the back, as well as on the sixteenth (today's par-4 7th). An eighty-three isn't a bad score from the tips at Augusta National.

The club's tradition from inception was to forgo a slope rating and hole handicaps. The scorecard explained their philosophy: "The club does not undertake to establish handicap ratings for the various holes. It is suggested that players employ the system frequently used in Scotland whereby strokes are allocated in numerical order. For instance, a three-stroke handicap would fall on every sixth hole and a six-stroke handicap on every third hole. The determination of stroke holes should in every event be arranged and agreed by contestants, in order to properly equalize the relative ability of players." The card also stipulated Augusta's out of bounds rule: "There is none—so long as ball remains on club property."

As he did on all of his cards, Ralph had his Augusta card attested to, this time by two club officials. It was signed by a superintendent, and by J. Reed Henderson, who wrote that he was bookkeeper and secretary. The superintendent who signed the card was none other than P. J. A.

Berckmans Jr. ("Allie"), a member of the family that formerly owned the nursery, who served as an early general manager of the club. Little did Ralph know how rare it would be to have Prosper Jules Alphonse Berckmans Jr.'s signature on his card serving as an attester.

The Berckmans family. The attester of Ralph's card is on the left, wearing a white jacket. *(Photo courtesy of Getty Images)*

Commenting about Augusta to *Golf Illustrated* a year after he played it, Kennedy raved about the same details modern golfers do when watching the Masters: "For floral beauty, the new Augusta National, occupying the former Baron Berckmans estate in the hills of northern Georgia, stands unrivaled. This Belgian horticulturist spent a fortune landscaping the tract and Bobby Jones's pet course is the beneficiary. It is a riot of color in the springtime when the honeysuckle, dogwood, azalea, wisteria, jasmine, magnolia, and daffodils are in bloom. The course itself has not proved as exacting a test as its designer, Dr. Alister MacKenzie hoped. He omitted bunkers for the most part, depending upon natural hazards and holes fashioned on the strategic rather than the penal principle." Ralph's description was accurate; the course only had twenty-nine sand traps when it opened. Years later, he would shorten his description of golf's Valhalla to "Augusta is the loveliest inland course in America."

The timing of Augusta National's opening was less than ideal, coming four years after the crash and a month after the forced bank closings in the heart of the Depression. Jones and Roberts's initial objective was to have one thousand members; they mailed letters to thousands of prospective members at prestigious clubs throughout the country, but due to the hard economic times, few could join. Trying to recruit during a time of stagnant growth and bank failures proved a challenge. As difficult as it is to imagine today, after two years of actively trying to recruit members, there were only sixty-six. While the tight-lipped club would not confirm whether Ralph was invited to join—since he knew Grantland Rice and Bobby Jones, had visited the property before the course opened, and was a member of a prominent club—the odds are good that he was in fact asked to join. The initiation fee would have been only a quarter of the amount it cost him to join Winged Foot a decade before.

Playing Augusta with no seeming effort was one of Ralph's greatest coups. While most golfers lust to play Augusta and cannot because of the makeup of its membership and the exclusivity of the club, for the connected Winged Foot man it proved no problem, securing an invitation three months after it opened and before the first Masters was held.

Sporting events and aviation feats were a welcome diversion from tough economic times. Although the country was in the depths of the Depression, it did not stop New York City from continuing to celebrate achievements, with ticker tape parades advancing up Lower Broadway from the Battery to City Hall. The city held three in 1933: one for the Italian General Italo Balbo and his crew for their feat of piloting twenty-five flying boats from Italy to Chicago; a second for Wiley Post after he flew around the world alone in eight days; and a third for James A. Mollison and his wife, who were intending to set a record for a westbound flight across the Atlantic. They flew from Wales and were bound for New York, although their biplane crash-landed in Bridgeport, Connecticut, short of their intended target when they ran out of fuel.

The steady golfer and his dutiful wife once again took the train out to Long Island in August to play Salisbury's No. 4 course in a hole-in-one tournament with fellow Winged Foot members Mr. and Mrs. J. B. Proctor. In a photo taken at the event, Mary Alice is standing behind her stocky, muscular husband looking like a forlorn flapper, clutching his arm; small and looking frail and hesitant, she is almost hiding

The Kennedys (left) and the Proctors at the Salisbury Links, Long Island, 1933. *(Photo courtesy of USGA)*

behind her confident mate, burying her face under a floppy white hat. The Proctors, wearing all white, appear to be a sophisticated couple.

While the Kennedys were on their summer vacation on Long Island, Lou Gehrig broke Everett Scott's record of 1,307 consecutive games. His "Iron Horse" name was wholly appropriate, as he shrugged off injuries that other players did not and played the previous fall with broken fingers. Gehrig had also decided to give up golf because he was convinced it interfered with his baseball swing. Lank Leonard, a syndicated comic illustrator, drew sketches gently mocking Lou's foray into golf, heading the five panels, "Another Noble Experiment."

Zip codes were a concept that had not yet arrived, as evidenced by the letter Ralph received from Richard G. Badger, the publisher of the Gorham Press in Boston, which was sent to him in care of the Eagle Pencil Company, New York City, inquiring about the possibility of

Ralph writing a book. Ralph had previously mentioned that he might want to write a book about his travel exploits, yet he never did, and there is no mention of the project with the Gorham Press gaining traction. If Ralph had written a book, he likely would have titled it *Ralph A. Kennedy: The Peripatetic Golfer.* This was the title he used to describe himself (years earlier Keeler referred to him as such), and he had it engraved on the cover of each of the six scrapbooks he created. His first scrapbook was titled, "The Story of a Thousand Golf Courses by Ralph A. Kennedy—The Peripatetic Golfer." Each subsequent book was titled with the same moniker, but changed to reflect "The Next 500" and "The Next 500," for each batch of courses he completed. The fancy word was perhaps an understatement for the linksman who never tired; the definition: "Peripatetic. Per-i-pa-tet-ic. Walking about or from place to place; traveling on foot."

Besides walking, trains, trolleys, buses, and ocean liners, Ralph found himself taking other unusual modes of transportation in pursuit of his achievement. While in the steel and coal-mining region south of Pittsburgh, he played in Uniontown, the birthplace of General George C. Marshall. The urban golfer found himself sitting on top of a donkey to navigate the hilly terrain as he made his way to the first tee at the Uniontown Country Club. He played the course's eighteen holes in one hour and forty minutes, shooting an eighty-two; then he played another eighteen holes at the nearby Summit Hotel Golf Course, all before dinner. While in Western Pennsylvania, he also played one of the great courses in golf, which is easily identified using only one word: Oakmont. Oakmont is shorthand for the Oakmont Country Club, and its name signifies both difficulty and excellence. Summing up its ambience and mystique, Walter Hagen said about the storied club, "It's as difficult to escape from the nineteenth at Oakmont as it is to get out of the cross-raked traps on the course." Six years earlier, when Tommy Armour won the 1927 U.S. Open at Oakmont, he was the professional at the Congressional Country Club in Maryland; and to celebrate his victory, the membership give him a dazzling Marmon Roadster. The picture of Armour standing in front of the grandiose car neatly

Tommy Armour with his sleek Marmon Roadster in front of the Congressional Country Club clubhouse. *(Photo courtesy of USGA)*

captures the essence of the Jazz Age in one iconic image, showing both the opulence of the times and also the degree to which golfers of the era had style.

Capping off a year that for most golfers would make a satisfying lifetime was a big push in the Chicago area in October. Ralph was in town for the World's Fair. His journey began from Grand Central Station, and he booked passage on an iconic train. The New York Central rolled out a special red carpet only once a day when their flagship service was running. Handing his luggage and golf bag to a redcap, it was down the red carpet for Mr. Kennedy and onto the railroad's foremost train, the *Twentieth Century Limited.* The swift steam-powered train was the height of luxury rail travel, offering air-conditioned Pullman sleeper berths, a roomy cocktail lounge, and fresh meals prepared by onboard chefs. The meals were served by nattily dressed waiters who wore all white, in a dining car filled with fresh-cut flowers, on china with white linen tablecloths. Passengers could get their hair cut by a barber onboard, have their shoes shined en route, and use the services of a train secretary who could assist in sending a telegram or in taking dictation. In the observation car on the rear of the train, passengers could relax on a settee and enjoy the views out the large windows while having a smoke.

Once in Chicago, the adept rail passenger used the Illinois Central to navigate his way around. He played a host of consequential courses in Chicagoland, including the Bob O'Link Golf Club (designed by Colt & Alison), the Calumet Country Club, the Flossmoor Country Club (site of the third PGA Championship, held in 1920), the Glen View Club (site of the 1904 U.S. Open), and Medinah's No. 1, 2, and 3 courses. It was with good reason the *Chicago Daily News* of October 11th gave him the nickname "Golfing Gadabout."

His pièce de résistance while in Chicago was playing at the expansive Olympia Fields Country Club, the first in the country to offer seventy-two holes of golf. Resembling a city more than a country club, among the other impressive facilities Olympia Fields contained were a hospital, a dining room that seated eight hundred, and its own ice-making plant. The club was so large it had one thousand caddies. Naturally, Kennedy played all four courses while there. At this point, it would be disappointing to learn that he did anything less.

What does a spirited golfer do after playing so much golf? Stay on the road and play more golf. Traveling to the South, the golfer with a knack for sartorial splendor fit in nicely in the well-mannered region. Under radiant sunshine, he uncoiled into his ball at the Gadsden Country Club, the Anniston Country Club, and the Briarmeade Golf Club. As Kennedy once commented, he played all manner of golf courses, including those on the fringes. His trip through the Heart of Dixie included the Marble City Golf Club in Sylacauga and the Goodyear Allweather Fairways Course in Gadsden. The latter course was a private one owned by the Goodyear Tire Company, with the company logo and a racing flag embellishing the front of their

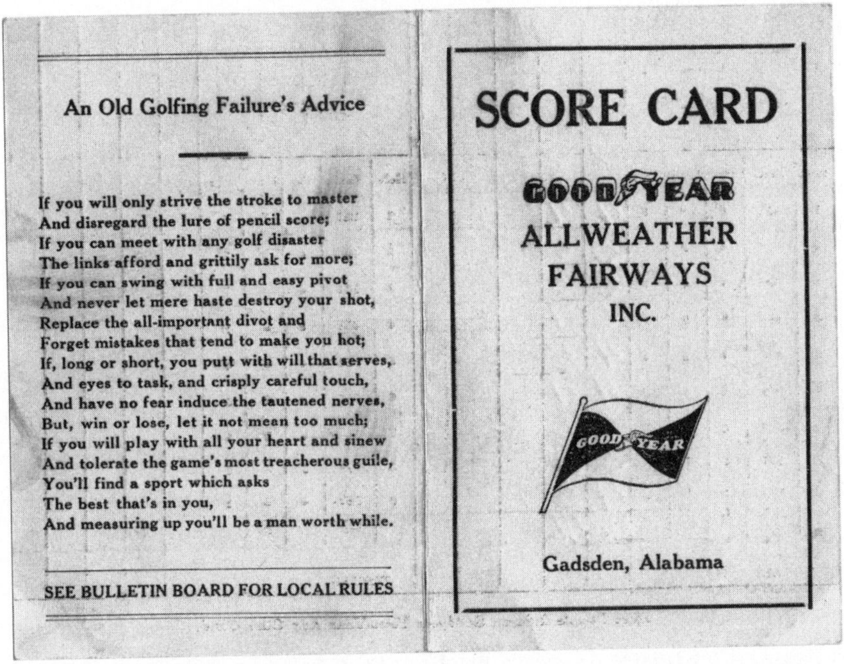

An Old Golfing Failure's Advice

If you will only strive the stroke to master
And disregard the lure of pencil score;
If you can meet with any golf disaster
The links afford and grittily ask for more;
If you can swing with full and easy pivot
And never let mere haste destroy your shot,
Replace the all-important divot and
Forget mistakes that tend to make you hot;
If, long or short, you putt with will that serves,
And eyes to task, and crisply careful touch,
And have no fear induce the tautened nerves,
But, win or lose, let it not mean too much;
If you will play with all your heart and sinew
And tolerate the game's most treacherous guile,
You'll find a sport which asks
The best that's in you,
And measuring up you'll be a man worth while.

SEE BULLETIN BOARD FOR LOCAL RULES

SCORE CARD

GOODYEAR

ALLWEATHER
FAIRWAYS
INC.

GOOD YEAR

Gadsden, Alabama

The card from Ralph's visit to the Goodyear course in Alabama; note the golf poetry on the left side. *(Photo courtesy of USGA)*

scorecard. Goodyear's card was quite creative and featured a golfing poem patterned after Rudyard Kipling's If on the back.

As revelers donned party hats and noise makers to ring out 1933, the Kennedys had reason to celebrate, coming off such a momentous year. Direct dial phone numbers were the new fascination, and the coming year was an appropriate one for the couple, since their home phone number encapsulated it in its last four digits: WAdsworth 3-1934. The automobile was continuing to gain traction at mid-decade, as were expanded roadways to accommodate them. As a result, the original Van Cortlandt Park course was changed, when both the Major Deegan Expressway and the Mosholu Parkways were routed through the course.

In January, Ralph was interviewed by George Trevor in *Golf Illustrated*. Describing the fifty-two-year-old as a heavy-jowled, auburn-haired, and pleasant-faced contact man, he tried to give his readers insights into the duffer, saying, "he was no 'twilight zone amateur,' he has refused free offers of balls and clubs and has declined 'all the whiskey he could drink'—a proposition contingent upon his displaying a certain brand of bourbon during his wanderings." Kennedy also had no illusions concerning the importance of his achievement. "It will not improve the breed of golfers, to paraphrase race-track lingo," he admitted, "nor make this world a better place to live in. It's just a hobby with me, about as significant as flag-pole sitting or oyster eating records, though I think a bit saner. I guess you would call me a nut—all hobby horse riders fall in that slightly goofy category. Anyhow, mine is a harmless diversion and swell for keeping a middle-aged chap with bay-windowish tendencies fit as a fiddle. A daily tramp across the links is more stimulating than the dull routine of setting-up exercises before an open window. Mind you, I'm proud of my record; in fact, it's become an obsession with me. After I've played 1,500 courses I expect to call it a day and let future generations shoot at it, but I said the same promise when I was gunning for the one thousand mark and here I am still plugging away—can't swear off any more than an old soak can renounce liquor. This kind of thing gets in your blood and there it sticks."

At the time of the interview, the game of golf was growing slowly; Trevor noted that there were 5,700 courses in the country in 1934, roughly the same number as at the start of the Depression due to course closures offsetting the growth in new courses. His interview also gives important insights into Kennedy: first, that he was a modest man and tried not to take himself too seriously; second, that Amherst's emphasis on a physical fitness regime had stuck with him long-term; and, last, in the category of the blindingly obvious, he was achievement-oriented and kept reaching for new heights once he obtained his goals.

Ralph always believed that he alone had the proof substantiating him as the record holder for most unique courses played, although he had rivals. Joe Kirkwood, the Australian-born professional and trick-shot artist, always claimed to have played more. Ralph liked to point out that the Aussie didn't keep records, and more important, although

Kirkwood visited courses when he held an exhibition, he didn't always play the course. Similar to the claim made by Charles Fletcher, the *Golfer's Handbook* wrote that Kirkwood had played "in every country in the world." Ralph had an amicable running feud with Kirkwood about the record and received a typed letter in March 1934 from Bill Corum of the *New York Journal*: "Kirkwood has gone to Australia and of course, all I know about it is what he told me. He also mentioned that he had a record of all the courses he had played. You two fellows should get together some time and settle it, not however, with me in the middle."

As odd as it seems today, since it is the most financially secure golf club in the world, Augusta National's difficulties continued after it opened. Because their membership drive was largely unsuccessful, the club had a difficult time making its mortgage payments, and they were letting lesser bills go unpaid due to lack of funds. During April, Cliff Roberts prepared a letter to the club's creditors asking that they not pursue payment for a period of time. Among those who thought the best option was to declare bankruptcy was Bobby Jones's father, Colonel Jones.

CHAPTER 10
Kindly Cancel My Subscription

By now, Ralph had established himself as a golfer far outside the norm and exhibited an enthusiasm that never waned. He behaved in a manner befitting a zealot, never ceasing in his pursuit: it rained and he golfed; it snowed and he golfed; he golfed in the sleet; he golfed when it was too cold to golf; he golfed when the winds were up and when the heat was unrelenting; he golfed when others were relaxing over morning coffee, and when they were unwinding in the afternoon, sipping cocktails; he golfed through dinnertime; he golfed long after twilight receded, when less obsessed golfers had already called it quits.

This single-mindedness propelled his momentum forward in 1934; it was a year of continual motion. A scorecard in the archives from the summer of 1934 at the Newport Country Club has two players listed: MAK and RAK. Accompanied by his wife, Ralph had completed play on the fourth of five founding clubs of the USGA. One of the organizing members of Newport was Theodore Havemeyer, who also served as the first president of the USGA. The trophy awarded to the U.S. Amateur champion each year is named after Havemeyer, who was an important figure in the early development of the game in America.

Newport hosted the first Amateur championship in 1895, and the first U.S. Open the same year. Interestingly, both events were played on what was then a nine-hole course; in the case of the Open, they played it four times in a single day to determine the champion. The influential club had a formidable set of early members and counted Cornelius Vanderbilt II and John Jacob Astor IV among their founders.

The USGA has a collection of over 20,000 scorecards from around the world in its library and archive. Ralph's Newport card is stored alongside other historic ones, including many filled out by Theodore Havemeyer and his brother H. O. Havemeyer when they played at Newport. Their early cards, dating from 1893 through 1896, are printed on rigid sheets of thick and sturdy cardboard, and list the names of the holes on both the front and the back. At the time the brothers played the nineteenth-century course, it was a design of Willie Davis, the first professional at the club. The front of each scorecard was intended for a golfer's first loop around the course, and the back of the card listed the same holes and was intended for their second nine. Interestingly, the earliest cards list only the hole names and do not indicate any par or bogey, nor do they show the length of the holes. One early scorecard, from 1893, highlighted the nautical theme of the course, with holes named as follows: Tower, Beach, Clubhouse, Reef, Life Station, Meadow, High, Burn, and Home.

The historic golf course has been revised several times since it was first built. In 1897, Davis expanded the course to eighteen holes, although some of the holes, which were laying on low ground, proved unsatisfactory. A. W. Tillinghast was brought in in 1921 and designed seven new holes and rerouted some others, completing the work in 1923. The course the Kennedys played on September 27th, 1934 (as his 1,250th course), was a full eighteen holes playing to a yardage of 6,541 yards from the tips.

Newport was not the only course Ralph played while visiting the Ocean State. He also got a chance to roll his ball on the smooth greens of T. Suffern Tailer's Ocean Links, as the scorecard called it, playing on a day awash in abundant sunshine, the electric blue waters of the Atlantic serving as the backdrop. The nine-hole course was built by C. B. Macdonald and Seth Raynor, and was also known simply as the Ocean Links. Built in 1921, the Ocean Links received praise from the *Brooklyn Daily Eagle*, which called the course the "last word in golf architecture," delighting in its mix of prototype holes and original holes. Dynamite was used to loosen the earth during the course's construction, and three of the greens were set directly along the ocean. The course's 460-yard 9th hole, a par-4 "Dogleg" hole, was given a par of four and a bogey of six, highlighting its difficulty for all but the most crack of players.

Married to an heiress of the Lorillard tobacco family, Tailer lived the life of an aristocratic gentleman and was an avid golfer and active in the horse racing circuit. A graduate of Harvard, he was a member of the prestigious Union Club in New York and worked on Wall Street. In addition to his residence in Rhode Island, he also kept homes in New York City; Tuxedo Park, New York; and South Dakota. As befitting a man of such privilege and wealth, Tailer was the only member of the Ocean Links, although he did allow members of the Newport Country Club next door playing privileges. C. B. Macdonald participated in Tailer's annual tournament held at Ocean Links, taking his "power yacht" up the coast from Southampton to Newport.

The *Eagle*'s course profile nicely highlighted how transportation was beginning to change, albeit for the wealthy only at this point: "As when golf and motoring became almost inseparable years ago, so may aviation play its part toward aiding the linksmen [to] reach a given point in a minimum period of time. Here again Newport will set the pace as in the early days of championships. That recent announcement of an airline service from New York to Newport, linking up the two in ninety minutes, as against a six hours' journey by rail, can scarcely make its appeal to golfers so fortunate as to be directly interested in visiting this exclusive spot."

Ralph and Mary Alice were frequent visitors to Long Island during the temperate months. Continuing a succession of great golfing seasons, Ralph played another Macdonald-Raynor course after they returned home, this time the Links Golf Club in Roslyn, Long Island, a course owned by the 1 percent of its era.

The year's itinerary also included a stop at the "Mrs. Graham Fair Vanderbilt Private Course." The course owned by the aristocratic lady didn't have its own scorecard, so the intrepid traveler took a blank generic scorecard and filled in the details and his scores nonetheless. Meticulous as ever, he had the superintendent sign the makeshift card to attest to his round. The nine-hole course played a total distance of 2,940 yards to a par of thirty-six and included three par fives and a 333-yard par four; Ralph shot two over par. He played another "private" Long Island course, as well, known as Greentree, located on the estate of Payne Whitney in Manhasset. Although the country was in dire economic straits, courses built for the use of one family were in vogue. It was Ralph's fourth visit to such a course; his first experience was at the Whitelaw Reid private course in Purchase, New York, which he played in 1927. Reid ran the *Herald Tribune,* although his fortunes were obtained partly by marrying well.

Although FDR was advancing a substantial amount of New Deal legislation, economic times continued to be very difficult. The Hooverville shantytowns that sprung up to provide rudimentary shelter in his predecessor's term remained a lingering problem. The Depression continued to present problems for the Eagle Pencil Company. As a result of reducing worker wages and hours, its New York factory was the subject of another strike in 1934. As a successful, college-educated traveling salesman, Ralph was lucky to avoid the problems besieging his fellow countrymen and colleagues.

Not only was he avoiding financial troubles, but he was, in fact, reaching new heights as evidenced by an important hand-delivered envelope received by Dr. A. B. Weaver at the Kentucky Hotel in Louisville while on his annual trip to the state. The letter inside, on official State House letterhead from the state capital, Frankfort, was on behalf of Kentucky Governor Ruby Laffoon. It was singularly good news, as the Honorable Ralph A. Kennedy of New York had received a commission to become a Kentucky colonel. Dr. Weaver was to let the golf fanatic know that he would soon receive his own notification under separate cover. A Kentucky colonel is a ceremonial title granted by the sitting governor, and those appointed become a member of the Honorable Order of Kentucky Colonels. The tradition originated in 1813, when political supporters were granted the title in the state militia. Ralph had played golf over a period of twenty years in the state and had thirty-four different courses in his scorecard collection. By chance, he happened to bump into Laffoon on one of his trips and, ever the raconteur, told the chief about his exploits in the state. Among other colonels Governor Laffoon would appoint—one year after Ralph—was the most famous of all: Harland Sanders.

Ralph made another jam-packed visit to Chicago in 1934, playing on the north and south shores of Lake Michigan and west of the city. He planned quite a trip and was on and off the train frequently, asking the professionals at nineteen additional courses to sign scorecards. His tried-and-true routine continued as it had for years: take the train out of the city in the early morning and hail a taxi to the course, where he would hire a caddie and walk the links. Then it was back into a cab and onto the next course, and if he had time and there was another nearby, he would do it again. Among the notable courses he played were the all-male bastion Old Elm Club, the Foulis brothers-designed Onwentsia Club (host of the 1906 U.S. Open), and the Seth Raynor-designed Shoreacres, all on the same day. He told the Windy City newspapers that he had just made his foray into Wisconsin and Michigan to play for the first time. He continued to use his Newspaper Club connections to gain access to some of the private courses. Ever the master of public relations, he also managed an interview with the *Chicago Daily News*: "'I was twenty-eight years old when I started this queer hobby,' Kennedy remarked between puffs of the inevitable cigar. 'Maybe I'm a nut but it's a harmless amusement, keeps a guy out in the air, and is more stimulating as a means of keeping fit than setting-up exercises.'"

The apex of his Midwest trip was a visit to the cloistered Charles Blair Macdonald-designed Chicago Golf Club in Wheaton. With only 125 members, the historic club has always been difficult to secure an invitation to. It was the last of the five founding member clubs of the

USGA that Ralph visited, as his 1,277th course, on Saturday the 13th of October. By the time of Ralph's visit, Chicago Golf Club had played host to the Walker Cup and U.S. Women's Amateur once, the U.S. Open three times, and the prestigious Amateur Championship four times.

Meanwhile in baseball, as the year came to an end, Lou Gehrig became the first athlete to appear on a box of Wheaties. He also won the Triple Crown, leading the league with a .363 batting average, 49 home runs, and 165 runs batted in. He tacked on an additional 154 games to his continuous game streak and negotiated his contract to be paid $31,000 for the following season. Ralph was pictured alongside Gehrig's teammate Babe Ruth in an illustration in the *New York World-Telegram*. Quite the famous golfer by now, he was shown next to Ruth and Walter Hagen and a number of other well-known athletes with a caption stating that they were all members of the hole-in-one club and that each was still trying for their second ace. To finish off another strong year of golf, Ralph visited the grande dame of Philadelphia's Main Line, the Merion Cricket Club in Ardmore, playing it as course No. 1,300.

As it turned out, Ruth would not return to the Yankees in 1935, ending an affiliation with the team that began in 1920. On April 21st, Gehrig was named the Yankees captain, a position that had been vacant for ten years. Lou would be inspired in his new role, turning in another impressive year, batting .329 with 30 home runs and 119 runs batted in, leading the Yankees in all three categories. "I guess I have been very lucky. Then I suppose I can thank my sturdy German ancestry for this iron constitution. Both my father and mother weigh over 200 pounds. We are a big-boned family," he told a reporter that year.

In the world of Ralph Kennedy, the *Atlantic City Press* led off the year's media coverage, calling him an unusual term of endearment: "golf glutton." Coincidentally, he visited Atlantic City the same year a board game featuring its streets was sold for the first time: *Monopoly*. He played a respectable number of courses in his usual places, including New Jersey, Connecticut, New York, Massachusetts, Kentucky, and Georgia, but his big campaigns for the year were in Vermont and Minnesota. He also crossed the border into North Dakota, playing at the El Zagal Temple Golf Course in Fargo. Although a course dedicated to the Shriners, "for the exclusive use of nobles of the Mystic shrine and their families," Ralph was able to play it nonetheless. The newly-appointed Colonel liked to cluster his courses together and play in bursts. He played thirty-one courses in Minnesota in twelve days, including two that Bobby Jones helped put on the map: The Minikahda Club, site of his 1927 Amateur victory; and Interlachen, site of his U.S. Open win in 1930. Ralph's trip to Vermont was even more intense: forty courses in nine days, albeit many were nine-holers. The veteran rail traveler took the Central Vermont Railroad throughout the Green Mountain State; among the courses he played were the Kingberry Club Golf Course, the Rutland Country Club, the Bellows Falls Country Club, and the Orleans Country Club.

Ralph's elevated press exposure continued in 1935. On Monday, March 11th, at 6:45 p.m. he appeared on Lowell Thomas's national radio program and received fan letters afterwards, several of which he pasted into his scrapbook. One listener commented that it was good to hear his "melodious voice." As a journalist, Thomas covered the First World War and eventually met T. E. Lawrence in Jerusalem. He is credited with creating the public persona "Lawrence of Arabia" in his coverage of the British officer. Thomas had a long career on the radio, broadcasting various shows starting in 1930 and continuing until 1976. He was the voice of Twentieth Century Fox's *Movietone* newsreels from 1935 until 1952, and NBC hired Lowell as their first nighttime news anchor in 1939. Broadcasting would make Thomas a wealthy man; in 1948, he earned the gargantuan sum of $420,300 for this radio work. He had enough money to build his own golf course on his 3,000-acre estate, the Quaker Hill Country Club, in Pawling, New York. It is no great mystery to learn that Ralph played the course (as No. 1,118) several years earlier, in June 1933, when it was only 2,390 yards and a par of thirty-five. The clubhouse at Quaker Hill contains something not typically found in one, a sound-proof studio, from which Lowell sometimes did radio broadcasts. Being featured on a national radio program by a respected journalist highlights how big a sensation the pride of the Eagle Pencil Company had become.

Later that same month, O. B. Keeler was pecking away at his typewriter again, cranking out an article in the *Atlanta Journal*, "Like Alexander the Great Mr. Ralph Kennedy of Winged Foot is looking for new worlds to conquer," complimenting the Winged Footer on his course streak. In a *Boston Post* interview, Ralph revealed that he had played Pine Valley again and shot a ninety-one, bettering his previous low of ninety-nine. He also recounted to the *Post* another of his entertaining stories, how "A colored caddie in Pensacola fished out red golf balls [from his golf bag] and then asked, are you bleeding? Did you kill a bird or a chicken with these?" Laughing heartily, he explained to the young man that he was not bleeding and did not kill anything, they were the balls he used at Winged Foot during the winter to play in the snow. This farther confused the caddie, who asked, "Shouldn't snowballs be white?"

In April, Ralph's former caddie, Gene Sarazen, scored a two on the par-5 15th hole at the Augusta National Invitation Tournament. In only its second year, it was not yet known as the Masters; Grantland Rice would be the first to use that term to describe the tournament several years in the future. Gene's double-eagle was the "shot heard 'round the world" and helped him eventually win the tournament. Nineteen-thirty-five was also the first year the

Ralph's second appearance on the *Saturday Evening Post*'s cover. *(Photo courtesy of Curtis Publishing)*

tournament was played in its current configuration, the two sets of nine holes playing in reverse order from when Ralph teed it up there.

Writing in the *New York Sun* in July 1935, George Trevor nicknamed Ralph "Golf's Lou Gehrig." Trevor had a knack for giving out monikers and was the first writer to use the term "impregnable quadrilateral," when referring to Bobby Jones's achievement winning the British and U.S. Opens and Amateurs in 1930.

The red-haired wonder appeared again on the cover of the *Saturday Evening Post* on August 31, 1935. This time, the illustration emphasized his ruddy cheeks; he is shown wearing a multi-colored tam-o'-shanter and a white dress shirt with a plaid tie. In his left hand he is holding a golf club and a scorecard and—to the delight of his employer—in his right hand, a pencil. His right hand is held in the air with his index finger extended, as if gesturing to another golfer, making a point. After its publication, Eagle sent a memorandum to all their salesmen trumpeting the free publicity they were receiving and encouraging them to use the magazine to help sell more.

Kennedy's appearance on the cover didn't please everyone. In one case, an irritable (though well fed) reader from the Bluegrass State sent the magazine's publisher a neatly typed, well-written letter at its headquarters in Philadelphia, dated August 27, 1935:

Gentlemen:

Kindly cancel my subscription to the Saturday Evening Post *immediately. It is with extreme regret that I make this request as I have been a subscriber to your very excellent magazine since 1867, and after our many years of pleasant relations I feel it is only fair to offer an explanation for my action.*

This morning, while enjoying a light breakfast of half a honeydew, cereal, fried eggs, mush, bacon, fried apples, waffles, honey, and coffee, the postman delivered your magazine dated August 31st. On looking at the cover I pushed aside my fifth cup of coffee and grabbed for my bottle of gin. I wish you to understand that I am a teetotaler, but during the long years of prohibition (due to a severe stomach ailment) I have been compelled—under advice of my physician—to take a modicum of gin before the evening meal. You will understand my extreme agitation. My faintness forced me to imbibe this devil's brew even before finishing my medium morning meal. The reason why I was so overcome is this: I am not only a Deacon in the Synagogue but also a member of the Louisville Board of Education and stand for honesty, sobriety, morality, etc., etc. The face of the person portrayed on the cover represents all of the things which I have fought with my last ounce of energy. The look in the man's eye indicates that he has not only entered upon the scorecard (with a typical Scotch pencil) a false score, but he is apparently endeavoring to collect a bet, the said bet evidently to be spent for strong drink. This is indicated not only by the flushed and florid color of the cheeks and nose, but even of the hair, tam, and necktie.

I could go on at great length but feel that if I continue I might say something which I would regret, therefore, I beg to remain,

Yours very truly.

P.S.

I am returning to you this copy of the Saturday Evening Post.

It is safe to assume that Ralph got a big kick out of such a strong reaction to his appearance, although he likely wondered as much as the present-day reader how so much could be read into the interesting expression on his face. No doubt Kennedy was also pleased with the mention of a pencil in the gin drinker's letter. The overly-caffeinated writer's prose is priceless, and we are lucky that he had a "light" breakfast consisting of only nine items, since a heavier repast could have run the emotional letter to another page or two. Unfortunately, he did not sign his impassioned correspondence, so his name is lost to posterity.

To close out the year, Ralph took a trip to the Midwest in October, visiting a handful of states. He made the short hop across the Iowa border to play in Nebraska for the first time. The school supply salesman was playing hooky on a Friday, spending the entire day at a smattering of courses in balmy autumn sunlight, wielding his mashies and niblicks at the Omaha Country Club, the Field Club of Omaha, the Happy Hollow Club, and the Harrison Heights Public Golf Links. It was his only visit to the state, although the *Omaha Bee* took notice of his brief visit with a small blurb spotlighting his foray into the Cornhusker State in their morning edition.

CHAPTER 11
Old Man River

THE DUST BOWL WOULD LAST almost a decade, raging through the middle part of the 1930s, sending Okies and other tattered families in search of a better life out West. The Harvard-educated president was using all the powers of his office to put the country back on solid footing. One of FDR's signature New Deal programs, Social Security, was implemented in 1935. His Rural Electrification Program launched in 1936, bringing electricity for the first time to a large number of Americans who still lived on farms.

In 1936, Lou Gehrig sat for an interview with Sid Keener of the *St. Louis Star-Times*; up until that point he had played 1,744 consecutive games. "But wouldn't you like to take an afternoon off and get away from the ballpark and the uniform?" Keener asked. "I should say not," Gehrig replied. "I don't know how much longer I can keep adding to my record, but I hope to add at least seven more seasons to my career." Gehrig came out of a game against the Washington Senators on September 26th in the second inning because his back hurt but kept his consecutive game streak intact. His 1936 season was another impressive one and among the reasons why he is considered one of the greatest ever to have played the game. He finished the year with a .354 batting average, hammered a league-leading 49 home runs, had 152 runs batted in, and justifiably won baseball's Most Valuable Player award.

Early in the year, Ralph traveled to the far western edge of Texas and played at the El Paso Country Club, a course easily accessible from the Santa Fe Railroad. The *Fraser's* guide wrote positively about golf in Texas: "Easterners probably think of Texas in vague terms of cattle, ranches and cowboys. But times have changed. Today Texas is one of the 'golfiest' states in the union." The El Paso Country Club had compacted cottonseed-hull greens when Ralph played it. The unusual greens were necessary because in certain parts of the West, it is so windy that greens made of sand are continually blown away. To create the cottonseed greens, woody fibers of the hulls are laid three to four inches in depth and then rolled to compact them; the more they were used, the better they became, because they were farther compacted by golfers walking on them. The USGA was a proponent of the greens in the Southwest and felt that they helped speed up the pace of play: they estimated that it took between forty and fifty minutes less time to play on cottonseed than it did on sand. Ralph was intrigued by the course and the cottonseed, although he highlighted one of their shortcomings: "Their only drawback is that a cigarette stub can set a blaze which water is helpless to combat. They burn for days and don't stop until the seed hulls are burned out."

For their 1936 summer sojourn, the Kennedys headed to the Canadian Maritime provinces, via a train through New England. Beginning in New Brunswick, they played seven courses, starting at the Algonquin Golf Club in St. Andrews, which has breathtaking views of Passamaquoddy Bay, an inlet of the Bay of Fundy, with its thundering waves and ominous tides. Then it was on to New Brunswick's largest city, also situated on the bay: Saint John, where they played the Portland Place Golf Course, the Donald Ross-designed Riverside Golf & Country Club, and the Ridgewood Golf & Country Club in South Bay. Ralph told the local newspaper that he thought Riverside was one of "the best," and he also commented that he loved visiting Canada because the people were more of his kind, due to his Scotch heritage.

It was back inland for a brief stop at the Sussex Golf Club, then on to Moncton, a railroad hub, where Ralph played the Lakeside Golf

Links and the Riverdale Golf Club. Venturing on, the duo turned east, with a visit to the Sackville Country Club. From New Brunswick, they traveled across the province line to Nova Scotia, where they played the Amherst Golf Club and then farther east still to the Truro Golf Club. Keeping up a pace that only true golf fanatics would love, they headed south to Digby to play the Pines Golf Club. The latter course was built for the Canadian Pacific Railway in support of their new Pines Hotel. Set in an idyllic location on a rocky bluff, the property overlooks the Annapolis basin, an inlet on the eastern side of the Bay of Fundy. The Stanley Thompson-designed course slopes toward a stream that runs through its center; its uphill 278-yard 11th hole presents the unsuspecting duffer with a unique challenge: two bunkers that together form the shape of a question mark.

Traveling northeast, the couple also stopped at the Antigonish Golf Club before crossing over to Cape Breton Island to the northern reaches of Nova Scotia. Their first stop was the nine-hole Lingan Country Club in Sydney, followed by a visit to the Highland Golf Club in the old coal-mining town of Dominion. The Kennedys' final stop on the scenic and remote island was the Beinn Bhreagh Golf Club—"Beautiful Mountain" in Scottish Gaelic—a name given by Alexander Graham Bell to his estate, which was located there. Bell loved spending time on the rugged Cape Breton because it reminded him of his native Scotland.

Perhaps not surprising for someone born in the town where the Boston Marathon begins, Ralph kept up a blistering pace, one worthy of a long-distance runner. From Cape Breton Island, the couple completed the loop south, stopping at the nine-hole Pictou Golf & Country Club, before being whisked across Northumberland Strait to the smallest of Canada's dominions. He enjoyed smashing his drives on five courses on Prince Edward Island: the Charlottetown Golf Club and the Stanhope Beach Inn Course in Charlottetown, the Gregor's Hotel Golf Club, Shaw's Golf Club, and the Summerside Golf Club. In addition to gorging himself on the abundance of local mussels, oysters, and lobster, the golf nomad king picked up twenty-three additional courses on his Maritime trip.

Ralph's handicap had come back down to a twelve by 1936, a number he would keep consistent over the next half-dozen years as he adjusted to the new ball and played frequently. His little tussle with Kirkwood continued to play out in the newspapers, with the *Sydney Mail* making the case that their hometown boy had played more courses. "Peculiar Record," was the headline. "How many courses have you played during your golfing career? This is a question that would, after fifteen minutes' deliberation, be easily answered by the majority of golfers in Australia. But Mr. Ralph Kennedy of New York would have a difficult task if he did not keep a tally. For this fifty-three-year-old golfer has played on no fewer than 1,436 courses, and he has the cards duly certified to this effect. Of course, many of these courses are only over nine holes. Kirkwood's figures might possibly be better than those of Mr. Kennedy, though the famous trick-shot maker has spent months travelling the world, whereas Mr. Kennedy's task has been accomplished in the U.S.A."

The *Mail* mentioned that Ralph played many nine-hole courses, which he did, although they seemed to be implying that this lessened his accomplishment. Although it is not as impressive as if he had played only eighteen-hole courses, the fact is, the effort required to seek out and travel to a nine-hole course is the same effort required for a course of eighteen holes. Certainly, it is less strenuous and taxing to only play nine, but it did allow Ralph to play more courses in a limited period of time than he otherwise would have been able to. By comparison, not even Lou Gehrig played every inning of every game; although his consecutive game streak is fully documented, he failed to complete plenty of games over the years because of injuries or because he needed a rest. There was in fact only one season, 1931, where he played every inning of every game.

Another of FDR's ambitious New Deal programs, the Works Progress Administration (WPA), benefited Ralph. If millions of people are being put to work to jump-start the economy, why not have them build golf courses? Through 1936, the WPA helped fund and build sixty-one nine-hole and thirteen eighteen-hole courses. One of the most prominent was the new Bethpage Black course, which Ralph played upon his return from Canada. Designed by A. W. Tillinghast, the course opened to praise, as evidenced by the fact that Ralph waited to play it as one of his milestones: course number 1,500. It is too bad the USGA eliminated the half-par hole convention years earlier, since if ever there was a hole that called for a par-4 ½ it is the Black Course's uphill par-4 15th hole, where the terrain rises to the green so steeply that at least two extra clubs are required to reach it on what was already a demanding hole of 413 yards.

Ralph returned to Illinois again in 1936, this time to the capital city. He topped his own accomplishment of playing four courses in one day when he played six different ones in one day on October 10th in Springfield. The spry New Yorker played seventy-two total holes: two eighteen-hole courses and four nine-hole courses, behaving as if he had actual winged feet.

Ralph was a long-time member of the NYAC and had by now been a member for thirty-two years. He was a frequent visitor to their elegant limestone clubhouse, "City House," which sits in a prominent position on Central Park South. When Tillinghast commented that he knew he could construct Winged Foot as a mighty course because NYAC members were men of brawn, he didn't know Ralph Kennedy personally, but he may as well have been commenting about him specifically.

After the 1936 season, Gehrig's streak numbered 1,808 consecutive games. "Two thousand games would be a breeze . . . 2,500 seemed like a reasonable target," he said at a press conference. Babe Ruth commented that it was foolish for Gehrig to keep playing every day. Ruth said, "I think Lou's making one of the worst mistakes a ballplayer can make by trying to keep up with that iron man stuff, he's already cut three years off his baseball life with it . . . He ougtha learn to sit on the bench and rest . . . They're not gonna pay off on how many games he's played." Never the best of friends, Lou was quite irritated with the Babe's comments. Gehrig stayed home the following January, resting while others were in Florida playing golf. Ruth, by then retired, was a three handicap, playing golf 240 days a year.

Franklin Roosevelt continued to battle a difficult economic environment in January 1937, when he said in his second inaugural address, "I see one-third of the nation ill-housed, ill-clad, ill-nourished . . . the test of our progress is not whether we add more to the abundance of those who have much; it is whether we provide enough for those who have too little." Roosevelt continued to push through spending programs, and in New York City the WPA funded a project to remove thirty-three miles of surface line tracks that were previously used by trolleys and rail lines, as the automobile was making them obsolete.

The coming year would be a big one for both Gehrig and Kennedy. Lou would play 157 games, and Ralph, 101 new courses. The latter began the season in the Deep South, visiting New Orleans once again in February for a National Education Association conference. Since schools were large buyers of pencils and other supplies that Eagle sold, attending conventions was a part of his normal routine. Never missing the opportunity to find a new course, he played the City Park No. 1 course, one that was newly built with federal money from the Emergency Relief Administration, a predecessor organization of the WPA. The *Times-Picayune* had a feature article about the nomadic golfer, calling him "Roving Ralph Kennedy," and they included a picture of him standing tall, wearing his tam-o'-shanter and plus fours. He had by now developed an eye for what he liked in course design and noted that he put a question mark by the 13th hole on his scorecard because he thought it such a queer hole; he was of the opinion that the green was slanted in the wrong direction.

Departing Louisiana, he trekked back east, hugging the Gulf Coast to play in Biloxi (the Country Club), Gulfport (the Great Southern Golf Club), and Pass Christian (the Pine Hills Golf Course), Mississippi.

During his annual spring visit to Kentucky, Colonel Kennedy played the Fort Knox Golf Course before traveling south to play the Hopkinsville Golf & Country Club. The *Kentucky New Era* used eloquent prose to take a jab at the obsessive player on the trip: "So golf's Old Man River is still rolling along, seeking new courses to add to his list, collecting golf courses as he travels for a pencil company. His is a bizarre fad." That same spring brought a dramatic aviation disaster. During the mid-afternoon of May 6th, the silver-skinned flagship dirigible of the Zeppelin Company—adorned with a large Nazi swastika emblem—sailed over the Kennedy apartment on its way to dock in Lakehurst, New Jersey. The spectacle of the *Hindenburg's* explosion and the death of thirty-six in horrific circumstances put a permanent stain on lighter-than-air transportation.

As the summer settled in, it was time to go back across the border to escape New York's sweltering heat and heavy humidity. Visiting Canada again, this year Ralph was focused on the courses of Quebec province. Twenty-two courses made the cut on Ralph's itinerary, including the oldest golf club in North America, Royal Montreal. Founded in 1873, the club received its "Royal" designation from Queen Victoria eleven years later. In addition to being the oldest, Kennedy also ranked it as the toughest of all the Canuck courses. After playing it, he offered a gathering of women who came to hear him speak discouraging advice, "Never play golf with your husband unless you are pretty good."

The postal service had a different type of round in mind when they carved their creed into the marble of the imposing post office on Manhattan's Eighth Avenue. Stretching for nearly two full city blocks, it reads, "Neither snow nor rain nor heat nor gloom of night stays these couriers from the swift completion of their appointed rounds." In September, the unstoppable golfer played a round in miserable conditions in an NYAC tournament held at Winged Foot. Heeding his own inner compass, which was in synch with the post office creed, the iron-willed Kennedy would not quit. It was raining so hard during the tournament that almost all the golfers walked off the course. Only four finished, and the trouper Ralph was one of them, backing into the championship because he was one of the few who finished, winning the "veterans" category.

Nineteen thirty-eight saw meaningful rules changes, specifically related to the stymie. The USGA began a trial on a new rule that allowed a ball within six inches of the hole to be lifted. Prior to this change, it was only permissible to lift a ball that was not within six inches of the

U. S. G. A. Rules govern play with exception of the following:

LOCAL GROUND RULES

Penalty for lost ball, or ball out of bounds, distance only.

Players will observe out of bounds stakes on Holes Nos. 1, 2, 7, 17 and 18.

Hole No. 4, a ball to left of fence is out of bounds.

Roadways and paths are hazards.

Ladies and Junior members are not permitted on the course Saturday Afternoons, Sunday Mornings, Holidays or Tournament days, with the exception that such members may have the privilege of the course Saturday Afternoons after 4 o'clock, starting only at No. 1 Tee.

Foursomes shall have equal rights with twosomes; singles and more than foursomes having no rights, must always give way to a properly constituted match.

Players unable to maintain their position on the course by reason of lost balls or slow play must permit following matches to pass through, and, *after signalling, must let them through.*

Players "cutting in" at any point must give way to those playing the regular course.

The use of regular tees, greens and traps for practice is positively forbidden.

The imaginative scorecard from Ralph's 1937 visit to the Columbus Country Club in Ohio. *(Photo courtesy of USGA)*

cup (and was more than six inches from the opponent's ball.) The fourteen-club rule was also instituted the same year. At one time, Lawson Little burdened himself by carrying up to thirty-one clubs. Apparently benefitting from the stricter rule, he went on to win the U.S. Open at the Canterbury Golf Club in Cleveland two years later.

Ralph visited the Georgia Low Country again, stopping in the genteel city of Savannah to play another company-owned course: the Union Bag Athletic Association (course No. 1,719), a basic nine-hole layout built for employees of the Union Bag and Paper Company, which had a large facility there. The company had an inclusive policy, and anyone who worked at their large mill could play the course. In an interesting side note, the Lowell family made its second indispensable contribution to civilization. The son of the patent holder for the Reddy Tee, William Lowell Jr., worked for Union Bag and was responsible for the invention of the first six-pack carton.

There was continued unrest at the Eagle pencil factory in New York in June, when another strike was called to protest a 10 percent cut in salaries. The factory was already on reduced hours due to the effects of the Great Depression, operating only twenty-four hours a week. A group of 150 people picketed the plant and fought a "pitched battle" with forty policemen at the main entrance when they blocked the way for employees trying to enter the premises.

It was not uncommon for the pungent smell of graphite and the woodsy aroma of cedar to waft along the East River near the Eagle factory. Eagle produced more than its best-selling No. 2 pencils at the hulking facility; they produced hundreds of varieties of specialized pencils for draftsmen, carpenters, artists, golfers, and other tradesmen. They also produced pens, pencil holders, pencil sharpeners, self-filling fountain pens, crayons, erasers, compasses, ink wells, and rulers. Ralph was in fact much more than a pencil salesman, although it doesn't make as splashy a headline; he sold a whole variety of school and office supplies.

Daily routines and customs in the middle part of the twentieth century reflected the different mode of life: it was common for doctors to make house calls; paperboys stood on street corners and in railroad stations hawking the news of the day; baseball was a game played in the warm sunshine of the afternoon, rather than at night; men's fashions included removable collars on shirts and straw dress hats in the summertime. In the fall, the smell of burning leaves filled the air. Throughout the year, the rhythmic sound of train whistles blowing in the distance was widespread. Clotheslines with clean laundry swinging in the breeze were a regular sight as Ralph crisscrossed the country. Electric clothes dryers were offered for sale for the first time in 1938, bringing a relatively affordable appliance to the mass-market. Kennedy's travels were in a slower-paced, less connected world, where local businesses were dominant.

It was back onto the rails as Ralph returned to Massachusetts during the summer, and among his stops was the Toy Town Golf Course in Winchendon. Toy Town was named by Paul E. Converse,

The Toy Town Golf Course, Massachusetts, 1929. Note the square-style green. *(Author's Collection)*

who was the driving force behind making the entire town over in the images of toys. *McClure's* did a feature story about Winchendon and noted how passengers stepping off the train entered a town that was almost entirely toy-themed. There was a Toy Town Tavern (a hotel), a Toy Town chocolate store, and a Toy Town golf course. The short golf course sits on top of a hill outside the village and features small greens. It was designed by Donald Ross and was 5,692 yards long when Ralph played it in August as part of his vacation, as course No. 1,821.

Ralph played another private, company-owned course in 1938, the eighteen-hole Pennsylvania Railroad Golf Club in Havertown. It was one of twenty-five courses in the Commonwealth on his dance card that year, along with the Susquehanna Valley Country Club, the Shamokin Valley Country Club, the Otzinachson Country Club, and the Aronimink Golf Club. The husky New Yorker was captured in print throughout the year, with local newspapers eating up his story. He was pictured in both the *Kingsport* (Tennessee) *Times* and in the *News* (Frederick, Maryland) wearing plus fours, a long-sleeved button-down dress shirt, and a snappy bow tie. He told the *News* reporter that he enjoyed the recordkeeping and planning associated with his unusual hobby: "My people were Scotch, and I was methodical enough to have everything down on paper from the beginning."

Headline writers nationally continued to invent catchy names for Ralph's long journey; the *Baltimore Sun* touted that the "Pencil Man has Courses Record" in 1938. The first signs of ALS hit Lou Gehrig the same year, and New York's headline writers were quick to notice. "Father Time Scouting Gehrig," the *New York Sun* declared in March, citing that "The end of the trail was nearing for the Iron Man." Gehrig was wearing sneakers when he went with some teammates to watch the St. Petersburg Open golf tournament in Florida. Pitcher Wes Ferrell noticed Lou slipping on the grass as they walked and knew something wasn't right. Gehrig played well throughout the season, but not up to the level of his prior years. The Yankees would go on to once again win the World Series, this time defeating the Chicago Cubs, with Gehrig returning to Wrigley Field, the site of his Commerce High School triumph many years earlier. He played all 157 games for the season, although his batting average dropped to .295.

After the World Series concluded, Ralph traveled to Chicago and played at the Tam O'Shanter Club (course No. 1,838), an appropriately named course. The course itself wasn't particularly distinctive, although a tournament hosted there was. Organizing and marketing a high-profile golf tournament was the brainchild of George S. May, a Chicago businessman who began his career as a Bible salesman. May assumed ownership of the Tam O'Shanter course one year before Ralph visited. The English golf writer Henry Longhurst described May as one of the people most responsible for making golf a spectator sport in the United States. For a period of time in the 1940s and 1950s, May's tournament regularly offered more prize money than any other, attracting strong fields. Longhurst described the environment at May's tournaments as having a "circus atmosphere," and slot machines were among the entertainments he provided for golfers on the course.

The large-scale, Art Deco Rockefeller Center development—located between Forty-Eighth and Fifty-First Streets, on a twelve-acre site in the heart of New York City—was completed in 1939. Its centerpiece was the seventy-story RCA (Radio Corporation of America) Building, appropriate for the era because radio was still such a dominant form of communication. The buildings were equipped with all the latest technology, including high-speed elevators and air conditioning. To emphasize how important a role radio played in the pre-television era, the prior fall Orson Welles's "Martian" radio broadcast sent Americans into a panic when aliens landed in Grover's Mill, New Jersey.

Almost fourteen years to the day since *The Great Gatsby* was published, on April 14, 1939, a new novel appeared capturing the zeitgeist of the times, this time with a much grimmer tone. John Steinbeck's *The Grapes of Wrath* chronicled the misery of those in the country's interior and their forced migration west in search of work.

As his ALS got worse, Lou Gehrig could not continue to play. In 1939, the beginning of what would have been his fourteenth full season, he played only the first eight games before taking himself out. On May 2nd, the Yankees were scheduled to play the Detroit Tigers; the team was staying at the Book-Cadillac Hotel, and it was there that Gehrig approached manager Joe McCarthy, asking to be taken out of the lineup. McCarthy's reaction sums up the situation perfectly: "It's a black day for me and the Yankees." Gehrig's last consecutive game turned out to be April 30, 1939, his 2,130th, played at Yankee Stadium. On exactly the same day, the World's Fair officially opened in Flushing, Queens. The theme of the World's Fair was "Building the World of Tomorrow." The AT&T pavilion featured a popular attraction for visitors: the ability to use a phone to make a free long distance call.

During his playing career, Gehrig was often overshadowed by his more colorful teammate Ruth. Gehrig was not as well liked by the sportswriters, who said he lacked color. Although fans never warmed to him to the same degree they did to Ruth, he garnered tremendous respect. On June 29th, during a game in Philadelphia against the Athletics, manager Connie Mack asked Gehrig to step onto the field before the game, even though he was not in the lineup. The crowd stood and cheered for a full *eight minutes* as Lou wiped tears from his eyes. July 4, 1939, was one of the saddest days in sports history; at Yankee Stadium, the thirty-six-year-old Yankees captain gave his "Luckiest Man" speech. At first, he was so overcome with emotion that he could not speak. When he did begin, head bowed, he spoke for less than three minutes. Gehrig was the first Yankee to have his number (four) retired. In his career with the Yankees, he hit 493 home runs, had a batting average of .340, and had 1,995 runs batted in.

Ralph's emphasis on the year was the Great Lakes Region. His first area of focus was in Wisconsin, where the intrepid golfer played eighteen courses across the Badger State. His travels were hither and yon, teeing it up in towns that would throw a contestant in a spelling bee out of whack: Oconomowoc, Baraboo, Oconto, and Waupun. The grand tour included a visit to the Wisconsin Dells, a beautiful region along the Wisconsin River replete with rock formations and a gorge with cliffs up to one hundred feet high. He played the melodic Berry's Dells Golf Course and the Dell View Golf Club in Wisconsin Dells. The Milwaukee Country Club—a vintage Colt & Alison track—was on the agenda, as well, as he ventured north along Lake Michigan, finishing off at the Green Bay Public Golf Club.

The golfer with unyielding vigor then journeyed across the state line to play thirty-one courses in Michigan, beginning in the Upper Peninsula at the Escanaba Golf Club in Delta County. He then boarded the ferry to Mackinac Island, where he played the Mackinac Headlands Golf Course in Mackinac City, as well as the Grand Hotel Golf Club. He also played the historic Wawashkamo Golf Club on Mackinac Island, which was founded in 1898 and designed by Scotsman Alex Smith, an émigré from Carnoustie, Scotland. The course's unique third green features an oddball "circus ring" design: an earthen mound with long grass on it completely encircles the green.

A case study of Newton's first law of motion, once he began, Kennedy kept moving. Among his areas of concentration in Michigan was Grand Rapids, where he scurried to play seven courses, once again knocking off six in one day. Before hitting his tee shot on the 110-yard

The "circus ring" hole at the Wawashkamo course in Michigan. *(Photo courtesy of David Owen)*

third hole at the Indian Trails Municipal Course, he asked his playing partners if they had ever seen a hole-in-one. None of them had. Reminiscent of Babe Ruth pointing to the outfield before hitting a home run in the World Series seven years earlier, Ralph stepped up to the ball and miraculously knocked it in the hole.

Detroit was an important stop for any traveling golfer, and the wandering linksman delved into the city on this trip, excited to visit. The *Fraser's* guide had whetted his appetite with its description of golf in the Motor City: "Detroit has developed its golf along possibly more exclusive lines than any other city. Among the many courses are some of the finest and most expensive in the country, notably the Detroit Golf Club, occupying the most valuable land of any golf club in the U.S.A. Wealth is in evidence at the clubhouses and no money has been spared to make the links the last word . . . The hotel accommodation in the city is not surpassed anywhere in the country." Detroit was the fourth largest city in the country in the '30s and '40s, and one with a rich heritage in both the golf world and with its buildings of architectural distinction (not to mention jazz). In addition to the grand Book-Cadillac Hotel—built in the Italian Renaissance style—the city had a train station designed by the same designers of New York's Grand Central and a library designed by Cass Gilbert (designer of the Woolworth Building). Ralph played the verdant and well-kept Detroit Golf Club (the North and South Courses, both designed by Donald

The Lake Lure Golf Course in the North Carolina mountains seen with sand greens. *(Author's Collection)*

Ross), as well as the Oakland Hills Country Club, site of the 1924 U.S. Open. To finish off his Michigan golf, it was on to the Port Huron Golf Club and the Black River Country Club in Port Huron, before he crossed the border into Ontario, where he played thirty-nine additional courses as his golf marathon continued.

The mountains of North Carolina were also on the sweeping agenda later in 1939. Ralph visited the courses around Asheville and Cashiers, which he termed "some of the best layouts in the country." His tour included the High Hampton Inn & Country Club, the Beaver Lake Golf Course, the Hendersonville Golf & Country Club, and the Lake Lure Municipal Golf Course. The latter course featured a log cabin clubhouse built by the WPA.

The late summer brought terrible news, when on September 1st, Adolf Hitler launched his *blitzkrieg* by invading Poland. Ralph had planned to take a six-month leave of absence in 1940 to play in the British Isles, but the war spoiled it. He and Mary Alice had planned ahead for a big vacation to Europe and bought installment stock in a building and loan association a few years prior. Their investment matured and paid them $500, although they were unable to use it immediately for their original purpose.

The Sunday newspapers on June 16, 1940, brought farther unsettling news. The German army had breached France's Maginot Line and was advancing across Europe. In New York, it was a seasonably cool day with low clouds hanging in the sky. It was Ralph's fifty-eighth birthday, and he always like to play a special course to celebrate. He was approaching his 2,000th unique course and seemed desperate to find a local venue he hadn't played yet. He chose a course that was not yet open, the Golf & Beach Club in Northport, located in Suffolk County on the Long Island Sound. They allowed him to celebrate his millennial milestone before the course was fully grown in by opening it for him and then closed it immediately thereafter. The short, flat, nine-hole public course, situated next to a veteran's hospital, was below his usual standards for a milestone course, and, seemingly embarrassed by it, he never mentioned it by name.

The ardent golfer played a substantial amount of golf later in the month on his vacation with Mary Alice. As the calendar flipped to July, the duo boarded a ferry and chopped through the clear waters of the chilly Atlantic to Nantucket Island. The radiant sunshine followed them to the Martha's Vineyard Country Club, and continuing his run of golf courses that presidents have played, Ralph visited the Hyannisport Club as course No. 2,008. Hyannisport is an Alex H. Findlay design and is famous for being the club the other Kennedy clan frequented, as their family compound abuts the course. A Philadelphia newspaper in 1940 featured a small article with the headline "Golf Papa Still at It," although they were not referring to Ralph, but instead to Findlay, who helped bring the game to America fifty-two years before. He was then seventy-two-years old, and they declared that he had played 2,388 courses with a goal to play 2,400. Unlike Ralph, Findlay did not keep his course scorecards, but his was a milestone number Ralph would clearly have to keep his sights on if he wanted to set the record.

Kennedy played from pillar to post that summer, chasing the ball around several dozen courses in the space of a month, enjoying *all* the courses on Cape Cod. From Cape Cod, the duo traversed Northern New England and went back across the Canadian border, visiting New Brunswick again to play the Woodstock Golf Club, the Armstrong Golf Club, and the Fredericton Golf Club. The choirboy from New York told the local newspaper during his July visit that he didn't drink or smoke while on a heavy playing schedule; in fact, he said that he goes to bed at 9 p.m. while on a golfing tear. Considering the pace he was on, he must have been on his best behavior as he made his way back down the coast, playing eighteen additional courses in Maine, including a stop on a small spit of land between Sand Cove and Mt. Desert Narrows. He played the nine-hole Grindstone Neck Golf Course in Winter Harbor, an 1891 design of Alex Handy that affords views of the water from every hole.

Mary Alice was still playing the game, as documented by the Kebo Valley Golf Club scorecard (course No. 2,042), which has both RAK and MAK written in as golfers at the historic Bar Harbor club. The Kennedys continued traveling around the scenic Maine coastline and visited the Castine Golf Club, a Willie Park Jr. design located on Castine Harbor, on a spectacular bluff overlooking Upper Penobscot Bay. While Ralph was in the Penobscot Bay region to play the nine-hole Northport Country Club, the *Republican Journal* of Belfast crowned him the "Champion Golf Rambler."

With the war raging in Europe, and before heading home from their long trip, Ralph chipped and putted at the Marion Golf Club located near Plymouth, Massachusetts, the first course designed by George Thomas Jr. before he moved to California. A quirky course, all the par threes at Marion are blind due to the use of old stone walls from the farmland the course was routed through. In total, his summer golfing bender encompassed seventy-seven courses over twenty-seven days, or almost three courses per day.

The persistent and swift golfer also played a host of courses in New York's Mohawk Valley later in the year, including the Beaver Brook Golf & Country Club and the Donald Ross-designed Teugega Country Club in Rome, as his 2,084th and 2,085th, going around the tracks in a speedy forty-three and ninety minutes, respectively. Ralph continued to visit company-owned golf courses, playing the IBM Country Club in Endicott, New York. The front of the IBM scorecard was simple and contains founder Thomas Watson's famous motto for the company printed on it: "Think."

The 1940 census enumerator asked people a half-dozen questions related to unemployment, which remained stubbornly high at 14.6 percent. The census sheet listing the Kennedys contained a surprise. Beatrice E. Gorman, a single, thirty-nine-year-old from Washington, was listed as residing with the Kennedys. A nurse, she worked eighty-four hours the prior week, though it is unknown if she was living with the Kennedys because Ralph or his wife was sick at the time. Ralph's income as a "salesman" was reported at $4,700, well above the national average of $1,368. As focused a salesman as he was a golfer, he indicated that he had put in sixty hours the prior week. Their neighborhood remained a melting pot, and solidly middle-class. Other residents in his multi-story apartment building included a salesman, a singer, a store manager, a railroad conductor, a nurse, and secretary.

Although the obsessive golfer had played more than two thousand unique courses until this point, two of his most significant trips still lay ahead. Before returning to Ralph's master plan, the next chapter takes a diversion from the chronological progression of his journey to focus in detail on the golf he played in his home city, one of his most impressive achievements. While exploring Ralph's accomplishments in the Big Apple, it is also worth a brief indulgence to examine all the courses that have ever graced the populous city.

CHAPTER 12

Golf in the Great Metropolis

GREAT GOLF AND NEW YORK City are not mutually exclusive. The coastal metropolis has the climate, terrain, and—during Ralph's lifetime—open space for such golf. It is not a stretch to call some of the courses he visited pastoral and peaceful. The fairways and greens he tramped were varied, making for some interesting juxtapositions among the courses in his home city. While some were intensely urban or seriously flawed, an equal number were scenic, isolated, and among the best built at the time. Of particular note are the lost golf courses of Queens, which were designed by architects of the Golden Age working at the peak of their prowess, including those of Seth Raynor, A. W. Tillinghast, Devereux Emmet, and Alister Mackenzie. Although Tom Bendelow would go on to design over five hundred courses nationally, his early efforts were concentrated in and around the city, and he played a defining role in early New York golf.

Modern-day New York City was created in 1898 when the two existing city boroughs—Manhattan and the Bronx—combined with Brooklyn (Kings County), Queens, and Staten Island to form a unified entity. The textbook image of New York City is of a flat environment filled with concrete, glass, and steel. The reality of the city Ralph played in was quite different, since it was still transitioning from—as difficult as it is to believe—farmland and open spaces to the city we know today. The current high-density metropolis also obscures terrain containing hills and valleys, some of which feature beautiful open vistas of the many surrounding bodies of water New York is blessed with. As a Gotham resident most of his adult life, Ralph naturally played a lot of golf within the five boroughs. Performing a detailed examination of the courses he played provides an unprecedented look at urban golf there in the first half of the twentieth century and how it evolved over the years. Of the fifty-eight courses that have ever existed within the city limits, Ralph played an impressive thirty-nine of them. Unfortunately, the relentless need for housing, development, and roads doomed many of the links to short life spans.

Let's begin in the borough where Ralph first played golf, the Bronx. In addition to his early ventures at the first public course in the country, Van Cortlandt, he also played at Pelham Bay and the Mosholu Links in his early days. In 1936, he dug divots at one other Bronx course built with WPA funds: Split Rock, located in the northeast corner of the borough overlooking Pelham Bay on the Long Island Sound. Bobby

The Pelham Bay course in the Bronx, 1924. *(Photo courtesy of the USGA)*

Jones took an interest in WPA golf courses and visited both Split Rock and Pelham Bay the same year.

As for the borough of Manhattan (which is distinct from the island of the same name and includes nine islands and a small portion of landmass in the lower Bronx), Ralph played the only course ever located there, on Governors Island. The 172-acre island occupies a central position in the middle of New York Harbor, with unrivaled views of the glimmering skyscrapers clustered in Lower Manhattan, and of Ellis Island and the Statue of Liberty. In 1931, the enthusiastic golfer took the short boat ride from South Ferry on the southern tip of Manhattan Island over to the Governors Island Golf Club and played their nine-hole par-3 course, which surrounded Fort Jay, an old star-shaped fortification that dates back to Revolutionary War times. Governors Island was used as a military base since the nation's early days, and the club's membership was comprised of officers stationed at the installation. The unusual shape of the fort, combined with the small acreage available for recreation, created what has been described as a "crooked" course. Golf there dates from 1902 and continued into the 1990s, when the federal government decamped from the strategic isle. There is no record of a golf course ever existing on Manhattan Island, making the Governors Island scorecard unique in Ralph's collection and the only one he collected from his home county.

Brooklyn was a short distance from Ralph's home and office, and he played a trio of courses in the densely populated borough (by 1900, Brooklyn already had 1.1 million residents). His first foray into Kings County was to play the original Marine & Field Club, set on elevated ground overlooking Gravesend Bay and the entrance to New York Harbor. The multi-purpose club was incorporated in 1885 with an objective of "the cultivation of all lawful land and water sports." By 1896, golf was among the lawful pursuits of interest, and Tom Bendelow was retained to design their seven-hole course on acreage that was converted from farmland; the following year, the course was expanded to a 2,826-yard, nine-hole course. The Marine & Field's clubhouse was located along the beach about a half-mile away, and when the club first opened, horse-drawn stage coaches took members between the course and the clubhouse. Ralph and Mary Alice played the course early in his pursuit, in 1917, the year America entered the Great War.

Immediately adjacent to the Marine & Field Club was the Dyker Meadow Golf Club, also located in the southwest corner of the borough near Lower New York Bay. Dyker Meadow was built in 1896 as a private nine-hole course, and it was well regarded. To reach the course, *Golf Guide* recommended taking the Fort Hamilton electric trolley from the Brooklyn Bridge, or, alternatively, the fledgling golfer could get to the links by elevated subway train. A popular course, by the turn of the century the membership was two hundred strong with a long waiting list. The *Guide* spoke of the course in glowing terms, noting, "This is a nine-hole green and probably the best in the United States. The total distance is just over 3,000 yards and the turf is excellent through-out. The course runs right down to the beach and the hazards obtained by the undulating nature of the ground and two ponds are very desirable." The *Links* said the course was also accessible by U.S. Government boat, and that Harry Vardon and George Low held the course record of seventy-three. Not bad for an urban course in Brooklyn.

Marine & Field and Dyker Meadow both evolved and eventually merged into one course. Marine & Field was expanded during the First World War with some of Dyker's holes incorporated into its design, and with some new holes created on acquired land. A jumble of bastardized holes was created over the years that played as an eighteen-hole course—at one point, the old Marine & Field comprised the front nine, and Dyker the back nine. Hemmed into a dense urban environment, many holes were too long as par threes and too short to be par fours. In 1928, the Parks Department took over the operation of the private courses, renaming the entity Dyker Beach Park. John Van Kleek redesigned the course in 1935, using the combined land to make it a more orthodox course. Ralph played this combined course, which is similar to today's layout, in 1942. Patience was the order of the day when Ralph played at Dyker. Calling the course popular doesn't do it justice. Dyker hosted 90,000 rounds of golf in 1940, significantly more play than most courses ever receive in a year. On one particularly fine summer day, 847 golfers wanted to play, or two times the number it is possible to squeeze onto a course, even if a foursome were sent out every seven and a half minutes.

Kennedy also played the Old Flatbush course in Brooklyn three years after it was built, in 1928, as course No. 487. It was a good thing he played it early on, as the course didn't survive for more than a few years. Golf and the ever-expanding city were not a good match. In this case, Old Flatbush was a highly urbanized course wedged between buildings and roadways. Built on a small amount of land for a golf course, the 3,065-yard nine-hole course occupied only fifty-three acres. The course designer called the paradoxical endeavor a "novel situation." He described the oddity of trying to cram a course into such a densely populated area: "One of the tees [fifth] is built on a lot between two large apartments. A large public school is back of the fifth green and a church is on the side of the seventh. A main thoroughfare [Bedford Avenue] runs through the center of the course. Several streets end at irregular points on the borders of the land, and it required some strategy to get nine holes in, without crossing these or Bedford Avenue."

In the category of life being stranger than fiction, the land the course occupied was originally a potato farm. It was then used variously as a field for circuses—most notably Ringling Bros. and Barnum &

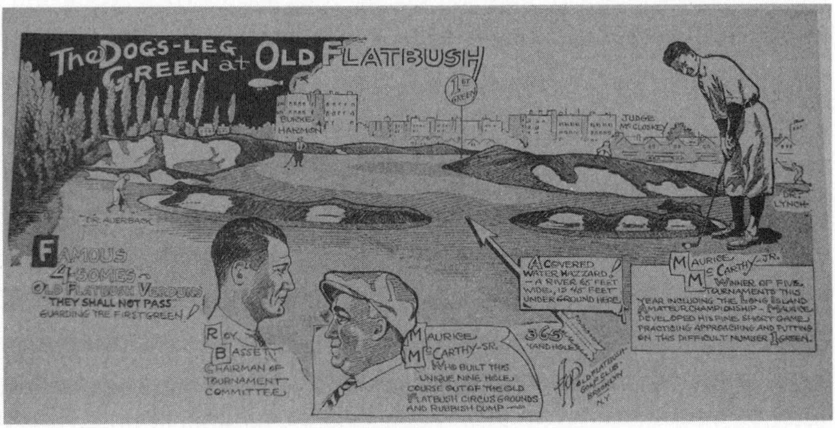

Brooklyn's Old Flatbush Golf Course. *(Author's Collection)*

Bailey—and also as a garbage dump. Construction of the course began in October 1924, and the ground was very difficult to work with: it was so hard that a crushing machine was used to break up the earth so that it could be contoured and grassed. The course designer was Maurice McCarthy Sr., who designed more than a dozen courses during this period, including the highly regarded West Course at the Hershey Country Club. Surviving pictures of Old Flatbush show a crowded urban environment with buildings set close to greens and tees. Its first hole, named "Elevation," featured a punchbowl-style green and white bunkers reminiscent of the "white faces" of Merion. The seventh hole, a par four of 360 yards named "Hope," had a green situated in front of a church, with large mounds of white sand piled up behind the putting surface as hazards (and, one presumes, also to protect unwary churchgoers from getting plunked with skulled shots). The *Brooklyn Daily Eagle* summed up Old Flatbush nicely, referring to it as a course "among apartment houses." Ironically enough for a course without trees, the word "Flatbush" is derived from the Dutch word meaning "wooded plain."

Given the inherent value of the land and the insatiable appetite for new housing, it was inevitable that the course would not survive, particularly after the city issued new proposed street routings that ran through the middle of it. The land was put up for sale in February 1931 and after it was sold was used as both baseball and football fields until Brooklyn College was constructed; it stands on the site today.

Ralph somehow missed playing the Brooklyn School of Golf in the 1920s. The indoor Brooklyn School had its own PGA professional, manufactured its own clubs, and kept long hours to serve the large borough's population. Ralph must not have considered it a real course because it was indoors, although a surviving scorecard in the USGA archives (not one of his) shows that it had eighteen holes and played 5,573 yards; its leadoff hole played an impressive 533 yards, especially considering the constraints imposed by city blocks. The card contains a stymie measure and reminded the metropolitan duffers to "Play Golf with a Conscience. Replace Divots," suggesting that it indeed had

Scorecard of the Brooklyn School of Golf. *(Photo courtesy of the USGA)*

grass. The Brooklyn School of Golf was not the only indoor course in the city; the Newspaper Golf Club played a match indoors in 1913, at the golf school of Joe Sylvester, which was located on 150th Street and Amsterdam Avenue in Manhattan. The event was a flop; the course was heavily criticized, and they never returned.

The borough in which Ralph played most of his city golf was Queens. The depth, breadth, and quality of golf courses that once graced Queens are nothing short of astonishing. The largest of all the boroughs, Queens (and Brooklyn) is geographically part of Long Island, so it isn't necessarily a surprise that it contains suitable terrain for golf, since the remainder of the 118-mile island is so rich in the sandy loam that is perfectly suited for good courses.

The Old Forest Park Course, straddling the Brooklyn border with Queens, was one of the earliest courses Ralph played, in 1913, as his fourth, accompanied by his wife. Designed by Tom Bendelow in 1896, the course was modified and expanded over the years and still exists as the Forest Park Golf Course in Woodhaven. When it opened, the city-owned course was true to its name, and heavily forested; among the notable hazards were a profusion of wild blackberry bushes scattered throughout the property. When the Kennedys played it, the course had a total distance of 4,907 yards and played to a bogey score of seventy-five and a par of sixty-eight. The tenth hole was 183 yards and a par three and one-half, and the fourteenth was a 365-yard par four and one-half. The course was landlocked then, as it is today, with the rules indicating out of bounds in multiple locations on four different roads surrounding the course, and in a cemetery near the eighteenth hole. Players were also warned on the back of the scorecard not to throw their lunch boxes on the course.

Ralph's collection contains a card from the Woodhaven Golf Club in Queens, one that he numbered as course No. 79 and played in 1917. Located less than ten miles from his office, this was again golf of the urban variety, and the scorecard gives the location of the various out of bounds, which included "the sidewalks of Simpson St. and Vanderveer Ave, and the side of street in gully." Although Ralph counted the course as another unique one in his sequential numbering of cards, the Woodhaven course never existed. The club itself was an association club similar to the Newspaper Golf Club, and they played their golf over the Old Forest Park Course; thus, course No. 79 wasn't a new unique one, and should not have been numbered as a new course played.

Where did erudite golfers play when they were seeking a tranquil oasis that served as a respite from the grind of city life? At the St. Albans Golf Club, which was considered the most exclusive golf club in Queens, if not all of New York City. Located northeast of today's John F. Kennedy International Airport, the Kennedys of Upper Manhattan played the manicured design—set on 137 acres—in 1921 as Ralph's

108th course. During this same timeframe, A. W. Tillinghast was brought in to resequence and renovate the course. Ralph played the redesigned Tillinghast course in August 1925 as a different and slightly shorter course, counting it as another unique one, which he was entitled to do based on his self-imposed rules, since it was a different layout. Babe Ruth played St. Albans frequently, and it was said to be his favorite course. Despite being a plum layout, it could not withstand the Depression and the war. The land was purchased by the Navy during World War II, and they built a hospital on the site.

Although traveling to Queens was a short trip for Ralph by bus or subway, the quickest way to travel to Bayside was on the Long Island Railroad, which had a station stop there. Ralph played the Belleclaire Golf & Country Club in Bayside in 1919. Members of Belleclaire engaged in not only golf, but a popular pastime of the era: motoring. Since automobiles were an emerging technology and a novelty, leisure seekers "motored" out to the (then) countryside for recreation. The club struggled financially, eventually changing its name to the Old Belleclaire Golf Club. Even with the new identity, the club didn't last a decade; it was renamed the Queensboro Golf and Country Club in 1927, and Ralph has a card from that course from 1929. The 1929 course played 6,228 yards, to a par of seventy-one, making it questionable whether it really should have been counted as a new course, since it was not renovated and was only slightly lengthened. An April 1931 newspaper headline described the problem that led to the course's eventual demise: "Queensboro Golf and Country Club Landlord Broke." Its 116 acres were sold to a developer, who used them to build one thousand homes in Bayside Hills to satisfy the needs of the ever-expanding population of Queens. The soil that was excavated for the development was removed to nearby Flushing Meadows for use in building the 1939 World's Fair.

Belleclaire was situated near one of the finest courses ever to exist in New York's five boroughs: the Oakland Golf Club, also located in Bayside. Incorporated in the nineteenth century, it was one of the earliest golf courses in the country, and the ever-busy Tom Bendelow built its initial nine-hole course on the site of an old estate. The *Golfer* commented on the original track in 1897, describing a rough, natural course that conjures up imagery we don't associate with the urban environment today: "The green is in a hollow behind an embankment and beside a stone pit. The eighth hole, named Heavenly Twins, has two deep ravines crossing the fairway. The first at sixty yards from the tee and the second precedes a plateau in the center of which is a green." A ravine located just thirty yards from the tee on the ninth hole was described as being a staggering forty yards deep. They continued, "A hill is next met with, following a fine level stretch. Apple trees and a stone barrier help to fatten the score." Their description of the topography and natural elements is as far as can be imagined from the densely populated neighborhood that exists there today, bordered by two interstate highways.

Quite a well-heeled club, its members included future New York Governor Alfred E. Smith, the steel magnate Charles Schwab, the financier Bernard Baruch, H. P. Whitney, and William K. Vanderbilt. The course was eventually expanded to eighteen holes in 1906, and Seth Raynor was subsequently enlisted in the early 1910s to redesign the course. He built a classic on the hilly property, including many blind shots and his usual prototype holes, including a Redan, an Alps, and a Home. Ralph was lucky to have finagled an invitation and walked the beautifully carpeted fairways in 1922, although he started off his round a bit rough, taking nine strokes on the opening "Toboggan" hole. The course only survived another thirty years; its 150 acres were put up for sale in 1952, when the insatiable appetite for land and the expanding highway system sounded its death knell.

Going through the subway turnstiles with his golf bag over his shoulder was a frequent occurrence for Ralph. Less than an hour from his front door was the Hillcrest Golf and Country Club in Queens, located between Kew Gardens and Jamaica. Organized in 1921, the club started with a rudimentary nine-hole course, and it later hired Devereux Emmet to expand it to an eighteen-hole course, built on only 110 acres. Ralph played it shortly after it opened in 1923. The *Brooklyn*

Daily Eagle announced a 1932 women's tournament to be held at the course with glee: "Some of the highest scores in golf history should be posted at the Hillcrest Golf Club in Jamaica next Tuesday. The stout ladies, you see, say that the slim ones have the advantage because they don't tire so easily. The slim ones say their huskier sisters have the brawn and strength that golf demands, and should therefore play better golf. And so they're going to team up and play a round." The club entered foreclosure in 1935, and the land was sold to St. John's University, which used it to build their Queens campus there.

As outlined previously, the 1939 World's Fair was partially built on landfill from the Belleclaire course. Another nearby course, the Pomonok Country Club in Flushing, hosted the PGA Championship the same year—to coincide with the fair. The oldest in Queens County, the club was started in the late 1880s as the Flushing Athletic Club, subsequently changing its name to the Flushing Country Club. The prolific Tom Bendelow was enlisted to build a nine-hole course in 1896. In 1921, the club was looking to upgrade to eighteen holes and found a suitable hilly piece of land nearby. They hired Devereux Emmet to build the new course, which they named Pomonok, after a local Indian tribe. The green ribbons of its narrow fairways were cut into the hilly site, creating several blind shots. Seven holes were of the "drive-and-kick" variety, short par fours that left a second shot close enough to kick the ball to the green. Some members were attached to the old nine-hole track and kept it in existence as the unimaginatively named Old Country Club. Ralph played Pomonok in 1924 and the Old Country Club in 1926. A rocky layout, the latter course's local rule No. 2 was "A ball lodged in a stone wall or stone pile may be dropped out one club's length, under penalty of one stroke." The Old Country Club failed during the Depression and was sold to developers in 1936. Pomonok survived until 1949 and then suffered the same fate.

Another Devereux Emmet-designed course in the borough was Queens Valley Golf Club, also located between Kew Gardens and Forest Hills. Queens Valley was established in 1916 as an 18-hole course; the club had a beautiful clubhouse made of field stones set up

The hilly terrain of the lost Pomonok golf course in Queens: 8th hole illustrated. *(Author's Collection)*

on a bluff, and the course's location was described as being in a picturesque, almost hidden spot. Ralph played the course in November 1924 as his 195th. Lou Gehrig also played at Queens Valley in an exhibition game, pitted against an amateur golfer, an archer, and two fishermen. They played an eclectic match of nine holes: the archer used a bow and arrow, Gehrig a baseball bat, and the fishermen competed using their rods and reels. The man firing the arrows won with thirty shots, beating Gehrig by one "stroke." Suffering the same fate as other courses in Queens, the 122-acre property was subsequently sold to build one thousand homes, a large shopping center, and a theater.

The courses of Queens were as varied as its immigrant neighborhoods, and Ralph played the bucolic Fresh Meadow Country Club in 1925, five years before it hosted the PGA Championship and seven years before it hosted the U.S. Open (won by Gene Sarazen, who also served as the club's professional for a time). An A. W. Tillinghast design built on farmland, Ralph loved the course and played it many times, including twice on June 29, 1925; he played it again in 1927, and eighteen years later in 1945. The course was described as having unusually narrow fairways, made even more challenging by the changing winds coming off the bay. Sadly, not even a Tillinghast pedigree, nor the fact that it hosted major championships, could save the course; its land was sold to developers in 1946, and the club itself moved to Long Island.

Ralph played two more Emmet courses in 1926: Nos. 1 and 2 at the public Laurelton Golf Courses in Queens. Yet again, the property they occupied was sold, and homes were built on the land in the 1930s. It is instructive to remember that New York was settled by the Dutch as a trading post and it has always focused on commerce first and foremost. Is it any wonder that profit repeatedly prevailed over pastimes as New York City evolved?

Not all the courses Ralph played have disappeared. Three city-owned courses still exist in Queens: the North Hills Golf Club in Douglaston, which he played in 1927, survives as the Douglaston Golf Course; and Kissena Park, which he played in 1935, is also still extant. Both provide needed recreation to the 2.3 million residents of the high-density borough today. Another early course, Clearview, in Bayside, which Ralph played in 1926, also survives as the Clearview Park Golf Course.

Queens was easy for Ralph to visit by subway; he could see the borough from his office at Eagle on the East River. The strap-hanging golfer paid his nickel fare and ventured out to the Jackson Heights Country Club in 1927. The course opened in 1919 as a short par-3 course; A. W. Tillinghast was brought in and recommended changes in 1923, around the time he was building Winged Foot. Ralph played the course after the renovations, in 1927, when it measured a negligible distance of 2,310 yards; it survived through the late 1930s, when its land was sold to build garden apartments.

With a first tee overlooking Powell's Cove along the East River, the Malba Field & Marine Club occupied land on the northern shores of Queens. A short nine-holer designed by local pro James Fraser in 1914, it was located just south of today's Whitestone Bridge, with views overlooking the East River where it joins the Long Island Sound. Ralph played Malba when it had been reduced to a par-7 course, playing an almost comical 1,134 yards. Although the club is still in existence, the golf course was converted to housing in 1945, becoming the Malba Gardens development, as the insatiable appetite for housing—spurred on by the GI Bill of Rights—continued. Ralph was not a fan of the course, and its loss did not cause him to shed a tear.

Another in the long string of courses Ralph played in Queens in 1931 was the Corona Park Golf Club. Located thirty minutes from Broadway, the course was incorporated the same year he played it. It had an ample 340 acres of land and a cute golf-themed telephone number: Havemeyer 9-FORE. Emphasizing that this was golf in an urban context, Ralph's scorecard indicated that the local rules permitted a ball laying on the railroad tracks on the first or tenth holes could be lifted without penalty. How well groomed the course was can only be speculated, although it must not have been pristine, as the scorecard is stamped on the front, "Play winter rules, players must tee up on fairways." Golfers play better when every lie is perfect, and Ralph certainly did. He shot a smooth seventy-four, playing it on a cloudless mid-September day; no doubt teeing up his ball helped his score. The course had a fleeting existence, disappearing within a few years when the World's Fair was erected.

Many of the world's best-known designers practiced their art in Queens. None other than the revered Alister MacKenzie designed a public golf course there. The Good Doctor laid out the Bayside Links on gently rolling farmland in 1931. Located in quite a good golf neighborhood, it was near the Raynor-designed Oakland Golf Course. Ralph played a predecessor course in 1919 as one of the first 100 courses he played. The original course opened in 1916 as an eighteen-holer; Kennedy played well given that he had only just taken up the game, shooting a ninety-seven. The original was sold off in 1921, and MacKenzie's Bayside Links was an entirely new course and was one of the first to use power-driven machinery in its construction. Ralph played MacKenzie's design the year it opened, 1932, the same year the architect was working on Augusta National. Constructed in the midst of the Great Depression on a low budget, the course

Advertisement for the Alister MacKenzie-designed Bayside Links. *(Author's Collection)*

was built on a scant ninety acres and contained only nineteen bunkers and no rough. Asked about his design philosophy for the course, MacKenzie told the *New York Times*, "I believe in pleasurable golf. No one wants to spend a lot of time looking for balls in the rough." Tragically, the course was sold off to developers in the 1950s, robbing future generations in the Northeast of the chance to experience one of his strategic designs.

The nineteenth Queens course the itinerant salesman played was the nine-hole Ocean Country Club in Far Rockaway, situated near the Atlantic Ocean. Organized in 1900, Ralph played it in 1933, and by 1938 the land was covered in houses. The penultimate course Ralph played in the golf-rich borough was the Kew Terrace Golf Links in Flushing, teeing it up in 1933. Not much is known about the course, which was located on Vleigh Road near the Union Turnpike, not far from where an overwhelming confluence of major roads intersects today, including the Grand Central Parkway and the Van Wyck Expressway.

The *New York Times* announced in 1930, "A handsome clubhouse is being completed on the new eighteen-hole golf course of the Idlewild Beach Golf Club, near the intersection of Rockaway Boulevard and Sunrise Highway, Jamaica, South, facing Jamaica Bay. It has a dining room on the open porch running the length of the bay. Barber shop, showers, and all men's lockers will be located on the first floor, which will have terrazzo floors and tile walls." Such was a description of the last course in Queens Ralph played, in 1933. He shot a nice score at Idlewild Beach, with a seventy-nine, and had a five-hole stretch where he was hot, playing Nos. 8–12 in par-par-birdie-par-birdie. According to the scorecard, the layout included lakes and played 6,317 yards, to a par of seventy-two. Among the advice offered on their scorecard: "The game ceases to be golf when rules are broken at pleasure."

Shifting to one of the city's islands, Ralph crossed New York Harbor multiple times to play seven courses in the most suburban of New York's five boroughs: Staten Island. He started with the Fox Hills Golf Club, in 1915, as course No. 16. New York City during the nineteen-teens was a very different city from today's urban jungle. To emphasize the point, while at Fox Hills, Ralph encountered "an ill-tempered bull tethered in a pasture within hooking range." Started as the Staten Island Cricket and Base Ball Club, the club added an eighteen-hole golf course at the turn of the century, designed by the omnipresent Tom Bendelow. *Golf Guide* felt that the club "Maintains one of the finest golf links in the state. The property on which it is situated has been called the ideal golf ground of America." Despite the course's strong beginnings, it failed during the Depression and was converted into military barracks during the Second World War.

The blue-eyed pencil salesman took the ferry across the busy harbor again in 1921. This time his destination was the historic Richmond County Country Club in Dongan Hills, one of the earliest golf clubs in the nation to be incorporated; it was chartered in 1888 as a multipurpose club involved in hunting and tennis. Although a nine-hole course was laid out by members in 1894, the course Ralph played was a revised layout of 1897. *Golf Guide* described its eighteen holes as "very sporty" and observed, "the course is over very rolling ground and affords many fine views of the ocean, the Upper and Lower Bays, New York City, and surrounding country." Richmond County survives as the only private course in the city today.

In 1931, the insatiable Kennedy returned to the island the Dutch named Staaten Eylandt to play the Tysen Manor Golf Club. The course opened the year before and only survived until 1943, when it was sold for a housing development. On the same trip, he played LaTourette in Richmond, which was then a nine-hole course; today it exists as an eighteen-hole course. His third stop was at the Silver Lake Golf Course, a John Van Kleek design of 1929, and his archived scorecard indicates that RAK shot a cracking seventy-seven. His final course of the trip was the private Mayflower Country Club in Huguenot, which survives today as the South Shore Country Club. His last visit to Staten Island was in 1933, when he battled Old Man Par at the Willowbrook Golf Club, located on Victory Boulevard. The club had a short life; there are no references to it after 1937.

In addition to all the courses outlined thus far, there were eighteen courses in New York City that no longer exist that Ralph did not play, although seventeen of them ceased to exist prior to his taking up the game. *Golf Guide* lists a New York Municipal Course, located on the tiny 253-acre City Island; established in 1912, it was "reached by auto to Pelham Park."

The Crescent Athletic Club, located in Bay Ridge, Brooklyn, was described as overlooking the Upper Bay of New York Harbor. The club was founded in 1884, and their course was laid out by Scotsman George Strath in 1896; its eighteen holes played a short 4,548 yards, although this was in the era before the Haskell ball. The course was gradually reduced in size beginning in the late nineteen-tens as land was sold off for houses; remnants survived until 1928, when it was abandoned. Although Ralph didn't play the club's course in Brooklyn, he did play their course in Huntington, Long Island, after they relocated there.

Another Brooklyn course that Ralph never got the opportunity to play was the Erasmus Hall Golf Club. Erasmus Hall was then a boys' school, which survives today as a high school. *Golf Guide* noted that their club was organized in 1898, " . . . and turns out each year a number of very promising young golfers," although it is possible that it was an association club only, without an actual course.

Ralph also never played the Knickerbocker Field Club in Flatbush, Brooklyn. Incorporated in 1891, the 2,041-yard, nine-hole course, located between Church Avenue and the Parade Grounds, survived less than twenty years before homes encroached upon it. He also missed the Sunset Park Club in Brooklyn, a six-hole course that was organized in 1899; it survived only until 1905, well before Ralph took up the game. The same applied to both the Eastern Parkway Golf Club and the Cliff Haven Golf Club, which also had short life spans at the turn of the century.

There were also several courses in Queens that predated Ralph, including The Richmond Hill Country Club near Jamaica, which was organized in 1896. The nine-hole course, which *Golf Guide* called "one of the most popular and best patronized in the vicinity," was destroyed in 1906 when the Long Island Rail Road built their Kew Gardens station. The Highland Golf Club's "very hilly and rugged" nine-hole course existed from 1903 through 1908 and was located near Kissena Lake in Queens. Similarly, the nine-hole Hollis Field Club breathed a short life, as did the Jamaica Golf Club. Another course Ralph could not have played was the Bayswater Golf Club in Far Rockaway, which started and extinguished in the first couple of years of the twentieth century. Likewise for the "short" Edgemere Golf Club, which was located on sandy ground nearby on the Rockaway Peninsula. The final course in the borough that was impossible for Ralph to play was the Queens Golf Club, a nine-hole layout of John Dunn, created during the last year of the nineteenth century. The course was located in today's Queens Village neighborhood and was in as unorthodox a location as possible, laid out so as not to directly interfere with trap shooting. The ill-conceived site they chose, "Interstate Park," was simultaneously used for competitive pigeon shooting.

There were also two courses predating Ralph's playing days in the Bronx: the original Century Country Club was a Tom Bendelow design in the Throgs Neck section of the borough; and the West Chester Golf Club, organized in 1895, was located on 167th Street at the corner of West Chester Avenue near the Bronx River Bridge. The latter club had three hundred members, and their "pretty nine-hole course" with "heavy turf" was laid out in 1897—playing a short 2,553 yards. Ralph just missed the opportunity to play it, taking up the game three years after the course disappeared. Too bad for Ralph, since the course's third hole must have been a sight to behold; named with a great play on words (especially with a Scottish accent), "Hellfersartin," it played what we can only imagine was an impossible 401 yards given the equipment of the time.

In Staten Island, Ralph's love of the game postdated the Harbor Hill Golf Club in New Brighton, which was incorporated in 1896 and went out of business in 1904. The short eighteen-hole course of 4,171 yards was described thusly: "turf is springy, the greens are excellent." The course's demise began when a property developer next door mistakenly plowed under several holes and the members began to fight about whether to reconstruct the course or sell the land, with the latter group winning out.

The only course that existed when Kennedy was an active golfer that he legitimately missed playing abutted Queens Valley in Forest Hills. It was a club with a multitude of names. The William H. Tucker Sr.-designed course dates to 1927, when it was built as the Antlers Golf and Country Club, "Organized by the leading Jews and Gentiles of the Borough of Brooklyn." It was their intention to build one of the "sportiest" courses in the country, and opening day was supposed to feature a match between Gene Sarazen and Bill Mehlhorn, but it had to be postponed because the course was not ready. It was not a good omen. The course eventually opened with only twelve holes, then the club reorganized as the Spring Hill Golf Club after the stock market crash, and it was subsequently sold in 1933 to become the Arrow Brook Golf & Country Club, which itself survived until 1939, when they leased their land to the World's Fair and never returned it to use as a golf course.

New York City is synonymous with a tumultuous environment, and the velocity of change and destruction of green spaces for recreation over the Kennedys' lifetime was consistent with the city's chaotic pace. The "Building the World of Tomorrow" that the 1939 World's Fair foreshadowed took a heavy toll on golf in Queens, with four different clubs contributing their land. The appellations contained in the city's lost course names give an evocative sense of what was lost: fields, meadows, forests, hills, and valleys.

The unstoppable golfer of yesteryear was fortunate to be able to enjoy so many of the city's fleeting courses before they disappeared.

CHAPTER 13

Golf in the War Years

Returning to Ralph's chronological journey, he had completed an active year in 1940, playing more than one hundred new courses. He continued to push ahead and now counted more than 2,100 cards in his collection after focusing his golf in the Northeast. Although his pace was about to slow because of gas rationing, restrictions on rubber, and a wartime economy, he kept plugging away where he could.

Ralph's hobby and occupation were simpatico. Obviously, being a traveling salesman afforded him the opportunity to crisscross the country on his employer's dime. His golf obsession also generated a lot of free publicity for the pencil maker; almost every article written about him mentioned that he worked for Eagle, including the *Saturday Evening Post*, which referred to him early in 1941, highlighting his milestone of 2,130 courses played. Scores of employees saw the small article, and the company newsletter encouraged his colleagues to use it in pursuit of selling more pencils.

His customary early trip to the South took him to the Carolinas, where the *Roanoke Beacon* interviewed him after he finished course No. 2,134, the Plymouth Country Club. The portrait that emerges makes him seem like a model golfer—they called him "affable and friendly without braggadocio." The Southern writers continued to invent colorful descriptions of Ralph. The *Savannah Morning News* dubbed him "The sturdy Scot, peddler for the largest pencil manufacturer in the country" and noted that he had a ruddy complexion and happy disposition. They also commented on his vigor: "He is unaffected by the grueling punishment he gives his legs and feet." At his next stop, the *Macon Telegraph* referred to him by his honorary title, calling him Colonel Ralph Kennedy.

Losing his battle with ALS, Lou Gehrig passed away tragically on June 2nd at the age of thirty-seven. His legacy is one of far more than the impressive statistics he left behind; it is one of grace, integrity, perseverance, and demonstrating how to keep dignity intact when life presents a "bad break."

Ralph again concentrated his play during his summer vacation in the cooler North. He played seventy-four courses over the span of twenty-three days in New England and Eastern Canada, including fourteen courses in New York, fourteen in Quebec, thirteen in Massachusetts, eleven in Maine, seven in Connecticut, seven in New Hampshire, five in Ontario, and three in New Brunswick. During his visit to Springfield, Massachusetts, he explained to the local newspaper why he loved the game and played so much: "Golf is a mental cathartic. It purges the mind of worries." No doubt he was worry-free by Labor Day, having played so much golf.

Ralph had shifted from a reliance on public transportation to occasionally driving his own car to the golf course. In Upstate New York, on his way home from a long trip, he was in a minor accident with a truck operated by the West Virginia Pulp and Paper Company. The company apologized to Ralph and wished him well in his travels playing new courses. Quite a literate bunch, an officer of the company sent him a letter with the following optimistic thoughts: ". . . all of us hope that you will emulate Old Man River and Tennyson's Brook and keep rolling until you have played at least 5,000 courses." Kennedy was not wearing a seat belt when he had his automobile accident because they were not in widespread use yet; manufacturers didn't begin putting them into cars until the 1950s.

The United States was an economic powerhouse in the middle of the twentieth century; among other impressive statistics, it produced

63 percent of the world's oil in 1941. After the Pearl Harbor attacks of December 7th, the government halted production of many nonessential products so that factories could be redeployed to support the war effort; this included the production of golf equipment. Titleist stopped producing golf balls in 1942 and retooled their factories to produce gas masks; production of balls wouldn't resume again until 1945. The war also created problems for Eagle, since a key component of pencil production—graphite—was in limited supply. At the time, almost a billion and a half pencils were being produced in the United States annually. The company had to switch from using the best graphite, which came from Madagascar and Ceylon, to an inferior product sourced from North America.

The fifty-nine-year-old Kennedy registered in the Selective Service again in 1942, as he was required to do, although he did not serve in any capacity. His brother registered again, as well, and served active duty. Robert H. Kennedy was given the rank of Colonel in the Army Medical Corps and operated as a surgeon from 1942 to 1946. He also served as the consulting surgeon of the 2nd Service Command based on Governors Island. At the end of the war, he received a commendation ribbon and the Legion of Merit for his meritorious conduct and extraordinary achievements between January 1945 and January 1946. Bobby Jones volunteered for the Army Air Force even though he was exempted through a medical disability. He served active duty, including going ashore at Normandy the day after D-Day.

Wartime life did not go on as normal for residents of the country's biggest city, as the daily newspapers brought news of victories and setbacks with every new edition. Afraid of U-boat attacks, New York imposed a "dimout" during the war, painting the tops of street lights black, dimming traffic signals, and turning off the lights in Times Square. Restrictions were placed on Automats during the war, as they were on other restaurants and retailers. Mayor La Guardia declared Tuesdays and Fridays were to be "meatless" to help the city cope with shortages. Hardly a major sacrifice, among other limitations, the

A Horn & Hardart Automat. *(Author's Collection)*

comfort foods of chicken à la king and baked ham were only available five days a week at Horn & Hardart.

In addition to being a financial and fashion center, New York City was a magnet for prizefighting in the forties. Boxing matches proved a welcome diversion from the privations of the war economy. Sugar Ray Robinson, Jake LaMotta, and Rocky Graziano fought important bouts in the city, and during the middle of the war there were seventy-four fight clubs in the metropolitan area.

New York's immense harbor was put to good use during the war. Occupying a total area of twelve hundred miles with 430 square miles of water, it had six hundred ship anchorages; eighteen hundred docks, piers, and wharves; one thousand warehouses; and forty active shipyards. An astonishing 575 tugboats served the clogged waterways. The city was teeming with soldiers and sailors; more than three million troops transited through New York during the global conflagration.

Membership at Augusta National was stressed because many of its members were serving their country. Bobby Jones had the idea that the club could contribute to the war effort by raising cattle on the course when it was closed for two years. Augusta National raised one thousand turkeys and roughly two hundred head of cattle during the mid-forties and harvested pecans from its trees. German prisoners of war held at Camp Gordon nearby, part of General Erwin Rommel's Afrika Korps, built a wooden truss bridge—a pre-cursor to the Nelson Bridge—over Rae's creek near the 13th tee. In town, the Army commandeered the Forrest Ricker Hotel, converting it into a hospital. The hotel's golf course survived but became known as the Armed Forces Golf Course.

Ralph continued to postpone his planned trip to the Home of Golf because of the war. He told a newshound, "It is my information that all of the Scottish golf courses had been destroyed except the Old Course. This was done by the home folks so there would be no convenient landing places for enemy troops or parachute troops floating in from Germany." Despite putting off his big getaway, the war didn't prevent the Kennedys from taking brief vacations. The high point of a summer trip at the end of July 1942 was a visit to the Myopia Hunt Club in South Hamilton, Massachusetts. Myopia is a special place to play golf, with its classic New England yellow-clapboard clubhouse, polo field, and old-world charm. Horses and hounds mix quaintly with the golf, which is of the highest order. Myopia hosted the U.S. Open four times by the time Ralph visited: in 1898, 1901, 1905, and 1908. Hosting the 1898 U.S. Open puts Myopia in a small fraternity of only five elite courses that were venues for the championship in the nineteenth century. A smaller fraternity still, the club is one of only two—along with Newport—that hosted the U.S. Open as a nine-hole layout. While away in Massachusetts, the Kennedys missed New York City's first surprise blackout and air raid drill.

Ralph's most unusual press coverage of his entire endeavor came in 1942, when there was a full-page feature about him in the *Dziennik dla wszystkich*, the "Polish Everybody's Daily." The largest circulation Polish newspaper in the country, it was published out of Buffalo, and a verbose columnist caught up with him when he was in the lakeside city to play the Park Country Club.

Radio enthusiasts heard Ralph's voice crackling over the airwaves again as he was interviewed by Lowell Thomas for a second time in

1942. Americans packed into theaters to watch movies throughout the global conflict and heard Thomas's authoritative voice each week narrating the *Movietone News*. While visiting Pawling, Kennedy again played Thomas's course, Quaker Hill, as No. 2,300. This time, he teed it up at a revised Robert Trent Jones Sr. layout, and his card was attested to by none other than Lowell Thomas.

Trolling around the reaches of his home state, Ralph visited the Finger Lakes region again in the fall. As the printing presses at the *Herald-Journal* in Syracuse churned out the newspaper of the day on October 3, 1941, they brought the encouraging news that the Navy had sunk five Japanese battleships in the Pacific. Closer to home, they let their readers know that "Golf's No. 1 Marathoner" was in town to play at the Bellevue Country Club and the Lafayette Golf & Country Club.

With gas rationing in effect, Ralph concentrated his efforts closer to home, playing the nine-hole Fenwick Golf Club in Old Saybrook, Connecticut, where golf has been played since 1894. Katharine Hepburn was a regular player at Fenwick and had a home on the property adjacent to the course. Fenwick is set on the Atlantic shoreline, on a narrow peninsula of land on Long Island Sound at the mouth of the Connecticut River; set in a classic New England nautical milieu, its setting includes views of two eighteenth-century lighthouses overlooking the sparkling water. While Ralph was in the small coastal state, a reporter for the *New Haven Register* penned a small article about him after bumping into him on a crowded Hartford bus (carrying his clubs, of course), as he was on the move searching for new links.

As battles raged around the globe, they stymied Kennedy's activity; and between 1943 and 1945, his pace of play slowed considerably, averaging less than fifty courses per year. In the latter war years, it became tough to play because there was a shortage of balls due to restrictions on the use of rubber. The sixty-year-old kept his swing in form by playing in local tournaments, including those sponsored by the NYAC and the New York Stationers, as well as in the Senior Westchester Championship.

The war brought substantial change to the landscape of golf courses, impacting Long Island particularly hard. Despite its natural advantages, the exceptional Lido Golf Club would not survive. The course ran into difficulties during the Depression, and the land was subsequently sold; the Navy eventually took over the hotel and golf course to house troops.

The war years also took a heavy toll on another highly regarded Long Island course: C. H. Alison's Timber Point, which also ran into misfortune during the Great Depression. It was sold by the original owners in the early forties, and Suffolk County eventually acquired the land for use as a public facility. The sprawling complex at the Salisbury Links also began to have difficulties during the Depression, and the war put added pressure on it. It would not survive as a privately owned club and was taken over by Nassau County, becoming part of their park system, with homes subsequently built on a portion of the property.

Although African Americans were serving with distinction in the war effort, the 1943 PGA Constitution included a new element that highlighted the continued racial divide in the country. Section I, Article 3, of the constitution and bylaws contained the following clause: "Professional Golfers of the Caucasian race . . . who have served at least five years in the profession . . . shall be eligible for membership." The exclusionary change to the bylaws was added curiously enough not by a delegation from the South, but by the delegation from Michigan. Their logic was less than impeccable, and they defended it by saying, "Show us some good golf courses established by Negroes."

Not all of Ralph's golf during the mid-forties was in the Northeast, as he still ventured out on the rails for business. There was something about the Midwest that motivated him to play multiple courses in one day. During 1943, he played four eighteen-hole courses in one day in Decatur, Illinois, less than forty miles from where he played six in one day in Springfield seven years earlier. He was clearly bitten hard by the golf bug, and at times his behavior bordered on obsessive-compulsive. On the other hand, as a road-warrior away from home often, there were limited options to pass a full day nine hundred miles from home in rural Illinois, and playing golf literally all day probably wasn't a bad alternative to puttering around aimlessly.

Media coverage of Ralph during the late war years continued to focus on his occupation; for example, on July 11, 1944, the *Hartford Courant* ran with the headline, "Pencil Salesman Covers Nation's Golf Courses." They appraised news readers of his intriguing journey: "There are lots of stories about the traveling man, but the one about Ralph Kennedy of New York is different. Kennedy is a pencil salesman and he covers the country. He's been around for thirty-one years. As he goes around he plays golf on weekends. To show that he hasn't missed many weekends, nor many golf courses, he has a collection of cards, 2,376 at last count. Every week is a thrill for him, but two of them especially stand out—the times he made his holes-in-one." Picking up on the theme, three months later the *Savannah News* called him one of the most colorful names of his journey, the "Pencil Peddler Extraordinary."

During the war, there was a shortage of caddies, and as a result Ralph started to carry his own clubs. However, as he entered his sixties, he found it increasingly difficult to do so, so he came up with an ingenious idea: playing with only one club. Ralph had acquired a "Novak special," as he called it, referring to the adjustable club that Joe Novak patented in 1929. Both the *Atlanta Journal* and the *Macon Telegraph* referred to him as playing with only this club, set in a 3-iron configuration, in April 1945. At the East Lake Golf Course in Atlanta, he shot a ninety-five using it, and in Macon he used it to shoot a ninety-two.

Harry S. Truman took over as president on April 12, 1945, after FDR died three months into his fourth term. Truman's decision to drop two atomic bombs on Japan in August formally launched the horrific atomic age, as the world was a long way from the Victorian Era Ralph grew up in. Ralph was on the links at the Nemours course of the DuPont Country Club in Wilmington on V-J Day as the Japanese surrendered.

One benefit of the hostilities was that they had a dramatic impact on employment, replacing the misery of the 1930s. The economy reached full employment, hitting a low of 1.2 percent unemployment at the peak of the global conflict. As GIs began to return home, air travel was still not a ubiquitous form of travel, but it was becoming increasingly important. Pan American had an active Clipper service in operation after the war, with flights—listed in the newspaper each day—leaving New York bound for London, Lisbon, Paris, Shannon, and Bermuda. Air travelers at the end of the war didn't board banal numbered flights; they took KLM's "Flying Dutchman" to Amsterdam and TWA's "Sphinx" to Cairo.

Ralph took an early spring trip to central Ohio in 1946, and among his stops was a visit to the Moundbuilders Country Club in Newark. Incorporated in 1910, the course was laid out by Tom Bendelow on hallowed ground, and it was unlike any other Ralph played. The club is named after the earthworks, or large mounds, the course was routed through, which were built by a prehistoric Native American civilization. The commanding mounds range from three to fourteen feet in height and form one of the largest sites of its kind in the world, creating interesting boundaries and hazards throughout the course. Pictured from a birds-eye view, there is a large circular

The illustrative scorecard from the Moundbuilders Country Club in Ohio. *(Photo courtesy of the USGA)*

mound measuring a half-mile in diameter that encloses twenty acres of the course; an adjacent octagonal mound is even larger, enclosing fifty acres. The course design incorporates the mounds into the holes, with shots required over and around the grassy hazards. The layout Kennedy visited had an 18th hole that played as a 381-yard par 4 with a green set behind one of the mounds forming the circle. The imaginative scorecard for Moundbuilders shows spirited ancient people depicted as golfers dancing among the mounds, wielding primitive stone and wooden axes. Moundbuilders was another club that used slot machines to help finance their club's survival during the Second World War.

Ralph's visit to Moundbuilders was just a prelude to a year to remember. He was approaching another milestone, his 2,500th course, as his effort to pile up unique golf courses was unflagging. With the Axis Powers defeated, he was eager to resume a more active golf schedule. One of his new goals was to play in all forty-eight states, and he set an ambitious schedule for the year, focused on golf in the Western states. Ralph Kennedy's golf spree was about to reach a fever pitch.

CHAPTER 14

Motoring out West

THE BIGGEST GOLF TRIP OF Ralph's lifetime began on the 29th of June, when he and Mary Alice left for a cross-country odyssey. The scope of the epic journey on which they were embarking would make 1946 their annus mirabilis, a twentieth-century golfing equivalent of the Lewis and Clark expedition. In letters he sent to ask for help in arranging for courses to play, Ralph wrote that he and his sweetheart of thirty-eight years would be "Motoring out West." An automobile trip was a new adventure for the Kennedys, and, no longer tethered to a train schedule, they had the freedom to drive where they wanted to explore the vast Western continent.

The country they were about to explore was evolving in the postwar period. Although suburbanization was about to accelerate, spawned by the mode of transportation they were using, it had not yet proliferated; people predominantly still lived in cities or small towns. It was also a time with a different approach to service: gas station attendants wore spiffy uniforms, checked a car's oil and water, cleaned the windshield, and offered free maps. Speed limits, which had been reduced to 35 mph during the war to save rubber, were raised again, allowing the Kennedys to motor at a comfortable pace. Among the gas stations available on their long journey was Tydol; in addition to its "Flying A" gas, it also marketed 100 percent Pennsylvania oil. Other "service stations" along the way were operated by Esso, Sinclair, the Union Oil Company, and Chevron, which sold Red Crown gasoline.

Polio was approaching epidemic proportions as the Kennedys departed on their trip, although progress in other areas of medicine continued. Led by penicillin, by the mid-1940s, antibiotics had become widely available. As they set off, pneumonia and influenza were no longer ranked in the top five causes of death in the country, and tuberculosis was also down dramatically as a killer. An evolving threat was being injured or killed in a motor-vehicle accident, which, for the first time, was among the top ten ways Americans died.

Ralph began their transcontinental trip with a handicap of nineteen, as printed in the list the MGA published that year in the *New York Times*. The list was appreciably shorter than it was before the war as the ranks of golfers were thinned because of the number of men who had been serving their country. Although some gas stations offered their own credit cards, the couple did not take any general-purpose cards with them because they were not yet commonly used; standard practice was to use cash or traveler's checks. Bringing a wad of cash, the Kennedys packed for an extended road trip, and Ralph brought his Novak Special with him. Mary Alice brought her clubs but only played occasionally on their long vacation.

Their ambitious journey would take them across the Mississippi through seventeen Western states and two Canadian provinces, through the Badlands, the Black Hills, the Rockies, the Cascades, the Sierra Nevada, Yosemite, the Great Salt Lake Desert, Death Valley, the Sonoran Desert, across the Rio Grande, through the High Plains, to the Colorado Plateau, Pikes Peak, and the Great Plains. It was the first and only time they ever visited many of the states, including California, Oregon, Washington, Nevada, Utah, Arizona, Idaho, New Mexico, and Colorado.

Traveling before the advent of the Interstate Highway System, they took two-lane state and local roads and, where they could, U.S.-numbered highways or routes. To begin their journey, it was a short drive to the George Washington Bridge to cross the Hudson River and connect to the mainland. Following Route 22 into Pennsylvania, they continued through Easton, Allentown, and Bethlehem before reaching Harrisburg. The Pennsylvania Turnpike began outside Harrisburg and carried cars through to just outside Pittsburgh, a distance of 160 miles. The roadway was opened only six years earlier and was built using New Deal funds provided through a highway building program and the WPA. In some ways, the Pennsylvania Turnpike represented the first modern highway that the interstate system would come to resemble. When it was opened, it had no speed limit, and, unlike its predecessors, which followed old winding road paths, the new highway was wide and spacious, crossing the Alleghany Mountains in a more direct route. West of Pittsburgh, the Kennedys took another half dozen state highways in Pennsylvania and Ohio before they reached their destination.

Their first stop was the Orchard Hills Country Club in Bryan, Ohio, on the 1st of July. The stop was a short one, since Ralph's scorecards show that later the same day he played the Auburn Country Club in Auburn, Indiana, forty-five minutes west on Route 6. The following day, it was down to Fort Wayne, Indiana, an hour away, to play the Orchard Ridge Country Club. From there, following the route of the Lincoln Highway, it was up toward Lake Michigan to play at the Christiana Country Club in Elkhart, before settling in for the night.

After a solid stretch of driving on Route 6, skipping golf in Illinois, it was time to play a couple of college courses: the University of Iowa Golf Course in Iowa City and the Iowa State College Golf Course. From Ames, it was due north on Route 69 to Minneapolis, where Ralph played at the Meadowbrook Golf Course, the Oak Ridge Country Club, the Theodore Wirth Golf Course, and the Orono Orchards Golf Course. A writer for the *Minnetonka Herald* in Wayzata, Minnesota, took note and pecked out a small story on his typewriter as the ardent duffer was now off and running.

Back on the road through Minnesota, it was easy motoring on the highway that traverses the prairies, Route 212, into South Dakota. Their movements through South Dakota were tracked city by city. On

July 7th, the *Daily Capital Journal* announced the "Hobbyist in Pierre Sunday." He was passing through after playing in Redfield in the eastern part of the state. As they headed west out of Pierre, crossing the Missouri River, the land forms were changing and they were entering a harsh landscape, one characterized by buttes, eroded terrain, and a barren plateau. The *Rapid City Daily Journal* reported to its readers that the couple had arrived in their fair city and, as the headline noted, that the "Renowned Golfer to Play around Meadowbrook." A visit to Mount Rushmore was in order as the Kennedys passed through the Badlands, and while in the region he played in Deadwood, a boomtown from the gold rush that swept the Dakota Territory in the late nineteenth century. The local newspaper noted that he played the Tomahawk Course near Black Hills National Park with only a 3-iron; as was his modus operandi, Ralph praised the course.

Continuing their westward trek, after a short ride they were in Wyoming, a state Ralph had not visited since he played in Riverton fourteen years before. Transiting from the Black Hills to Sheridan, it was through more prairies and grasslands, and as they approached the end of the 250-mile leg, they got their first glimpse of mountains rising in the distance. For the next thousand miles west, they would be driving through, in, and around the jagged landscape. The classic western town of Sheridan offered two rounds of golf: the Kendrick Municipal Golf Course and the Sheridan Country Club. Mary Alice joined her husband as they played both courses; Ralph used only his Novak club, and they hired a Native American "Indian guide" as a caddie. Kendrick's scorecard reveals a great deal about the dusty course, which had more than its fair share of sand and dirt and therefore required special instructions. It let players know to "clean out cups, don't throw sweeps, place sweep on departing side." Sweeps are presumably brooms stationed at each green that allowed players to smooth out irregularities on the sandy surfaces. Apparently not the best conditioned course of the thousands Ralph played, it also had a local rule that stipulated that a "ball on the fairway beyond 100-yard stake may be moved a club's length, not nearer hole, and placed on natural tee." Although located 1,600 miles from the game's rule makers, the club took a purist approach to playing. A prominent warning to golfers included on the card was "No conceded putts. Ball must be played from where it lies on all putting greens and MUST be holed out." One final reminder was included for good measure: "No high heels on greens."

The scorecard from Ralph's visit to the Sheridan Country Club in Wyoming. *(Photo courtesy of USGA)*

Rumbling on to their next state along U.S. Route 87 took them directly past the site of the Battle of the Little Bighorn, where General George A. Custer was killed. It was time to go full-throttle one hundred and twenty-five miles north, passing through the Crow Indian Reservation and over the Bighorn and Yellowstone rivers, before arriving in Billings, Montana. Billings sported three courses, and Ralph made a tee time at each—the Billings Club Public Golf Course, the Hilands Golf Club, and the Hiltop Golf Club—dodging afternoon thunderstorms as the summer heat was rising.

Relentlessly soldiering on, it was an additional one hundred and fifty miles west to Bozeman—the majestic peaks of the Gallatin Range greeting the vacationing New Yorkers—where Ralph teed it up at the Bozeman Country Club. Butte was an additional ninety-minute journey farther west, occupying an idyllic setting nestled in a bowl high up in the Rockies. The Kennedys were now in the heart of the West, in Big Sky country. It was fitting that they stopped at the Butte Country Club on July 16th, since it was the course where earlier in his career Joe Novak served as the professional, and Ralph was now touring around with one of his clubs. The Kennedys satisfied their wanderlust by continuing farther north to play the Deer Lodge Country Club in sparsely populated Deer Lodge, Montana.

The intrepid couple did not book hotel rooms in advance, partially because their agenda was flexible, but also because it was difficult to reserve ahead of time. Sheraton became the first national chain to introduce a centralized toll-free (although not an 800) number to make reservations, but that was far in the future. To plan ahead, they sent for brochures from hotels at which they were thinking of staying. The Sunday newspapers in New York contained ten full pages of small advertisements from properties across the country touting their unique charms. The prospective traveler was urged to write to the manager of the hotel, motel, or resort for a copy of their printed brochure. Alternatively, they would simply pull up to properties with a vacancy sign out and check in for the night.

Continuing north by northwest, the next destination was the Missoula Country Club, then it was on to Kalispell in northern Montana to play the town's Municipal Golf Course. New golf courses beckoned as the pair was pulled farther north to play the Whitefish Lake Golf Course, followed by a visit to the Waterton-Glacier International Peace Park straddling the Canadian border. Crossing the 49th Parallel into Alberta, the day was fully occupied playing the Calgary Golf & Country Club and the Earl Grey Golf Club. Progressing back in a south by southwesterly direction, the motoring couple arrived at the westernmost Canadian province of British Columbia to play the Cranbrook Golf & Country Club and the Kimberley Golf & Country Club.

Zigzagging between the United States and Canada, almost one month into their journey, the Kennedys were visiting another state for the first time—Idaho—crossing the skinny northern tip, shoehorned between Montana and Washington. Ralph's only round in the state was at the Hayden Lake Golf Club on the edge of the Coeur d'Alene Forest. As reported by the *Coeur d'Alene Press*, the man with the body that never tired played with his trusty Novak set as a 3-iron.

Their stay in the Gem State was a brief one. Forty-five minutes farther west brought their maiden visit to Washington, to play the

Manito Golf & Country Club in Spokane, host of the 1944 PGA Championship. The course was the first of a half-dozen Ralph was about to play designed by Arthur Vernon Macan, who worked as an architect during the Golden Age. An Irishman who attended Trinity College and the University of London, he was educated as a lawyer but gave up the profession to design golf courses. Macan's oeuvre is primarily in the Pacific Northwest, and he had a distinct design style, centered on making putting surfaces challenging, or, in his own words, "Greens should not be flat but hogbacks, undulations and crowns should be incorporated to defy the backspin players." It is unlikely that Ralph was penalized by the greens, since it would have been difficult for him to generate backspin on his ball using only a 3-iron.

Two more course cards were added to the growing collection before leaving Eastern Washington: the Indian Canyon Golf Course and the Spokane Country Club. The couple then sauntered across the state, traveling hundreds of miles through the diverse terrain, including passing through the barren Scablands, through fertile farm country, and across the snow-capped Cascade Range. The area that the lifelong city dwellers had trekked to was remote and filled with western character. The country was far less homogenized in 1946 due to a variety of factors, including the lack of interstates, and this allowed them to go slower and enjoy the local flavor of the wide range of communities they visited.

Finally reaching the Pacific coastline, the couple continued up into Canada, to the western edge of British Columbia, to play the Shaughnessy Heights Golf Club in Vancouver, another Macan layout. It was Ralph's first and only visit to Canada's westernmost province and his first return to the Pacific's shores since his 1930 trip through the Panama Canal to South America.

The following day, it was a short journey across the Lions Gate Bridge to West Vancouver to play at one of the best courses he would visit on the trip: the Capilano Golf & Country Club. Ralph was returning to a Stanley Thompson course after a long absence. Capilano was built over a four-year period from 1932 to 1936, and Robert Trent

Jones, then just beginning as a designer, assisted Thompson and routed the holes.

The club's sprawling clubhouse occupies an impressive piece of real estate at the crest of the property, nestled between two mountain parks. The course is built on a steeply sloping hillside amid six thousand acres of thick coniferous forest populated with Douglas fir, western hemlock, cedar, and cypress. The long view offered from the tee on the sixth hole is one of sheer beauty, overlooking the mile-long Lions Gate suspension bridge, with the azure blue waters of Vancouver harbor and the city skyline in the distance. From his prior visits to Western Canada, Ralph had retained vivid memories of holes at Thompson's other designs at Banff and Jasper Park. Added to the noteworthy list was another hole with which he was particularly impressed, Capilano's demanding par-5 finisher, which Thompson made a brawny one, featuring blind shots, hidden bunkers, and a tricky, elevated green.

When they were done sightseeing in the beautiful coastal seaport, it was a short ferry ride over to Vancouver Island, reaching the westernmost point in their journey. In the provincial capital of Victoria, he played at a pair of Macan courses: the Gorge Vale Golf Club and the

The idyllic Capilano Golf & Country Club in Vancouver. *(Author's Collection)*

Royal Colwood Golf Club. After completing the two, they boarded another vessel to splash across the electric blue waters of the Haro Strait and Puget Sound. Once back on American shores, the next course played, under temperatures in the fifties and stereotypical cloudy skies, was the Cedar Crest Public Golf Course located north of Seattle, in Snohomish County. He then played a pair of courses in Seattle beginning with another Macan design, the Broadmoor Golf Club, followed by eighteen holes at the Seattle Golf Club. The 14,410-foot Mount Rainier dominated their views looking east as they continued southbound past Tacoma. Their next destination was the small agricultural town of Chehalis, Washington, to play two additional tracks: the Dunahoe Golf Course and the Chehalis Golf & Country Club. The last course played in the state was the Coweeman Golf Course in the logging town of Kelso on the state's southern boundary.

As they crossed the Columbia River into Portland, four courses were on the agenda: the Alderwood Country Club (host of the U.S. Amateur in 1937), the Columbia-Edgewater Country Club (another Macan-designed course), the Colwood Golf Club, and the Portland Golf Club (which hosted the PGA Championship less than a month after Ralph played it). Continuing back east slightly, it was to the Mount Hood Golf Club in Welches, located in the Salmon River Valley of Mount Hood National Forest. From there, it was back down the coast to play the nine-hole Coquille Valley Country Club in Coos County, fifteen miles inland from Bandon, Oregon. The traveling salesman was used to a life on the road living out of a suitcase, and it was a good thing, since the couple rarely stayed for more than one night in the same town on their long journey.

California beckoned, so it was down scenic Highway 101, across the salmon-rich Rogue River, and into the Golden State for the first time. The five-hour drive south through the Redwood Forest led the duo to the nine-hole Benbow Golf & Country Club. Then it was on to the capital of Sonoma County, to play the Santa Rosa Golf & Country Club. The Kennedys didn't linger long in wine country, since Santa Rosa was Ralph's 2,499th course and his next round was going to be a memorable one. They breezed through Marin County, across the Golden Gate—bypassing San Francisco—continuing through San Mateo and Santa Cruz counties.

Red finally visited Pebble Beach, on August 8th, to tee it up at the course he built the trip around, playing it as course No. 2,500. The day began with morning fog, but after it burned off, it was a mild, sun-drenched day. Napoleon once said that geography is destiny, and he was correct when it came to golf on the Monterey Peninsula. Ralph appreciated the majesty of Pebble Beach, where the pale blue skies provided the ideal backdrop for the sweeping views from the lush cliffside fairways. The navy blue waters crashed violently against the jagged coast, sending up plumes of white foam as the peppy golfer walked the verdant fairways above. Soaking up the ambiance of the region fully, the Kennedys spent the night in Pebble Beach at the Lodge.

How do you top a round of golf at Pebble Beach, a highlight in the life of most golfers? By playing a golf course par excellence the next day. August 9th was one of the most important golf days of Ralph's life, as he played the exclusive and flawless Cypress Point Golf Club as course No. 2,501. As Providence would have it, he was again blessed with California's abundant sunshine, this particular cranny of the state offering a special radiance. He was immediately impressed and said that the last four holes at Cypress Point were the finest he'd ever seen, "With only Merion Cricket Club in Philly even close." The Kennedys celebrated their visit to Cypress Point with cocktails; Ralph was drinking scotch and soda, and Mary Alice champagne. His visit to the breathtaking peninsula was filled with scenes from nature; he mentioned that he saw "Stags at Cypress Point and Pebble Beach, who reared their magnificent heads and stood menacingly until their does and fawns had time to escape." Visits to the Del Monte Golf Course and the Monterey Peninsula Country Club rounded out his stay in one of the best golf regions of the world.

Because he wanted to play Pebble Beach as his 2,500th course, the couple had diverted south to play on the Monterey Peninsula, and they now returned north to San Francisco to check off additional courses.

The par-3 15th at Cypress Point, Pebble Beach, California. *(Author's Collection)*

Traveling back up the San Francisco Peninsula, he played at the Los Altos Golf & Country Club.

The concentration of great courses he played in a short period of time in the Bay Area was reminiscent of the quality of golf he played in the Hamptons in 1929. Within the span of a few days, he stepped gingerly around both the Olympic Club's Lake Course and its Ocean Course, the California Golf Club of San Francisco (another Macan track), and the San Francisco Golf Club. He had the opportunity to contrast the design of San Francisco (an early Tillinghast work) to Winged Foot and found many similarities in the strategic nature of the course, including the pristine bunkers and the artful routing. He also noticed some striking differences, most notably in the jarring elevation changes the property has. It was a pleasant two-block walk from his accommodations in the northern part of the city for his final round in the region at the Presidio Golf Course, which sits near Fort Point at the entrance to San Francisco Bay.

The *San Francisco News* picked up his trail on August 14th and reported, "The era of the flagpole sitters, goldfish swallowers, etc. etc. may come and go but there is one era that marches on indefinitely—the era of the marathon golfer. This is not the type of marathon golfer who endeavors to set a mere dawn-to-dusk record. No indeed." Noting that Kennedy was a stocky New Yorker, they called him a well-groomed businessman, an image borne out by the picture of him that appeared alongside the article, wearing his Sunday best. Asked about the golf he had played thus far in California, Kennedy admitted he enjoyed many courses but saved his most effusive praise for Cypress Point. "The Olympic Club is a fine test of golf but I've got to credit Cypress Point as the most spectacular of the more than 2,500 golf courses I've played so far. I've never seen such breath-taking beauty. The variety of the layout, the condition of the entire course and the beauty and the wildlife make Cypress Point the grandest I have even seen."

There is no optimal route to follow to play golf throughout the West without doubling back along the way. Thus, to play in Nevada and Utah, the Kennedys took a thousand-mile diversion, following the Lincoln Highway route. Departing the Bay Area, it was east, to cross the Sierra Nevada, taking the relatively efficient Route 40 through Sacramento and Truckee, their car struggling to climb through the 7,000-foot-high Donner Pass, as they made their way into Nevada, continuing through to Reno (where they stopped as he played the Washoe County Golf Course, another course built with WPA funds). The salesman had his foot on the accelerator as they rolled an additional 400 miles northeast, transiting the baked and arid Great Basin Desert, passing through Elko to the Utah border. Continuing up a desolate stretch of Route 40, the twosome motored across the Great Salt Lake Desert. After crossing the high desert, they were in the 4,000-foot-high Salt Lake City at the edge of the Wasatch Range Mountains.

The Mountain West impressed the couple from the East with its beautiful vistas. Back in 1929, *Fraser's* described Salt Lake City as being "in a striking situation near the lake, at a high altitude. The climate is dry and healthy." On August 20th, Ralph played the city's nine-hole Nibley Park Muni, and the tenacious duffer's goal was to collect a complete set of cards in the home of the Mormon Church. Ralph was blessed with good genes and stamina, and whether his body was aching by this point after having played for more than fifty consecutive days is unknown, although he never complained about it. While in Salt Lake City, he chased his little white ball around the Bonneville Municipal Golf Course, the Country Club, the Forest Dale Municipal Golf Course, and the Fort Douglas Club, staying at the elegant five hundred-room Hotel Utah, which was built in the Renaissance revival style.

From Salt Lake City, it was more than four hundred miles southwest to their next stop back in Nevada, this time taking the isolated southerly roadway through the infertile but charming terrain to Las Vegas along Route 91. The Las Vegas the couple visited was not a glitzy megatown. Its population in 1940 was a mere 8,422 people, and although it grew rapidly over the next decade, by 1950 its population was still less than 25,000. Several iconic properties in town had yet to open, including the Desert Inn, the Tropicana, and the Stardust. The Flamingo

A postcard depicting Las Vegas at the time of the Kennedys' visit. *(Author's Collection)*

was nearing completion along the Los Angeles Highway "Strip" when they visited and opened four months later. Ex-bootlegger Bugsy Siegel oversaw its final stages of construction. Although gambling had been legal in Las Vegas since 1931, at the time of the Kennedys' sensational trip it was more famous as a quickie divorce location. With one of the most liberal divorce laws in the nation, after establishing residency for six weeks, a couple could legally separate, as contrasted with New York, where, at the time, the only grounds for divorce was adultery.

Ralph told the *Las Vegas Review-Journal* that he used only a 2-iron to play the nine-hole Las Vegas Municipal Golf Course, or "El Rancho" as he called it, on the 22nd of August. Among the rustic desert course's rules were "A ball lying in a hole, or on a mound made by a burrowing animal shall be dropped without penalty." Before setting out across Southern Nevada, the veteran travelers topped up their car's fuel tank and filled the radiator with water. They were about to cross the bone-dry and remote roadways through the Mojave Desert on their way back into Southern California.

Ralph repeatedly said he played on the Devil's Golf Course in Death Valley, located only a couple of hours from Sin City. Death Valley is an expansive area of three thousand square miles, situated 250 feet below sea level, known for its extremely low humidity and withering heat. There is no scorecard in the Far Hills archives for the Devil's Golf Course because it is a metaphorical course; it is simply a name given to the large salt pan that lines the valley bottom. The National Park Service once joked that "only the devil could play golf" on the jagged surface. It is more likely that the sporting Kennedy stopped in the valley en route, dropped a ball or two, and pitched and putted over the rough terrain just to add another notch to his belt. Ralph knew it would add a colorful dimension to the repertoire of anecdotes he used to entertain dinner guests.

From Death Valley, he chauffeured Mrs. Kennedy onward to Yosemite, to play the nine-hole Wawona Hotel Golf Course, built at an elevation of 4,000 feet in the Sierra Nevada Mountains. The next morning, Ralph steered their gas guzzler southwest to Fresno in

California's Central Valley, playing the University-Sequoia Sunnyside Club on August 26th. As he departed the massive agricultural region, it was finally time to visit the City of Angels. The population of Los Angeles was growing rapidly when the Kennedys visited; by 1940, it was already America's fifth largest city with a population of a million and a half people. This was quite a contrast from the year when Ralph first played golf, 1910, when it had a population of only 319,000 and was the seventeenth largest city. At the time of their visit, there was only one McDonald's on the expansive continent; the original, in Southern California, was operating in San Bernardino, selling mostly barbeque, served by carhops. The conversion to the Golden Arches and a hamburger menu was still two years away, as was the founding of In-N-Out Burger in the city's Baldwin Park neighborhood.

If a golfer is going to travel across an entire continent, they may as well play the best courses the country has. Ralph began his Los Angeles-area golf orgy by playing a trio of posh courses on the city's west side, beginning with a ride up the foothills of the Santa Monica Mountains on Sunset Boulevard. First up was the George Thomas Jr.-designed Riviera Country Club in Pacific Palisades. His only prior exposure to a Thomas course was the nine-hole Marion Golf Club in Massachusetts, and he was now about to immerse himself in the respected designer's work. It was up early on the 28th and a short journey down Wilshire Boulevard to sweep off the dew at the Los Angeles Country Club (LACC). Like Winged Foot, LACC is a 36-hole complex with a memorable meandering clubhouse. His day began on the South Course, a design of William Bell—later modified by Thomas—and then it was time to tee it up at one of the masterpieces of his trip, the classic North Course. The fabled links is routed through rolling hills, around thickets of trees, and over the distinctly Southern California hazard of barrancas. Thomas's sand traps look like they were designed by an artist rather than a golf architect.

Continuing his Thomas course schooling, he visited the Bel-Air Country Club, located three miles from LACC, set in the Santa Monica Mountains overlooking UCLA. The traveling golf celebrity enjoyed his day in the Zen-like setting, and in a sign of Ralph's stature in the world of record-setting amateur golfers, one of the club's members, Clark Gable, asked to meet him (the two had something in common: Governor Laffoon also appointed Gable a Kentucky Colonel). It was a visit to remember, made even more special because his scorecard was signed by Joe Novak, the inventor of the club with whom Ralph was touring the West, who served as the professional at the elite club.

Stringing together quite a collection of upper-crust private courses, on the same day he played Bel-Air, he played at Grantland Rice's winter club, the Lakeside Golf Club of Hollywood, located adjacent to the movie studios. Lakeside's card let players know that they were to play by strict rules: "There are no 'unwritten' or local 'understandings.'" Their card also reminded players to level their footprints in the bunkers, since rakes were still not used on golf courses. Remaining near Hollywood, Kennedy was fortunate enough to arrange a round at the Wilshire Country Club in the Hancock Park neighborhood. Ralph was never a golf snob, and in addition to the masterful collection of private links he enjoyed, he also played the Harding Course in Griffith Park, a 1926 design of George Thomas Jr. Knocking down golf courses like they were bowling pins, Ralph made additional visits to the Pasadena Municipal Golf Course, the Annandale Golf Club, and the San Gabriel Country Club. He also played the other Oakmont; this one, the Oakmont Country Club, was located in Glendale.

As the calendar turned to September, the Kennedys rolled into San Diego. A visit to the West Coast wouldn't be complete without paying homage to the Clambake, and Ralph included the Rancho Santa Fe Golf Club in his itinerary, the original host course of the Bing Crosby Pro-Amateur Tournament. The *San Diego Union* mentioned that on September 3rd, Ralph played at the La Jolla Country Club (another William Bell design), and he told them that the course was most interesting. Golf at the San Diego Country Club rounded out his visit to the Pacific Coast city, playing as their characteristic vibrant yellow sunshine washed over him.

After completing play in California, the Kennedys made their way to two states they would also be visiting for the first time. Arizona and New Mexico were territories when they were born, having been admitted as states in 1912. The 170-mile journey on Route 80 took them along the Mexican border and through the Imperial Valley. As soon as they crossed the Colorado River, they stopped so he could play in Yuma. On September 4th, the day's recreation was at the Las Palmas Golf Club. The heat was stifling when he played in the desert environment, although perhaps he was suffering from delirium based on the length of his trip and the unrelenting heat when he said, "It was 115 in the shade and (I think) 185 on the fairway. Put grape leaves in your hat, they told me, and I did." He only played nine holes at Las Palmas and shot a forty-four. He also said that he refreshed himself with the off-putting combination of "warm water and salt tablets cached at each tee."

Although "air cooling" was starting to become more common in hotel rooms, it was by no means a standard feature, so the couple did not linger in the broiling Southwest summer. Continuing on Route 80 through the parched desert, they next stopped in Litchfield Park to play the Wigwam Country Club. Proceeding east brought them directly into Phoenix, where Ralph teed it up at the Phoenix Country Club. Decamping from Phoenix, it was north to Williams, Arizona, in Coconino County, a town of two thousand residents west of Flagstaff, set on a high plateau at 6,700 feet of elevation on Route 66. Ralph played the nine-hole Williams Country Club, a course designed in the 1920s by railway workers, located in a thick forest of ponderosa pine, fir, spruce, and aspen. The town takes its name from "Old Bill Williams," a trapper and mountain man who operated in the area. After *el gran jugador*'s quick round, it was one hour north for a little sightseeing at the Grand Canyon, and then, back down to the Flagstaff Country Club, whose card described it as "a beautiful, sporty, nine-hole course among the big pines at an altitude of more than 7,000 feet."

Although he would not identify which course it was, when asked years later what were some of the worst courses he ever played, Ralph said, "There was a course in Arizona that was truly a cow pasture with slabs of wood, like gravestones implanted perhaps every twenty yards to show where the fairway ended and the rough began. The grass was about ten inches high in both sectors, but on the so-called fairway you could tee it up."

The Kennedys picked up Route 66 in Flagstaff and followed it to Winslow, past the Painted Desert, through Native American lands, and then across the border into Gallup, New Mexico, to play the Gallup Country Club, situated at an elevation of 6,500 feet. Continuing east on Route 66, it was back across the Continental Divide. The landscape was unfamiliar to the couple born in New England; they were now motoring through the parched ocher landscape of broken mesas, wide deserts, cacti, and enchanting wilderness, before crossing the Rio Grande and arriving in the high-altitude city of Albuquerque. He repaired ball marks at two courses in the city that was established by the Spanish more than 240 years before their visit: the University of New Mexico Public Golf Course and the historic Albuquerque Country Club.

Albuquerque Country Club opened in 1914 with a five-hole course featuring gravel fairways and sand greens. Winds in the area were strong enough to blow balls off the greens, so when the course was extended to nine holes, the greens were converted to oiled sand. In 1927, the club's professional constructed a new course. He used five teams of horses and eighty-eight men to build a new set of nine holes, which featured grass fairways and greens made of cottonseed hulls. It would be several more years before the greens were converted to grass. The course went on to install an irrigation system during the Depression and took on debt to do so. Like Moundbuilders and Idle Hour, the club allowed slot machines to be placed in the clubhouse, the proceeds of which were used to help pay off their debt. When the debt was paid off in 1941, the club celebrated not only by burning the mortgage document, but also by burying the one-armed bandits out on the course.

There was one final course to visit in New Mexico before reaching an additional big milestone of the trip. It was north again, to play the Santa Fe Municipal Golf Course on September 11th, before heading through Taos, destination: Colorado, the heart of the Rocky Mountain region and the last of the nation's forty-eight states that Ralph visited, teeing it up at the Pueblo Golf & Country Club on September 13th. Exiting Pueblo, they rolled north to Colorado Springs and the Broadmoor Golf Club, set in the Cheyenne Mountain foothills at 6,400 feet of elevation with views of Pikes Peak. Ralph was a fan of Donald Ross courses, and the Broadmoor's East Course, designed by the Scottish émigré in 1916, was one that made a special impression on him.

The final stop in Colorado was in the capital city, and if Ralph's sixty-four-year-old body was showing any signs of strain after two and a half months on the road, it was difficult to tell by the amount of golf he played in Denver. Whereas Phileas Fogg was at the point of completion in his circumnavigation after eighty days, the couple from Washington Heights was far from done four-score days into theirs. The tenacious Kennedy played at the Overland Municipal Golf Course, the Wellshire Municipal Golf Course, the Cherry Hills Country Club, the Denver Country Club, and the Lakewood Country Club.

Taking U.S. 24 out of Colorado, the Kennedys set their sights on Manhattan, although this time it was the one in Kansas. There were two more states to tackle before heading home. He played the Manhattan Country Club on September 21st, but not before stopping at a handful of towns along the way. *Fraser's* colorfully described golf in Kansas as follows: "The state has a dry and mild winter climate, but lacks wooded areas. Artificial afforestation is being carried out by the government. In the early days nearly all the emigrants carrying 'prairie schooners' passed through Kansas on their way to California and Utah. Practically every town of any size in Kansas has a golf course, many of which are as sporty as could be wished for."

Ralph played in a succession of villages and hamlets as they traversed the prairieland. To say they were visiting small-town America was an understatement. The city block that the couple lived on had more inhabitants than each of the towns they visited. By this point, his bride was done golfing, so the implacable golfer played alone at the Meadow Lake Country Club in Colby (1940 population: 2,458), the Stockton Golf

Club (1940 population: 1,418), the Osborne Golf Club (1940 population: 1,876), and the Beloit Golf Club (1940 population: 3,765).

The vacationers stopped in Topeka so Ralph could play the Topeka Country Club (designed by Tom Bendelow and Perry Maxwell) and the Shawnee Country Club. It was Ralph's first time back to Kansas since his ever-so-brief visit there during his four-state-in-one-day feat in Baxter Springs in 1931, and the barnstorming golfer was making the most of the visit, to say the least. The last course he played in the state was the Smiley's Armour Golf Course in Kansas City, Kansas, before crossing the border to play four courses in the city of the same name in Missouri.

Talking Route 40 eastward across the state, and showing no signs that they were eager to get home, the sexagenarians stopped in any town they could along the way. In the middle of Missouri, that included Boonville, where Ralph romped around the Kemper Military School Golf Course. Appropriately enough for a trip focused on the Western states, they finished just west of St. Louis, the Gateway to the West. It was finally across the wide banks of the Mississippi, and at long last they were homeward-bound to the Manhattan of granite and steel. Having left during the middle of the summer, they were now returning home to autumn weather on October 9th. The Kennedys' Western trip of 1946 was monumental; they traveled 13,997 miles (the number is so precise because they tracked it with the car's odometer) and were gone for over one hundred days. As Keeler had previously referred to him, "Ralpho of the Iron Arm" played an exhausting one hundred and twenty-one different courses as part of his biggest trip ever on their fourteen-week vacation.

One would think that after playing so much golf, Kennedy would take a break. Not so. The *Pibroch*—the newsletter of the St. Andrew's Society of New York—of October 1946 highlights an event held at the Blind Brook Club in Westchester County. A group of about fifty golfers is pictured in front of the clubhouse wearing suits and ties. Front and center, smack dab in the middle of the picture, standing next to the bagpiper with a big grin on his face, is Ralph Kennedy.

CHAPTER 15

The Next 500 Courses

Not content to play only local courses upon his return, Ralph's extended Western trip didn't dampen the voracious golfer's enthusiasm for faraway junkets. Back on the road within a month, the traveling salesman took a thousand-mile trip to play in Florida in mid-November of his big year. The *Florida Times Union* called him a "divot digger," and Kennedy pronounced the Ponte Vedra Club "one of the finest courses I have ever played." In addition to his big Western push, Ralph continued to plug away and collect new courses along the East Coast in the postwar period. He had not yet lost his mojo and would play 384 courses in the coming three years, a blistering pace of more than one new course every three days.

Long-distance calls still required human assistance, and as the year came to a close, AT&T reached its peak employment of operators, with an astonishing 350,000 of them manually operating switchboards for Ma Bell. To put the number in perspective, it was more than the total populations of San Diego, Fort Worth, Miami, or Atlanta.

Life in Truman's America was good. As the calendar turned to 1947, Frank Capra's *It's a Wonderful Life* debuted in theaters. The Eagle Pencil Company was running newspaper advertisements in New York, looking for "girls" who could earn $28 a week doing light factory work. The long war was over, the economy was growing, jobs were plentiful, and the middle-class was becoming more mobile—fueled by the rise of the automobile. Levittown began to sprout on the site of potato fields in Nassau County, Long Island, as Americans began to migrate out of cities into the countryside. Government programs helped to accelerate the trend, since they allowed buyers to purchase homes with little or no money down. Although it allowed GIs to buy into the American Dream, suburbanization would unfortunately have a negative impact on historic golf courses.

Ralph turned sixty-five in June and began to collect Social Security twelve years after the safety net program was first launched. At the end of July, he received his first "old-age benefit." The average amount paid to seniors was $25 per month, with a maximum of $85 per month. Remarkably, you could still make a living as an iceman after the Second World War; one in three households continued to use "iced boxes," which still required delivery of fresh ice.

Ralph played golf his whole life wearing relatively formal clothing: long pants or knickers, long-sleeved shirts—often with a tie—and a tam-o'-shanter, playing in the era before baseball-style hats were worn. He never wore shorts. Professional golfers, like amateurs of the day, dressed well in all aspects of their lives, including when they played golf. Jimmy Demaret, always known on tour for being a colorful dresser, was the first professional to wear shorts while playing, in 1947, at George May's All-American Tournament at Tam O'Shanter. He was joined by Freddie Haas Jr., who also wore them, although Demaret didn't use particularly good judgment. The strapping Texan wore tight short-shorts, which showed a visible bulging in an area where it was not seemly to show a protuberance. He was asked not to wear them again, and professional golf attire has never looked back.

"Rambling Golfer Here," the Peterborough newspaper announced in midsummer, as the NYAC member was in Ontario to play a trio of courses: the Peterborough Golf & Country Club, the Beaver Meadow Golf Club, and the Kawartha Golf & Country Club. The article included a picture of the road warrior holding his Novak set as a 3-iron, the only club he used to play the three courses. He must have been quite adept at manufacturing shots with the club, particularly the knock-down shots required to hit par threes or approaches to the greens with such a low-lofted clubface.

The rising medium of broadcast television was slowly making inroads into sports. The year's U.S. Open, held at the C. B. Macdonald-designed St. Louis Country Club (which Ralph played in 1936), was the first to be televised, although it was only shown locally on station KSD-TV.

A hometown newspaper described Ralph quite accurately in 1948 as the "Most Elaborate, Globetrotting Golfer," referring to him as a school-supply salesman. The centerpiece of an early spring trip to Atlanta in pursuit of the royal and ancient game was a visit to the newly-opened Peachtree Golf Club, a club Bobby Jones founded (he co-designed the course with Robert Trent Jones). The fact that Ralph played two months after the club opened—on April 3rd—highlights how well connected the Winged Footer remained with his continued ties to the legendary golfer.

The *Minnesota Star* reported in May 1948 that the Gotham golfer had recently completed playing the Tom Bendelow-designed Edina Country Club. It was for good reason that Bendelow received the nickname "The Johnny Appleseed of Golf," since he designed early courses from coast to coast in the United States and Canada. Bendelow was a religious man and did not swear or drink alcohol, although, like Stanley Thompson and Ralph Kennedy, he did fancy big cigars. Edina was one of a dozen courses Kennedy played on his trip to the Land of 10,000 Lakes. The newspaper did feel it necessary, however, to qualify his accomplishments: "Kennedy is by no means a golf nut or dub."

Ralph played only eighteen holes on a short visit to the Keystone State in 1948, split among two nine-hole courses. He began at the private Phoenixville Country Club and then took a taxi to the public Meadow Brook Golf Club near Valley Forge. The Phoenixville course has a pedigreed designer: its nine holes were laid out by High Wilson, the designer of Merion, one of only a handful of the talented architect's layouts. Picking up on the *Star*'s theme, the *Daily Republican* in

Phoenixville described Kennedy's quest as "a mild form of insanity." It was good that Ralph had a mild case, because if he had a more acute form, he would have experienced some of the worst medical care given. Although there were meaningful advances in many areas of medicine over Ralph's lifetime, there was little related to mental health by the 1940s. Conscientious objectors from World War II were sometimes put into "insane asylums" or "lunatic asylums," and as a result, the poor conditions inside were exposed to the broader population. They were, in effect, custodian institutions that did little to care for patients. Although Dr. William Mayo had predicted as far back as 1935 that a pill to "cure" mental ailments would soon be available, it was not, and procedures such as lobotomy surgery and shock treatments were standard.

For his sixty-sixth birthday, Ralph chose the Country Club of New Jersey in River Vale as course No. 2,700, the *New York Sun* reported in June. Never one to let the weather affect his plans, later that summer Ralph competed in the U.S. Senior Amateur Championship at Apawamis and shot rounds of ninety-eight and one hundred and three. The *New Yorker* recounted how the thoroughly drenching tournament was played in weather more suited for porpoises than for golfers. At the time of the article, Kennedy told the magazine he had played all the courses in New York, New Hampshire, Rhode Island, and Maine and that he was missing only one in Massachusetts: the Petersham Country Club. He also boasted that he stored his signed cards in a bank vault, safe from "fire and theft." Mrs. Kennedy, accompanying her husband of forty-one years on their summer vacation, drew a distinction from her rabid mate; she is quoted as saying, "I'm not crazy," letting them know she had "only" played six hundred courses.

People of color continued to be excluded from the game after the war. In July 1948, a group of black golfers brought a suit in federal court against the City of Baltimore. The city limited them to one shoddy nine-hole course, while whites had access to three eighteen-hole courses kept in good condition. It was one of many lawsuits brought over the years by black golfers in the city, who continually asserted that the restrictions put on them amounted to limiting their choices to one Jim Crow course. Ralph played the nine-hole course in question, Carroll Park, two decades earlier, when it was a white-only facility and had sand greens, before it was converted to a segregated facility.

Tournament golf remained low-stakes in the late forties. Ben Hogan won the 1948 U.S. Open held at the Riviera Country Club and collected $2,000 in prize money. When Winged Foot's Claude Harmon won the Masters the same year, his check was only $500 more than Hogan's.

Americans had money to spend as the economy shifted from war-time production to consumer products. The breakthrough technology product of the coming year, 1949, was a new vinyl disc that could play music on a turntable for twenty-five uninterrupted minutes: more commonly known as the 45-rpm record. When Ralph first played at Van Cortlandt Park during the Model T era, less than 15 percent of households owned a car. Motor-vehicle ownership was about to pass the 50 percent mark when Oldsmobile released a new model as the decade wound down, the "88," a streamlined automobile with a Rocket V-8 engine.

O. B. Keeler continued to tell Ralph's story in the *Atlanta Journal* and quoted the New Yorker, who was still traveling throughout Georgia playing nine-hole courses: "You've got some pretty fair golf courses in Georgia . . . maybe you've forgot the count, but I've played 139 different golf courses in Georgia, and some of them rather lately." Keeler also mentioned that Ralph was now number four on the "championship list" at Winged Foot (the same number Gehrig had worn on the back of his pin-striped uniform), ranking his seniority at the club. Still traveling light, playing with a 3-iron only, Ralph referred to the stylish resort near Brunswick, Georgia, in flowery prose: "The Jekyll Island layout has wonderful prospects: sand dunes, all hazards. Stubby pines that look like the Cedars of Lebanon, bent down by the wind."

Architect William Mitchell remodeled the Van Cortlandt Park course in 1949. For the first time, four holes were designed on the other side of the railroad tracks, as was first suggested by the Gotham golfers back in 1914.

To escape New York's suffocating humid summers in the days before air-conditioning, the Kennedys had a tradition of spending August in the cooler climates of New England and Eastern Canada, and 1949 was no exception. By now, they used their time to track down and play newly built courses, or those that had somehow escaped them on previous visits. Petersham did not remain the only course in the Bay State that Ralph missed for long. The go-getter ticked the picturesque course off his list when the couple visited in August. Located only thirty minutes from Amherst, it was a fitting final venue. Settled in 1733, Petersham has all the elements of a classic rural New England village: rolling meadows, farms, bucolic ponds, old-growth forests, a white church with a tall spire, colonial houses, a country store, and, in the middle, a town common. After completing the nine-hole Donald Ross design, Ralph now had a complete set of cards from his birth state.

Continuing his travels up into Canada, the *Sudbury Daily Star* of Ontario termed Ralph a "New York State Industrialist," referring to him as tanned and muscular, with a wiry frame. "Be on the lookout for a good looking middle-aged New Yorker," it warned its readers. He played seventeen new courses in the province, downplaying his obsession: "It's just a hobby. Some people like to fish, others hunt. I like to travel from one place to another and play on a different course each day. Sometimes I do several in one day. It gets one around the country more than anything I know of." Apparently fond of Big Blue's courses, Ralph played two more: the nine-hole IBM Country Club in Toronto, and their Robert Trent Jones-designed course in Poughkeepsie.

The media had been covering Ralph's travels for almost twenty-five years now, and their reporting had not waned. The *New York World-Telegram* wasn't far off in their assessment, touting in a headline, "He's Played Everywhere." That same month, the *Elmira Advertiser* added that the "Likeable New Yorker" was well groomed and in the pink of conditioning when he again visited Upstate. They also ran a picture of him putting his golf bag—which still contained only a handful of clubs—into the trunk of his car. Thinking big, he told them that he was going to bequeath his scorecard collection to the Smithsonian

Institution in his last will and testament. The Smithsonian was contemplating adding a golf section to their museum, and Ralph was hoping to form the nucleus of their card collection. At the time, his will gave instructions to bequeath the cards to the James River Country Club in Newport News, Virginia, which operated a golf museum, the oldest in the country.

While in Elmira, the couple stayed at the Tom Sawyer Motor Inn, and Ralph played the Elmira Country Club, a course with a special pedigree. Its front nine was designed by Willie Dunn Jr. (designer of the original Shinnecock Hills and Ardsley Casino courses), and its back nine was designed by A. W. Tillinghast.

As the middle decade of the century began, television viewers in New York City who were tuned to Channel 11 at 7:00 p.m. on January 25, 1950, did not watch the nightly news but instead watched a well-dressed Eagle Pencil salesman who was number four on the championship list at Winged Foot. A television pioneer, as well as a pioneer in the world of golf, Ralph appeared on the tube twenty-two years after the first set was sold and before many well-known shows existed, including *The Today Show*, *The Tonight Show*, *Captain Kangaroo*, *The Honeymooners,* and *Sesame Street.* Jimmy Powers, a writer and editor for the *New York Daily News*, also served as an early television journalist and had his own program on local station WPIX. He interviewed Ralph on his eponymous show, which appeared for fifteen minutes in prime time. The script for the program shows that Powers was interested in Ralph's marathon sessions, prompting him to talk about how he played forty courses in Vermont in nine days and thirty-one courses in Minnesota in nine days. Considering that the world Ralph was born into was one without electricity, both he and technology had come quite a way in a short time.

Ripley's Believe it or Not was also interested in featuring Kennedy again, and in a letter they asked him to tell them "what golf togs you usually wear," so they could draw an accurate illustration. Although he was approaching his sixty-eighth year, he hadn't slowed his pace very much. Having played exactly one hundred courses since his sixty-sixth, he played his 2,800th course on his birthday two years later, picking the course at Rutgers University in New Jersey.

As they had the previous year, Ralph and Mary Alice again dedicated the month of August to Canada, playing another thirty courses in Quebec and two additional in New Brunswick. After a fourteen-year absence, they returned to Nova Scotia, and Ralph's mid-August visit was featured in the *Spectator*, his tally now up to 2,893 courses after completing the Eden Golf & Country Club in Bridgetown. Traveling so far and wide allowed the Kennedys to experience some of the continent's most scenic and historic locales, including the Annapolis Valley, where he played at the Ken-Wo Country Club and the Annapolis Royal Golf Club. It was then across the peninsula to play at the Bluenose Club in Lunenburg, a nine-hole track set on a small cape that juts out into the cobalt blue waters of Lunenburg Harbour, with backdrops of the colorful old colonial city and its maritime harbor full of wooden masts and sailing ships bobbing gently in the water. The senior citizens finished off their trip visiting the Brightwood Golf & Country Club, a Donald Ross-Willie Park Jr. design in Dartmouth, across the harbor from Halifax.

Returning home from his summer vacation, Ralph made his second prime-time television appearance. He was again a guest on the Jimmy Powers Sportscast, as it was now called, this time broadcast at 6:45 p.m. It was a nascent time for television broadcasting. As the media and communications capital of the country, New York had a total of only seven local stations available, their transmissions picked up by VHF antennas on fat and primitive black-and-white television sets whose innards were filled with tubes.

The *La Grange Daily News* (Ohio) apparently didn't have a lot to report on in the harvest season. Either that, or Ralph really was a big deal, as they printed the following headline on their front page on October 14, 1950: "World Famous Golfer Stops Here." Although he owned a car, Ralph still preferred to take trains and buses where he could. They noted that he caught a bus from their terminal en route to Columbus; he was again on his way to the center of the Midwest.

Ralph had a penchant for playing multiple courses in a twenty-four-hour period, especially in the Land of Lincoln. He was back in the heart of Illinois to add quickly to his course count and to dazzle the locals, this time in Peoria. His conquest of 1950 included five in one day: the Country Club of Peoria, the Madison Park Municipal Golf Links, the Newman Park Municipal Golf Links, the Mount Hawley Country Club, and the Northmoor Municipal Golf Links, playing nine holes at each.

The newspaper brought bad news while Ralph was on his Midwestern trip—his longtime friend O. B. Keeler had died at the age of sixty-eight. Commenting on Keeler's death, the highest praise of all came from Bobby Jones, who said, "He was my dearest friend." Bobby gave Keeler credit for helping him through his days in tournament golf: "The play and the result were as personally his as mine. There is no way to measure the worth of such a companion when one is in the midst of a taxing endeavor." The *Atlanta Constitution* captured Keeler's love of the game perfectly in the headline of their obituary saluting him, "O. B. Keeler Walks Life's Final Fairway."

The *New York Herald Tribune* kept its readers up-to-date on their hometown wonder as the New Year dawned, featuring the following headline in a story about Ralph: "Golf course collector compiles unassailable mark." Despite what he told the newspaper in Ontario about it only being a hobby, the description provided to his local scribe was closer to the truth: "Damn thing began as a hobby forty years ago, now it's a mania." The *Herald Tribune*'s Al Laney bumped into Ralph, who was swinging a 7-iron, in the golf shop at the NYAC. "The most hopelessly unassailable record in sport," he called Ralph's achievement, although the modest Kennedy replied that he was "Just an ordinary guy working for a living."

The working man was already hatching plans for his final big splash. His travels in the late forties had increased his course count, and he was now approaching another big milestone: 3,000 unique courses. He was also about to add a new mode of transportation to his portfolio, ready to take flight for the first time in pursuit of his longtime quest.

CHAPTER 16

The Glamorous Traveler

FORTY YEARS AFTER HE BEGAN to keep track of his golf, Ralph planned the most far-reaching trip of his life across the Atlantic to play in the British Isles, as he was approaching the culmination of his long quest. He had originally thought about going to Scotland in the early 1930s, but due to tough economic times, he put it off. Then, he had planned on spending six months there in 1940 and was going to play St. Andrews as his 2,000th course, but that changed when "Hitler teed off against the Maginot Line." His historic expedition would be realized in 1951, and he had an ambitious itinerary. While visiting Europe to round out his golfing education, he planned to immerse himself in the courses of Old Tom Morris, Alister MacKenzie, James Braid, and H. S. Colt, among other famed architects. As the pinnacle of his lifetime of golfing expeditions, he planned to play a hallowed ground as his 3,000th course, one unlike any other: The Old Course at St. Andrews.

The handwritten notes in his scrapbook list the courses he planned to play while overseas, noting the distances between them. Among his desired destinations in Scotland were Turnberry, Gullane, Royal Burgess, Troon, Erskine, Pitlochry, Montrose, Carnoustie, Gleneagles, Muirfield, and the Old Course at St. Andrews. In addition to the courses clustered in the lowland portion of Scotland, he also wanted to play in the Highlands, including at Nairn, Dornoch, and on the Isle of Skye. Since Ralph was a planner, he wrote to many different sources in the British Isles seeking travel advice, including *Golfing Magazine* (Edinburgh); his personality was such that he liked to have a comprehensive road map in place when he traveled. Proud of his Scottish heritage, he mentioned in his letters that his grandparents were born there. One of the replies he received back, from the British Travel Association, noted that it would be a stretch to try and play at Dornoch, since it was over four hours from Gleneagles in the center of Scotland, or, as they put it, "it would be a trifle strenuous." The Brits obviously didn't know who they were dealing with, trying to talk him out of the trek north.

Golf in the British Isles evolved from different traditions from those in the United States, and Ralph wanted to make sure he could gain access to the links he wanted to play while in foreign lands. In preparation for his big trip, he took a belt-and-suspenders approach, making sure he was prepared for any contingency. It was the custom to be introduced to play at golf clubs in Great Britain and Ireland, so he pursued many avenues to ensure that he would be welcomed. He obtained letters of introduction from the USGA, the Metropolitan Golf Association, the President of Winged Foot (James Shields), and *Golfing Magazine*. The letter of introduction from the President of the MGA told prospective readers, "Mr. Kennedy is a well-known sportsman and a fine gentleman." Shields commented, "Not only is Mr. Kennedy a good golf player but he is also a good after-dinner speaker."

Airline traffic had risen to thirty-one million passengers worldwide by 1951, surging after the war with the advent of newfound prosperity and continued advances in commercial aviation. Flying during this period was still not a common experience, as it was not yet the epoch of jet airliners. To emphasize the point, the 1949 Walker Cup team's voyage to Winged Foot was on an ocean liner. Air travel was at slower speeds than it is today; planes flew at lower altitudes and therefore were more susceptible to being impacted by bad weather and turbulence. Airline accidents were a regular occurrence.

There were more than two dozen commercial aviation accidents in 1950, including an Air France flight with forty-six fatalities; a Northwest Airlines flight in Minneapolis with fifteen fatalities; a Northwest Airlines flight that disappeared over Lake Michigan with fifty-eight people losing their lives; a British European Airways flight that crashed while landing in thick fog at London Airport (not yet named Heathrow), killing twenty-eight; and a TWA Constellation flight that suffered catastrophic engine failure, leading to fifty-five lost lives. Closer to home, one of Ralph's colleagues at the Eagle Pencil Company was killed in 1936 when a Pan Am Clipper he was on flipped as it was attempting to take off, swerving out of the way to avoid a small boat that had driven in front of it.

Within this context, it is understandable that Kennedy was a nervous flyer. He was so nervous, in fact, that he checked with his insurance company before departing to make sure they would pay on his policy should anything calamitous happen. He received a letter back from New England Mutual confirming that his policy had "No aviation restrictions." In preparation for the big trip, he packed four trunks of clothing and equipment and went to Perera Company in Rockefeller Center to get his foreign currency, or, as they called it, foreign money.

His first planned stop was Scotland, where he intended to play a sizable number of historic and important courses. He booked passage on British Overseas Air Corporation (BOAC) to fly from New York, making landfall at Prestwick to visit the Scottish courses. He then planned to take the train to London, where he would play select courses in the area, before continuing on by flying to Dublin, where the plan was to play several more courses. His final leg would be across Éire by bus, flying back to New York out of Shannon on the West Coast.

In an interesting twist of fate, on the very spot where Ralph played the Idlewild Beach Golf Course in 1933, he was now flying to Europe, out of Idlewild Airport. Perhaps inevitably, the course did not last long in the urban environment of Queens. The city acquired the land in 1941, and construction of the airport began in 1947. Ralph shot one of his best scores at Idlewild Beach, carding a seventy-nine, on what was now concrete and a sprawling new 5,000-acre aviation complex. By the time of his visit to the airport, his handicap had ballooned to twenty-five, as the impact of poor eyesight and his sixty-nine years began to slow him down.

Flight BA 514 departed Idlewild at 5:30 p.m. on Saturday September 1st, bound for Prestwick, but not before a scheduled stop in Boston an hour later to pick up more passengers. Ralph flew on BOAC's double-decker Stratocruiser, a piston-powered propeller plane. The Stratocruiser was manufactured by Boeing and evolved out of their wartime B-29 Superfortress bombers. The plane had the ability to cruise at up to 30,000 feet with a maximum ground speed of 340 mph, although BOAC flew their aircraft at only 25,000 feet, at a speed of 275 mph. Ralph's trip was considerably slower than today's jet travel; the nonstop flight from Boston to Prestwick took twelve and one-half hours. Although the plane had performance and

The luxurious BOAC lounge on their Stratocruiser. *(Author's Collection)*

safety issues, it was the height of luxury travel. A wide-body aircraft, it carried only eighty passengers in pressurized comfort. BOAC served complimentary seven-course meals on their flights, prepared in a state-of-the-art kitchen and served by stewards and stewardesses off shining silver trolleys.

By 1951, Ralph was a well-known amateur golfer, and his trip attracted attention. His flight on BOAC was a big deal, and the airline issued a press release and hired a photographer to make sure that the moment was captured. For his departure, Hollywood couldn't have scripted a more picture-perfect image from the glamorous age of early air travel if they tried. Ralph is pictured at Idlewild walking up an external staircase to board the Stratocruiser, wearing his finest suit and a fedora. A fashionable handkerchief is sticking out of his pocket, and a tan raincoat is slung over his left arm. Channeling his inner Clark Gable, he is turned backward, hand aloft, as if waving at the adoring crowds, flashbulbs popping in rapid succession.

Departing Boston at 7:40 p.m., the flight reached Scotland's Prestwick Airport at noon on the 2nd of September. Ralph was immediately excited, since the Prestwick Golf Club—which sits along the Firth of Clyde—is close by and visible from the small airport. Golf would wait another day, Sunday being a rare day of rest as he adjusted to the new time zone. He was now in his ancestral homeland for the first time, a kingdom filled with lochs, dells, and firths, with landscapes of mountains and dales, where the locals wear kilts and speak with an agreeable intonation, rolling their *r*s.

The glamorous traveler boarding his flight to Scotland at Idlewild Airport. *(Photo courtesy of USGA)*

His first course in the home of golf was a fitting one: Prestwick, host of twenty-four British Opens, including the first twelve contested, beginning in 1860. Prestwick demanded a different style of golf than Ralph was generally used to playing in the United States, one played along the ground and honed under the trying conditions of stiff winds. It was also his first exposure to the original versions of the various prototype holes he had played so many times on Macdonald Raynor-designed courses, including the original Alps and Cardinal. He also got a quick education in courses routed through sand dunes, as well as those with pot bunkers, Scotch broom, heather, gorse, burns, rabbit scrapings, tight lies, and firm fairways. The first tee shot at Prestwick is one of the best in the world, the quintessential tester to acclimatize him to links golf. Like many courses in Britain, Prestwick is located adjacent to a train track and railway station. A short par-4, the hole runs parallel to the rails that sit on the other side of an old stone wall. Without a warm-up, golfers are keen not to slice over the wall, although an approach pulled left heads toward the gorse and leaves a trickier angle to the green. Welcome to Scotland, Mr. Kennedy.

Many of the clubs he visited in Scotland, like Prestwick, were true links courses, set along the sandy dunes land next to the ocean. The logistics and planning of his trip was orchestrated around one primary goal—to peak at the Old Course at St. Andrews as course No. 3,000—and Prestwick provided the ideal introduction to how the centuries-old game was played along the seaside.

Following his round at Prestwick, he played the Troon Golf Club immediately adjacent, and then the Ayr Corporation Municipal Golf Course in Ayr (their Belleisle course, designed by James Braid). For this leg of the trip, Ralph hired a chauffeur, Archibald Cowan, who also occasionally served as his caddie. The duo motored south, down the winding roads of the Ayrshire Coast to play at Turnberry, a dramatic course with its signature lighthouse adjacent to the 9th hole sitting on the Firth of Clyde, high up on an isolated crag. Turnberry had been greatly impacted by the war, as parts of the course were turned into landing fields for the Royal Air Force, and it had to be rebuilt after the war.

From Turnberry, they headed back up the Ayrshire coast toward Glasgow, playing the lesser known Fereneze Golf Club, a moorland course south of the city. This was followed by a round at the Erskine Golf Club, set along the River Clyde west of the city, a course designed by Willie Fernie, James Braid, and Alister MacKenzie. This completed their play on the country's West Coast, so they drove into central Scotland, where Ralph got his first glimpse of the breathtaking inland scenery and purple-hued mountains that abound there.

He spared no expense on his big trip and stayed at the Gleneagles Hotel in Perthshire, playing the James Braid-designed King's and Queen's courses, moorland designs set in the foothills of the Highlands. He then paid a visit to the Pitlochry Golf Club, enjoying the beautiful mountain scenery and sweeping views. His accommodations were at the old-world Dundarach Hotel, an elaborate building with gables built from locally quarried stones, where he traded stories with the locals while enjoying a few pints. Capping off his visit to the central region, he visited the Blairgowrie Golf Club, situated at the base of the Grampian Mountains, playing their Rosemount course, one designed by James Braid and Alister MacKenzie. For a man proud of his Caledonian heritage, he immensely enjoyed the stirring scenery in the interior of the country, with its spacious vistas and dramatic glens set in an unspoiled environment.

He did not heed the advice of the British Travel Association, and even at age sixty-nine Kennedy didn't find anything to be even a trifle strenuous. Not to be talked out of a great golf course, Ralph made the long journey to Dornoch, passing through the most dramatic of the Highland scenery, and he was rewarded for the visit, teeing it up at one of the most special courses in the world. Although golf was first played in Dornoch in 1616, the current links evolved out of one designed by Old Tom Morris. The out-and-back layout plays along a broad raised beach and has panoramic views of gently rising mountains in the distance. He timed his trip to coincide with the blooming of the gorse, the golden yellow flowers a joy to look at, although not so much fun to touch should your ball unexpectedly fly into the thorny evergreen.

Not exactly roughing it in the Sutherland region, he stayed at the first-rate Dornoch Hotel. On his way back down through the Highlands, he stopped in the Speyside region, one with a deep heritage in making scotch. He played at the Moray Golf Club (Lossiemouth) and the Nairn Golf Club, both set on the Moray Firth in Northern Scotland; his accommodations for the night were at the Victorian Stotfield House in Lossiemouth. From there, it was a short ride back inland to play the parkland Elgin Golf Club, before duffer and chauffeur headed down the East Coast.

Once in the county of Angus, much farther south (missing the courses of the Aberdeen Coast), he played some well-regarded courses, beginning with Carnoustie, where he achieved the mental state that golfers strive for but cannot will into existence: staying in the present. The canny New Yorker achieved the state of flow at Carnoustie, shooting fourteen strokes below his handicap from the back tees. He was not as lucky at his next two venues, the chilly seaside winds pushing his ball around at the Montrose Links and the Panmure Golf Club. Panmure would have its profile raised significantly two years later, when Ben Hogan used it to practice on prior to his British Open victory at nearby Carnoustie in 1953.

Ralph attracted media attention throughout his visit to the Isles. The *Dundee Courier Advertiser* was curious how he could achieve such a feat, and he mused, "I'm not a rich man, and golf is my only hobby." When asked a similar question by another British reporter, he replied, closer to the truth, "It's no hobby son, it's an obsession." His chauffeur proved invaluable, not only in helping him navigate through the remote reaches of a foreign land, but he was also helpful interpreting the thick local accents they encountered. Ralph complimented Cowan's all-around skills, noting, "He badgered golf clubs into giving me a rubdown when it rains." Kennedy talked to reporters so frequently after his rounds that his chauffeur became frustrated waiting for him; the crusty driver had a classic Scottish aversion to too much talking. When asked about Ralph's interviews with reporters, typically done over a glass of whisky, Cowan's assessment was, "He's bletherin' again! Just bletherin'!"

A short trip across the River Tay brought the duo into the Kingdom of Fife, then they scampered across the Firth of Forth to East Lothian, where Kennedy got another chance to feel firsthand some fresh Scottish breezes and endure pelting rain squalls, playing the course of the historic Honourable Company of Edinburgh Golfers—Muirfield. He also visited the North Berwick Golf Club and experienced the original Redan hole in all its glory, having to hit out backwards from the devilish bunker in front of the green because he couldn't hit forwards due to the steepness of the bunker wall. The final course played in East Lothian was the Longniddry Golf Club, situated on the Firth and designed by Philip Mackenzie Ross (the original H. S. Colt course was plowed under during the war and used for food production). Through his connections, he arranged to play at two of the oldest golf clubs in

Kennedy watching his ball soar off the first tee at the Old Course at St. Andrews, Scotland. *(Photo courtesy of USGA)*

the world while in Edinburgh: the Royal Burgess Golfing Society and the Bruntsfield Links. His caddie at Royal Burgess was a real character: an eighty-year-old with a gray waxed mustache who served in the Boer War; proud of his service, he carried Ralph's bag around, wearing all his commendation medals.

It was now time for the crowning achievement of Ralph's long golfing life, and he was close to the course he had longed to play for so long: the fountain head, as he termed it. He recounted his excitement: "Such a long and varied menu had only whetted my appetite for the main dish: St. Andrews." He picked convenient accommodations, staying at the Rusacks Hotel overlooking the eighteenth fairway of the Old Course. Monday, September 17, 1951, was his big day, and it dawned with agreeable weather. Fortified by a full Scottish breakfast and a stroll around the Auld Grey Toon, he was off to the appointed round. Ralph had an 11:00 a.m. tee time, and he attracted a crowd, including the local press and several photographers. He played the Old Course with Ellis Knowles, an American member of the Royal & Ancient Golf Club whom he knew from New York; Leonard Crawley, a former Walker Cup player; and John Beck, a former Walker Cup captain. He was nervous hitting off the first tee—as all golfers are—because of the gallery of spectators watching, and because it is the home of golf. Wearing a nice pair of slacks, a sweater, and his tam-o'-shanter, Ralph aimed at the railway bridge in the distance and hit a respectable drive down the first fairway.

Golfing in the royal burgh had Ralph's spirits soaring; as his lungs filled with the briny sea air, he clipped his iron shots on the ancient course's tight lies. On the famous 17th, the par-five Road Hole, the experienced golfer sent his blind tee shot soaring over the black railway sheds to bound into the fairway offset at an angle. Playing slightly better than his handicap, Ralph carded a ninety-three for the round.

After finishing one of the most significant rounds of his life, he enjoyed sitting in the pine-paneled St. Andrews clubhouse rubbing elbows with the aristocracy, anticipating the ceremony where the newly appointed club captain hits off the first tee with great fanfare:

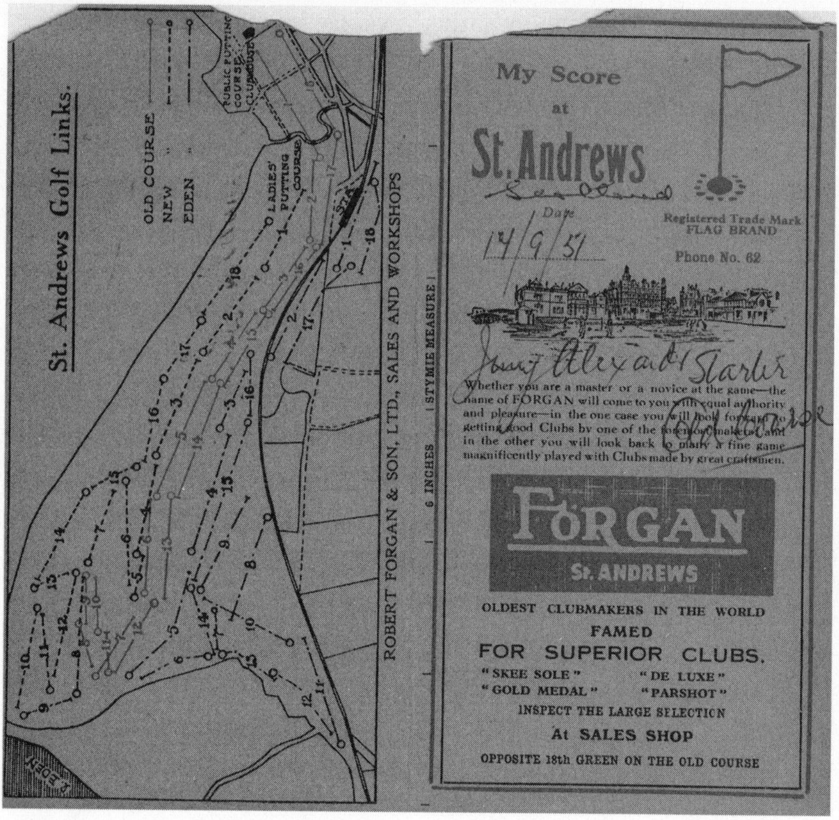

Ralph's St. Andrews scorecard. *(Photo courtesy of USGA)*

"Over a cottage pie Lord Teviot [a past R & A captain] and Sir George Cunningham [the outgoing R & A captain] told me of the ceremony that would take place two days from then." Ralph was aware of the event, as he had previously written to Ouimet to see if Francis could accompany him for his round at the Old Course, but Ouimet was unable to accommodate. Two days hence—by tradition, on the third Wednesday of September—Francis would drive himself in as captain of the R & A as a ceremonial cannon was fired; he was the first American to have the honor of doing so. As a consolation, Ralph was able to have Ouimet sign his 3,000th card to memorialize the round. After completing the Old Course, Kennedy also played the New Course at St. Andrews—one designed by Old Tom Morris that opened in 1895. Capping off a brilliant Scottish trip was another Old Tom-designed course located nearby, the Lundin Links.

The elderly golfer behind a gorse bush at St. Andrews, Scotland. *(Photo courtesy of USGA)*

Among the many souvenirs Ralph collected on his trip, one of the most memorable was a clump of heather from St. Andrews; its brittle remnants are stuffed into an envelope pasted into one of his scrapbooks. Before heading south to England, the intrepid New Yorker went on a shopping spree and bought several gifts for Mary Alice, including seven scarves and a tea cozy. He also bought himself a tie with the Kennedy clan crest on it. Visiting his ancestral home and playing so many famous links courses made the Scottish portion of his trip very satisfying. He was impressed with how much the game was ingrained into the Scottish culture and summed it up succinctly and poetically: "Its citizens would rather putt than prosper."

Ralph had played at a frenetic pace in the bonnie country, just as he had throughout his life, playing twenty-six courses over the span of seventeen days. The only location he was not able to visit was the remote Isle of Skye; because of his packed itinerary, he had to bypass the island's fledgling "hilly and very sporting" nine-hole "holiday" course, the twenty members of the Dunvegan Golf Course forever missing their opportunity to meet the renowned traveler.

Once his Scottish adventure was complete, Ralph boarded the London and North Eastern Railway for his trip down to London, arriving on the 20th. Continuing to live in high cotton, he stayed at the Rubens Hotel across from Buckingham Palace while he was in the capital. His time in England was limited, although he made up in quality what he lacked in quantity, focusing his efforts in Ascot and the Royal

County of Berkshire. He played Wentworth's East and West Courses, designed by H. S. Colt, and the Old and New Courses at Sunningdale.

Typical of the golf experienced around London, Sunningdale is a heathland course set on sandy soil and dotted with birch trees, pines, heather, and gorse. Golf is sometimes referred to metaphorically as a walk in the park; in the case of Sunningdale, it is literally true. The course is surrounded by deep woods and is idyllic and peaceful. It has a stately English clubhouse, a "Stockbroker's Tudor," and there are walking paths around the course where locals stroll with their dogs in peaceful solitude. Sunningdale has some deep Bobby Jones history. It was on Sunningdale's Old Course during a British Open qualifier in 1926 that Jones shot what was described as a "perfect" round of sixty-six.

Rounding out Ralph's schooling in heathland golf were three additional gems: the aristocratic and anachronistic Swinley Forest Golf Club in Ascot (another H. S. Colt design), and the Berkshire Red and Blue courses, built on Crown Lands and designed by Herbert Fowler and Tom Simpson. The spirited traveler had covered more than five hundred miles since landing in Prestwick. It was on his visit to the capital of the British Empire that the *Times of London* featured their comment about the ardent globetrotter, writing that "Metaphorical trumpets should sound and drums be beaten for such a conquering hero."

His tight schedule sent him quickly back to London Airport, where he took Aer Lingus flight 171 to Dublin on the 23rd, and it was a testing trip. Passing through a storm, the white-knuckled flight took three hours instead of its scheduled two, and as Ralph put it, they were "bouncing around like a ping pong ball on the jet air." He got off the plane and took a bus to play at the H. S. Colt-designed Royal Dublin Golf Club, where he "encountered the most phlegmatic caddie of my career." He capped off an exciting round of golf when he hit a blind shot over a hill and asked his caddie if he was on the green. "No," was the reply, "It is in the hole." He rounded out his Irish golfing experience by playing at the Portmarnock Golf Club, staying at the

Ralph (center), pictured with two fellow golfers, enjoying his time in Ireland. *(Photo courtesy of USGA)*

Claremont House in Dublin before taking the bus to Limerick and then on to Shannon.

The media on the Emerald Isle covered his brief stay in detail; when he stepped off his bus in Dublin, he asked a police officer where he could get a taxi. The officer responded that he would be happy to fetch one for him, calling him by name. The patrolman had seen a picture of Ralph in that morning's newspaper and recognized him. The *Irish Independent* called him an energetic American and noted that Mary Alice "had the craze too," since she had played 600 different courses. Ralph told them that he liked the way the game was played in Britain and Ireland, specifically the fact that match play was favored over each player keeping score. He noted that many of the cards had just one row on them where the players wrote down who won the hole, and they did not provide a space for each player to keep track of their own score.

The downstairs lounge of BOAC flight 505—from Shannon to Idlewild—on September 25th was thick with cigar smoke and abuzz with golf stories from the conquering hero, who was triumphantly returning home. His fellow voyagers were not the only ones infatuated with his story. To use modern parlance, the story of Ralph's trip to his ancestral homeland had gone viral. Through wire service reporting, readers as far away as Perth, Adelaide, and Brisbane were able to follow the peppy golfer's capstone trip in their local newspapers. Kennedy arrived back in New York the following morning at 7:00 a.m., returning with two new stamps on his passport and a nice collection of scorecards to take to the bank for his safe deposit boxes.

Tracing a line all the way back to his public speaking courses at Amherst, Ralph continued to be an engaging and sought-after raconteur. Upon his return to the States, he continued to speak at rotary clubs, schools, MGA events, and the St. Andrew's Society. One of his favorite tales was one he picked up in Scotland, of a golfer who, upon finishing his round, was asked by his partner for a rematch the following day. "Well, it might be arranged," he replied, "I was to be married tomorrow, but nae doot that can be postponed."

Ralph enjoyed playing in the United Kingdom and Ireland, since the long rolls on links courses suited his lack of length off the tee. He also had ample opportunity to use the part of his game he enjoyed the most (long putting), commenting, "Over here, our courses are comparatively easy until we are within seventy-five to one hundred yards of the green, then they are severely trapped and it takes a well-played shot to get home. The British courses are terrific until you are within about the same distance of the green. Then they are relatively easy; you can roll the ball up to the pin."

While Ralph's air travel was unadventurous, future passengers would not fare as well. Of the fifty-six Stratocruisers ever built, ten aircraft were lost, with 135 people perishing. Luckily for the flying public, the jet age was dawning, and in a few short years, travel would become much faster and more reliable, although not as adventurous or comfortable as Ralph's historic trip.

CHAPTER 17
The Final Leg

In addition to his European adventure, the resolute Kennedy also played sixty-three courses in the United States and Canada in 1951, focusing his efforts on the Eastern Seaboard. Colorful reportage of his wanderings continued, the *New York Journal-American* referring to him as the "pitching and putting pilgrim." The nationally renowned golfer was featured again in *Ripley's Believe it or Not,* belatedly highlighting his Springfield, Illinois, feat of 1936, when he played six courses in one day. He was illustrated wearing his golf togs of plus fours and his tam-o'-shanter.

As 1951 drew to a close, many facets of life that are more familiar to us today were emerging. The first direct dial cross-country call occurred in November, accelerating a decline in the need for hundreds of thousands of telephone operators. Television was beginning to replace radio as the preferred form of entertainment, and on October 15, 1951, *I Love Lucy* first aired. Although at one time it was the largest restaurant chain in the country, serving 800,000 people a day, by 1951 Horn & Hardart's self-serve format was beginning to wane. New Yorkers no longer appreciated the fact that they could get baked beans or creamed spinach served through an Automat. In a sign of things to come, in Salt Lake City the following year, Colonel Sanders opened the first Kentucky Fried Chicken franchise.

Ralph's focus also began to shift after his trip to the British Isles; no longer talking about his future conquests, he was now beginning to look back: "A few months ago, my wife unloaded about twenty-five hundred of the duplicates [scorecards] to the Golf Association's museum, on East Thirty-Eighth Street, of which I'm a committee member. My wife says they take up too much room." He also gave the USGA one of the balls he used at St. Andrews. Two years earlier, the USGA purchased a five-story brownstone in Manhattan's Murray Hill neighborhood, which they called *Golf House*. Other members of the USGA's museum committee included Bobby Jones, H. B. Martin, and Francis Ouimet.

We tend to not associate Manhattan with golf, since it is a densely populated island containing no courses. However, as we have seen, it played a significant role in the early development of the game. The USGA and PGA were both founded there, the USGA had its headquarters there for decades, and the city hosted ticker tape parades for golfing icons. A. W. Tillinghast had offices on Forty-Second Street, and C. B. Macdonald founded an exclusive private club for golfers in the metropolis: The Links, on East Sixty-Second Street. The Sarazen Golf Correspondence School operated out of Midtown Manhattan, on Forty-Second Street and Madison Avenue, offering a complete course of instruction for five dollars. Forty-Second Street was indeed the epicenter of New York City golf since the design firm of Colt, Alison, & Morrison also had an office on East Forty-Second Street. Slightly farther west on the wide thoroughfare was Devereux Emmet, who ran his design business from 11 West Forty-Second Street. Robert Trent Jones and Stanley Thompson also operated a New York City office out of West Forty-Fifth Street.

Now that he was a grandfatherly figure, the USGA *Journal of Turf Management,* using language appropriate to the day, called Kennedy a "portly man of medium size with a twinkle in his eyes." During his USGA interview, Ralph told the reporter that he does not "believe that intimate knowledge of a course and its local conditions is much of an asset in scoring." And he said that he generally plays a course better the first time he sees it than upon a return visit, citing as evidence Winged Foot. "My club handicap is about ten strokes higher than I can really play. I can't play Winged Foot and it burns me up because I helped found it back in 1921."

Having developed a great deal of perspective after playing more than 3,000 courses, he reminisced about the best of the best. He was a fan of Mid Ocean in Bermuda and mentioned the Broadmoor in Colorado Springs and Capilano in Vancouver. He reiterated that he was fond of Augusta, which he had played multiple times. His succinct description of why he liked it still rings true today: "Because it is tough and easy—tough for the good player and easy for the dub." Playing at Winged Foot for a good portion of his adult life gave him an appreciation of what was right and wrong in golf design, and he liked man-sized courses. His list of the finest included the Olympic Club in San Francisco, the Los Angeles Country Club, and two Devereux Emmet designs on Long Island: the Meadow Brook and Garden City Golf Clubs. "Sheer length and scenic beauty cannot be the true test. To me no finish tops that of Cypress Point, no single finishing hole equals that of Capilano and no course requires as many planned shots as Pine Valley." RAK had a knack for spotting greatness; almost every course he named that survives is ranked among the best in the world.

Breaking his unwritten rule of not criticizing courses, he noted some undesirable exceptions, criticizing the Malba Field Club in Queens as being particularly poor; and in an omen of things to come, he noted that it was a real estate development first, with a course thrown in as an afterthought to make home sales easier: "It had as many things wrong with it that man can conjure up." Another poor course he didn't identify: "I won't name the worst, but it's out in the Southwest. The grass is about two feet high, even in the fairway; in fact, they have stakes up to mark where the rough starts." He was not a big fan of penal sand traps and in shades of Walter Hagen at Salisbury said, "I rarely resist the temptation to take my putter and roll the ball out of the sand. A lot of traps we have now are just ball arrestors. That isn't golf."

As the year closed out, Ralph was honored at a Winged Foot "Night of Champions" dinner. They celebrated his accomplishment up until that point of having played 3,020 different courses. Also honored at the dinner were Tom Robbins, the reigning U.S. Seniors Champion; Claude Harmon, the Winged Foot professional and current Metropolitan Open and PGA Champion; and Joseph Gagliardi and Earl Ross, the Metropolitan Amateur Champion and runner-up, respectively. Winged Foot, with its focus on golf excellence, remained the perfect club for the golf-obsessed Kennedy to be a member of.

Golf rules were modified in 1952, and significant changes were implemented when the USGA and R & A both eliminated the stymie as they harmonized their rules. At the same time, they changed the penalty for hitting a ball out of bounds to two strokes, taking away the ability to reduce it to one stroke by local rule. As equipment and the general skill level of players improved, both of the game's governing bodies agreed to use the term "par" for all competitions, formally relegating bogey as a measure of a hole's difficulty to history.

Never short of cute titles, the *Brooklyn Daily Eagle* dubbed Ralph the "Son of Scotland" in January 1952. He explained the philosophy of his long odyssey to them: "I've gone on golf debauches. And I have played as many as seventy-eight courses in a month. I guess if this sort of thing doesn't kill you early, it'll never get you."

National Geographic approached him to write a full-length feature article for the magazine, paying him $1,000 for his effort. He wrote an entertaining account touting his exploits playing golf around the world. His standard-bearer stories were all there, including his four-state-in-one-day feat, his exotic travel to South America, and his new collection of yarns from playing in the British Isles. He mentioned that the United States now had the majority of golf courses, or 4,926 of the world's 7,500. He detailed his favorites again, including Pine Valley, Pebble Beach, Cypress Point, Yale, and Jasper Park. He also offered praise for the Mark Twain Golf Course in Elmira and the Robert Trent Jones Dunes Beach and Golf Club in Myrtle Beach. By now, architects were using earth-moving equipment and designing a different style of course than was built during the Golden Age. He was impressed with the shaping of the land and the fact that the Dunes Beach Club took advantage of the "Estuary known as Singleton Swash, which empties into the Atlantic, and Jones has contrived to work some part of the water into six of his eighteen holes."

Ralph at home with the safe deposit boxes containing his life's achievement. *(Photo courtesy of* National Geographic*)*

Not yet done with his playing days, Ralph was still making pilgrimages to the South. The proud Colonel visited Kentucky in March, playing the Lindsey Golf Course in Ft. Knox and the nine-hole Shelbyville Golf and Fishing Club, located midway between Louisville and Frankfort, as his 3,032nd.

On November 4, 1952, General Dwight David Eisenhower was elected president. It took virtually Ralph's entire lifetime before America elected a president who was as golf-obsessed as Ike was. He was periodically seen on the White House lawn hitting balls, and during his tenure as president, he played a substantial amount of golf: over eight hundred rounds in total. Ralph played at all of Ike's favorite haunts over the years, including Cherry Hills in Denver, the Gettysburg Country Club in Pennsylvania, Blind Brook and Century in New York, the Chevy Chase Club and Burning Tree in Maryland, Newport in Rhode Island, and, of course, Augusta National. As a member, Ike visited Augusta so frequently that his cottage on the grounds was nicknamed the "Little White House" during his tenure.

Spring was synonymous with Ralph Kennedy visiting the South, and on March 25, 1953, he was back in Georgia, playing at the Perry Country Club south of Macon, a nine-hole course that opened two years before. Adjusting to the challenging conditions with his usual determination, with water dripping from his nose and spectacles, he played in such a heavy downpour that he had to return to his car between shots in order to not become completely waterlogged.

The *Washington Post* wrote about him the same year, calling him an executive and highlighting the fact that he played the Argyle Country Club in Maryland as course No. 3,099 with only a 4-iron. Seeking out new links in the state he had somehow previously missed, he also played the White Flint Golf Course in Kensington and the Oakland Country Club; the latter course received funding from the WPA in 1937 when it was built.

Ralph's pace of playing new courses was finally starting to slow; by the time he paid his dime fare to take the subway down to the *New Yorker*'s cozy offices on West Forty-Third Street, he had played only five new courses over the prior four months. He was running into a new challenge since he had played so much: there was a lack of courses for him to play without traveling great distances. "The coziest athletic record we've heard of in some time was set by a dapper, dedicated man, just turned seventy," the respected magazine wrote. He told them that he had played all the courses in New England except three, two of which were on islands. He also said that he had played *all* the courses that existed in New Jersey, Maryland, Delaware, and Utah. He played almost all the courses in the Piedmont region, including every course in Virginia, the vast majority in Georgia, and all but two in both North and South Carolina. Bizarrely, he played all the courses in the Empire State except for eighteen courses around Rochester, noting, "I never seem to get to Rochester."

Ralph was invited to dinner at the Park Lane Hotel in Manhattan in July, an event put on by the USGA, featuring Grantland Rice as toastmaster. The dinner was organized for Ben Hogan, who was in New York being honored with a ticker tape parade for his Triple Crown achievement. To highlight a still-dominant mode of transportation, the Hogans arrived back from their Carnoustie trip on the ocean liner SS *United States*. Unfortunately, Ralph was out of town and was unable to attend, although he would see Rice at the Phi Delta Theta alumni club dinner, which was held in the city later that summer.

One of the final places Ralph had yet to conquer in the three-million-square-mile land mass of the continental U.S. was the coal mining region in the Appalachian Mountains of West Virginia. Mary Alice and Ralph drove down for his final burst of courses jammed into a short period of time, playing a series of nine-holers, concluding with the Tygart Valley Country Club in Elkins as course No. 3,142. His trip also included the Bluefield Country Club, the Mercer Country Club, the Sistersville Country Club, and the Morgantown Golf & Country Club. The couple also visited Virginia's Shenandoah Valley and played the Gypsy Hill Golf Links, the Ingleside Golf Course in Staunton, the Winchester Golf Club, and the Spotswood Country Club in Harrisonburg. He was well trained at Amherst as a "track man" and kept his body in top condition his entire life; the *Bluefield Daily Telegraph* called him "ruddy-faced and physically fit."

The *Portland Herald* in Maine concurred when he traveled up the coast to play again at the end of the summer, calling him, "Graying but powerfully built." They published a picture of him with his cousin, the two men standing on a tee box gazing out at the course. Ralph wore eyeglasses his entire life, and while he was in great physical condition, his eyes were increasingly giving him trouble.

Kennedy pictured with his cousin in Maine. *(Photo courtesy of USGA)*

Anticipating the end of his playing days, there was one final big idea: play his last round of golf with the President of the United States. His friend and fellow pencil salesman at Eagle, Walter E. Haggerty of Caldwell, New Jersey, wrote to Eisenhower's press secretary on July 8, 1953. Haggerty asked James C. Hagerty if "he could possibly fix up a date for Kennedy to play with him [Ike]. I have not said a word to him about it but I am sure that any week-end would be satisfactory. I'd just like to see a grand old golfer end up his career in a very special way." The following reply was received back on White House stationery from one of Ike's secretaries on July 24th: "I am sorry, however, that we cannot give you any assurance that such a game as you suggest can be arranged. Frankly, the president's time for recreation is so limited that it is impossible to make any plans of this nature in advance." Given Ike's enviable playing record, his secretary obviously wasn't being entirely truthful; in fact, two days before the letter was sent, Ike played a round at Burning Tree with Senator Prescott Bush. It is too bad that Eisenhower refused Ralph a round; it would have been the most fitting ending imaginable to his long journey.

Ralph traveled to the Finger Lakes region shortly after the summer ended. He played the Saratoga Spa Golf Course in Saratoga Springs, the Syracuse Yacht Club, the Brooklawn Golf Club, as well as the Oneida Country Club. Forty-two years, two months, and nineteen days after his streak began in Van Cortlandt Park, Ralph was approaching the end of his long journey. He was about to play his final new golf course. Due to his failing eyesight, golf's Iron Horse was taking himself out of the game for good on Sunday, September 27, 1953, a beautiful day in Central New York, the temperature seventy-three degrees with a cooling autumn zephyr blowing. His final scorecard shows the usual RAK written across the top. The course he chose for his final act was the Hamilton Inn Golf Club in Lake Pleasant, a nine-holer with a total yardage of 2,808 yards that opened in the mid-1930s. The designer of the final course he played is unknown. All that is known about the course's topography and routing can be inferred from the local rules on the scorecard: "1. All woods are played as out of bounds. 2. Ball in swamp on left side of first fairway may be lifted back without penalty. 3. Ball in cross ditch on number six may be lifted back without penalty." Playing with his friend Walter Haggerty, Kennedy shot a forty-four. Some things hadn't changed much in the long stretch of time. Although the USGA had recently eliminated the rule, fittingly, the card still had a stymie gauge on it. As was his custom for four decades, he had someone from the course

The scorecard from the final course, Hamilton Inn, Lake Pleasant, New York. *(Photo courtesy of USGA)*

sign his card to attest to the fact that he played there: Sandy Foreman signed as professional.

The front of the classic 1950s scorecard from the Hamilton Inn course features an illustration of a relaxed couple playing golf. A female golfer has just hit off from the tee; the bottom corner of her skirt is blowing up from the wind. Her playing partner, wearing checkered slacks, a fedora, and a nice sweater, is walking up to her from behind, golf club tucked under his arm. The final card has "Course # 3,165" written across the top, and it was his last conquest. Exhibiting perfect symmetry, Ralph's journey began in New York and was bookended in New York. He collected his first course on the Sabbath and played his last on the Sabbath, as well. Displaying a verve that was unequaled, between July 9, 1911, and September 27, 1953, he averaged playing seventy-five new golf courses a year.

Ralph estimated that his long odyssey had cost him $30,000 over his lifetime, or about $10 per course played. The USGA estimated that he walked the equivalent of fifty thousand miles in pursuit of the

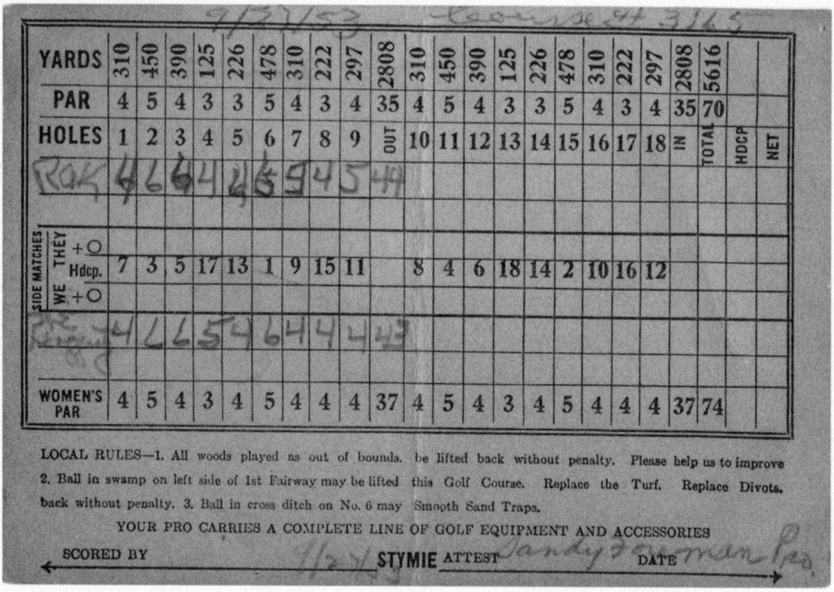

HOLES	1	2	3	4	5	6	7	8	9	OUT	10	11	12	13	14	15	16	17	18	IN	TOTAL	HDCP	NET
YARDS	310	450	390	125	226	478	310	222	297	2808	310	450	390	125	226	478	310	222	297	2808	5616		
PAR	4	5	4	3	3	5	4	3	4	35	4	5	4	3	3	5	4	3	4	35	70		
SIDE MATCHES THEY +O																							
Hdcp.	7	3	5	17	13	1	9	15	11		8	4	6	18	14	2	10	16	12				
WE +O																							
WOMEN'S PAR	4	5	4	3	4	5	4	4	4	37	4	5	4	3	4	5	4	4	4	37	74		

LOCAL RULES—1. All woods played as out of bounds. 2. Ball in swamp on left side of 1st Fairway may be lifted back without penalty. 3. Ball in cross ditch on No. 6 may be lifted back without penalty.

Please help us to improve this Golf Course. Replace the Turf. Replace Divots. Smooth Sand Traps.

YOUR PRO CARRIES A COMPLETE LINE OF GOLF EQUIPMENT AND ACCESSORIES

SCORED BY STYMIE ATTEST DATE

The final attested scorecard, No. 3,165. *(Photo courtesy of USGA)*

white—and occasional red—ball, or two times the circumference of the earth. Not to be overlooked, Mary Alice also played more than 600 unique courses alongside her husband during her lifetime.

He was completing his quest of marathon golf as the simple charms of Norman Rockwell's America were beginning to wane. In some ways, the world he finished playing in in September 1953 was still as it was when he first played, but in other ways our modern era had begun. The New York newspapers still had a "Shipping-Mails" section listing incoming and outgoing ships, but it was now accompanied by another section, which was growing increasingly larger every day: "Overseas Plane Arrivals and Departures." The last icebox manufacturer in the United States coincidently went out of business the year he played his final course. As a convenient service, milk delivery survived for a long time after refrigeration became ubiquitous, and for at least another decade after he finished playing, 30 percent of American households still had milk delivered every day. Ralph lived through a period that witnessed a large wave of immigration into the country. Twelve million huddled masses passed through Ellis Island between 1892, when it opened, and November 1954, when the island gateway was closed, a year after Ralph stopped playing.

Among professional golfers, the leading money winners in 1953 included Ben Hogan, Lew Worsham, Lloyd Mangrum, and Doug Ford. Hogan's total winnings from the Masters, U.S. Open, British Open, and two other titles during the season was $16,600. The era of big-money golf was still far in the future, although television was about to burst onto the golf scene. George May's tournament at Tam O'Shanter was the first to broadcast golf to a national audience. Always a marquee event on tour, his $25,000 prize was double that of the next-closest tournament. In the opposite of today's economic arrangement—where networks pay vast sums of money to broadcast tournament golf—in 1953, May had to write a check to ABC for $32,000 so they would cover the tournament, although by modern standards calling it coverage is generous. ABC's broadcast was for the final hour only on the last day, with one camera atop the grandstand on the eighteenth hole. In an act of serendipity, May's bet paid off; the tournament finished as Lew Worsham holed out a 102-yard shot from the fairway—caught live on TV—for a come-from-behind victory.

Golf in Eisenhower's suburban America. *(Photo courtesy of Curtis Publishing)*

The saddest item in Ralph's six scrapbooks is a letter sent to all Eagle salesmen dated November 30, 1953: "Our old friend, Ralph Kennedy has been having trouble with his eyes and finally had to have a cataract removed. Meanwhile, he sits around home listening to radio, and has developed a violent dislike for commercials." Despite his surgery, Ralph's eyes would never be good enough to allow him to golf again. His days of rising early to sweep the dew off the fairways were over; there would be no more crisp iron shots hit to the green; he would no longer savor the smell of freshly cut grass out on the course; he would no longer hear the satisfying sound of his ball rattling around the bottom of the cup; there were no more birdie putts to line up for the city dweller.

Later in the year, Grantland Rice died suddenly of a stroke while in his New York City office, working at the age of seventy-three. Ralph retired from Eagle in 1955 at the same age, having served only as an ambassador-at-large for the last several years. Employed by Eagle for over forty years, the contact man had focused his efforts of late on schools and railroads. Reflecting back on his career, he loved his product: "Eagle Number Two is the most popular pencil in the world. When I was on the road I used to say to customers I'm just a chaperon; the pencil is the salesman." Both Gehrig and Kennedy achieved their feats at a time when employment loyalty was at its peak. Gehrig and Kennedy worked for the Yankees and Eagle, respectively, their entire careers.

The 1950s represented a period of modernization in New York City, the country, and the world. Rapid change was underway, as were the Cold War and the beginning of the baby boom. The *Man in the Gray Flannel Suit* was published the year Ralph retired and was reflective of the times, as the country was increasingly becoming dominated by big business and a consumer-driven, more materialistic culture. Medicine continued to advance, and 1955 saw the first broad spectrum antibiotic, Tetracycline, patented. The Third Avenue elevated subway was closed and dismantled in Manhattan beginning in 1955. Ralph and Mary Alice's neighborhood was also changing, as the twelve-lane Trans-Manhattan Expressway and an added roadway to the George Washington Bridge were approved in 1957, having a massive negative impact two blocks north of their old Audubon Avenue apartment. That same year, both the Giants and the Dodgers broke their fans' hearts when they moved from New York to California. Having evolved from its roots as a mail and parcel company, American Express offered their first "charge card" in 1958, following the lead of Diners Club, which first offered one in 1950.

By 1957, *Golf Digest* contained advertisements for a half-dozen different motorized golf carts, as manufacturers were now marketing directly to consumers rather than attempting to sell through golf clubs. The Tag-a-lectric Cart Company of Pompano Beach, Florida, offered one- and two-passenger models for $395. The Victor Adding Machine Company offered two two-seater models that allowed a golfer to lay their clubs flat in the back. Even Sears offered their own electric golf carts, touting their ability to go for thirty-six holes without needing to be recharged. Carts would change the nature of golf to a large degree, eliminating a critical part of the game's charm. In addition to taking away the essential element that allows golfers to immerse themselves in the great outdoors, it also changed the way that architects designed courses. Forgetting the lessons taught by North Berwick, Dornoch, and Prestwick, it was no longer necessarily a short walk from green to tee. And the need to accommodate carts changed the aesthetics of the course because of the need to route a macadam or concrete path.

Ralph's old friendly nemesis and the inspiration for his odyssey, Charles Fletcher—who lived a long life—died in Ventura, California, in 1958 at the age of eighty-nine. In 1959, the iconic "Welcome to Las Vegas" sign was erected, Alaska and Hawaii were admitted to the Union, and another of Ralph's acquaintances from the old Newspaper Golf Club, H. B. Martin, died. His obituary called him a leading authority on golf and documented that at one time he was the publisher and editor of four golf magazines.

At the end of his life, Ralph began to glimpse golf's future, driven by telegenic stars who emerged as the decade progressed. In 1960, Arnold Palmer had one of his greatest years: he won the Masters with birdies on the last two holes, as well as the U.S. Open with a final round sixty-five; finished second in the British Open at St. Andrews; and won six additional PGA Tour events. Bobby Jones published *Golf*

Is My Game the same year, lamenting the loss of the stymie, devoting an entire chapter to the subject titled "Let's Have It Back!" He wrote, "It has been appalling to me to find that there are golfers of today who do not even know the meaning of the word stymie." Jones continued, "With the stymie in the game, match-play golf becomes an exciting duel in which the player must always be on guard against a sudden, often demoralizing thrust."

It was fortuitous of Ralph to retire from the sport when he did because he could go out in peace. One of the scourges of the great outdoors was invented as he gave up the game: the completely unnecessary, noise- and air-polluting leaf blower, which would ruin the ambiance and peacefulness of golf courses in the future. His timing was perfect.

CHAPTER 18

The Legacy

MARY ALICE DIED SUDDENLY ON February 11th, 1960, just a week shy of her seventy-seventh birthday; Ralph asked that donations be made to the American Heart Association in lieu of sending flowers. He told a New England newspaper in the summer of 1940 that he hoped that he could go on playing golf until he "drops dead on a golf course." Alas, it was not to be. The *New York Times* announced the death of the salesman almost exactly one year later, on February 20, 1961. Ralph had passed away two days earlier at the age of seventy-eight at the Fifth Avenue Nursing Home. Although the obituary writers didn't mention it, Ralph was always proud to have been named a Kentucky Colonel, listing it in his Amherst alumni biography each year. His long life—thirty-three years longer than life expectancy at his birth—was the result of all the advances in medicine, his focus on physical fitness, and because he was blessed with great genes. Ralph was survived by his younger brother, whose successful career in medicine continued: Robert Kennedy served as the Surgical Director of New York's Beekman Street Hospital and as a professor of surgery at Columbia Medical School; and was the author of over seventy-five articles in medical books and journals.

The UPI wire service (incorrectly citing his course total) honored the late Winged Footer on December 31, 1961, as part of their look back at noteworthy people who passed away during the year. In the world of baseball, they mourned the passing of Ty Cobb and Branch Rickey Jr. In the world of golf, they honored former U.S. Open champion Willie MacFarlane; and, in a nod to his Scottish heritage, Ralph Kennedy, "known everywhere for the 3,150 courses he played before holing out his last putt. We've wander'd many a weary foot, Sin auld lang syne."

Ralph lived long enough to see a Kennedy occupy the White House. One month before Ralph died, John F. Kennedy took office. Two months after Ralph's death, Russian cosmonaut Yuri Gagarin became the first man to travel into outer space. At the same time, a mode of transportation Ralph used to get to his courses, the streetcar, had largely disappeared; the last streetcar in Los Angeles was retired in the early 1960s. Railroads were also losing their prominent place in passenger transportation, displaced by the automobile. At the time of Ralph's death, the jet age was by now in full swing: American Airlines advertised that it had twenty-two non-stop jets on its schedule each day in New York.

It is easy to reflect back on the good-natured Kennedy's life and accomplishments with a sense of wonder. His impressive feat is difficult to fully appreciate in our automobile-centric modern times aided by the Internet, smart phones, and global positioning systems. A late bloomer, he didn't even take up the game until he was twenty-eight, and he played his 2,000th unique course when he was fifty-eight, a time when most men of his era began to slow down. He kept plugging away until his early seventies, showing extraordinary stamina, walking every one of his rounds.

A starkly different time, the Kennedys' epoch was one of operator-assisted telephone service and ocean liners. The language of Ralph's life featured vaudeville, old soaks, pole-sitters, teetotalers, togs, knickerbockers, and dubs. It was a time when the Miss America Pageant was an event; when Detroit, Havana, and Atlantic City were destination cities; when radio broadcasts from Lakehurst were news. He came of age as the automobile was emerging and when America was the world's top oil-producing country. He experienced Route 66 in its heyday and saw the ravages of the Great Depression and the impacts of the New Deal and the Works Progress Administration (the WPA was eventually involved in building or improving over six hundred golf courses). He lived when golf courses in New York City had wild blackberry bushes and apples trees. Automats were the McDonald's of his day.

In a letter to the *Golfer's Handbook,* Ralph called himself a "contact man," preferring the term over "salesman." The hearty contact man always kept his achievements in perspective: "What I do I know will neither improve the breed of golfers nor make the world a better place to live in. It compares to flagpole sitting or oyster eating—purely the answer to a personal choice of doing what is most satisfying." Ralph eventually donated not just his duplicates, but all his scorecards—weighing over one hundred pounds—to the USGA. Along with the scorecards, he gave them a driving iron and putter which he used when he first played golf, as well as a Ben Lomond niblick that had a concave face. In a 1957 letter, USGA Executive Director Joseph C. Dey Jr. told Ralph that "We regard your collection as one of the most significant in *Golf House.*" His "magnanimous gift" included scorecards signed by Bobby Jones, Walter Hagen, Byron Nelson, Tommy Armour, Bobby Cruickshank, and Willie MacFarlane. Herbert Warren Wind thought enough of Ralph's achievements to include the USGA's article, "The Dr. Livingstone of Golf," in his 1954 anthology *The Complete Golfer.* Ralph's article for *National Geographic* remains the magazine's only full-length piece focused on golf even to this day.

It all began when Michael Burke convinced Ralph that golf would be a good form of exercise. It became a life goal when he met Charles Fletcher back in the Bronx in 1919. It ended with "the most hopelessly unassailable record in sport," when he was finished off from poor vision, which finally defeated him two generations later. By the time he finished his long quest, Ralph had played over 2,500 courses in the United States, or more than half of all the courses in the country, and over three hundred courses in Canada. In his extended travels, he played a large percentage of the courses that hosted the U.S. Open, the U.S. Amateur, and the PGA Championship.

His pursuit of new links took him to a range of countries, including Bermuda, Peru, Ecuador, Canada, Scotland, England, Ireland, Panama, Cuba, and Mexico. Although he did not play golf in college, Ralph played more than his fair share of college and university courses in his travels, including those at Bucknell, Hamilton, Vassar, Spring Hill, Western Illinois State College, Mount Holyoke, Williams, Amherst, and the St. Bonaventure College Country Club; Yale, Princeton (Springdale), Rutgers, Iowa State, Ohio State, and Purdue; and the Universities of Illinois, North Carolina, Virginia, Michigan, Minnesota, Iowa, and New Mexico.

Although it is not practical to list all 3,165 courses Ralph played in his lifetime, without doing so it is difficult to give justice to the breadth of Kennedy's travels. Picking a small sample of the venues he played gives a feel for the extent of his achievements. No matter through what lens Ralph's odyssey is viewed, its scope is far-reaching. For NASCAR fans, Kennedy visited and teed it up in Bristol, Darlington, Daytona Beach, Dover, Indianapolis, Richmond, Talladega, and Watkins Glen. Although he never played in Continental Europe, Africa, Australia, or the Middle East, he did play in Melbourne (Florida), Amsterdam (New York), Paris (Kentucky, Maine, and Tennessee), Rome (New York), Venice (Florida), Vienna (Georgia), Geneva (New York), Lebanon (Indiana), Waterloo (Iowa), Algiers (Louisiana), Denmark (South Carolina), and Bethlehem (Pennsylvania and New Hampshire). He played at the Minute Man Golf Club in Lexington, Massachusetts, as well as in Concord, Trenton, Valley Forge, and Saratoga. He played in the homes of the military service academies: West Point, Annapolis, Colorado Springs, and New London, and on Parris Island, where Marine recruits are trained; and at several military complexes, including Fort Snelling, Fort Bragg, Fort Benning, the Picatinny Arsenal, the Naval Base in Norfolk, and the Aberdeen Proving Ground. And he visited and played golf in many of the historically significant cities of the civil rights movement, including Selma, Little Rock, Birmingham, Greensboro, and Memphis.

We look back with nostalgia at courses built by Tillinghast, MacKenzie, Macdonald, Raynor, Colt, Alison, Emmet, Thomas,

Ross, Macan, and Thompson, viewing them through our historical lens. Ralph lived through the Golden Age of golf course architecture as a contemporary, when many of the great courses were being built, and played them in their original forms shortly after they opened.

As a member of the New York Athletic Club and Winged Foot, Ralph had exceptional connections that allowed him to play at a wide variety of private courses. Those connections were enhanced by the myriad of journalists he knew, growing out of his associations from the Newspaper Club. Among his greatest accomplishments was playing Augusta National three months after it opened and meeting a member of the Berckmans family, as was playing some of the best courses in the world, including Cypress Point, Pine Valley, Pebble Beach, Pinehurst No. 2, Shinnecock Hills, the San Francisco Golf Club, the National Golf Links of America, the Old Course at St. Andrews, North Berwick, Dornoch, and Carnoustie.

Despite his many travels, he was underrepresented in Texas and Florida and never played many courses there, including the storied Seminole Golf Club near Palm Beach. Since he only visited the Far West once, he missed a great number of courses there, as well.

Ralph was born just after Reconstruction, when the country was still recovering from the Civil War, and lived until the dawn of both the jet age and the space age. The persistent salesman had a front row seat as America rose to become an industrial power. His life was enhanced by virtue of the fact that he lived in New York City. Cities go through inevitable cycles: they rise and fall, ascend and decline. Ralph was lucky to live in one of the great cities of the world during a period when it was vibrant and in the ascendency.

The world has come a long way from Ralph's prime days when the New York City Fire Department used horse-drawn fire engines, when ice was a precious commodity, and when stagecoaches took early golfers to and fro. Paralleling the development of the game in the British Isles, early golf in North America developed near railroads, and consequently alongside telegraph lines, which have long since disappeared. Our relationship with the automobile has also changed. We no longer go motoring for the novelty of it, and certainly not to receive free paper maps, nor to experience the joys of the Holland Tunnel. Today, neither taxi drivers nor service station attendants (if they exist at all) wear uniforms. Milkmen are largely gone, and train travel is infrequent, at best, for most Americans. We no longer ride on steamers as he did, and knickers have gone out of style. Havana has faded from being a preeminent city, as it was when Ralph and his brother visited. The Detroit Golf Club no longer occupies the most valuable piece of golf property in the country; today, the distinction would likely belong to the Los Angeles Country Club.

Looking back through Ralph's scorecard collection shows how much golf has evolved from its inception in our country when it was played by the elite—as seen by the strong influence the Vanderbilts, Morgans, Astors, and other powerful families had at the game's beginnings. As the population of the country grew and became more prosperous, the appetite for courses continued to grow: between 1950 and 1969, over 5,500 new courses were built, a sizable increase in just two decades. As the game evolved, it became more democratized, and in the 1960s for the first time there were more public courses in the country than private. Today, three quarters of existing courses allow public access.

The well-dressed, itinerant golfer—who wore a tam-o'-shanter but no glove—saw the game evolve from sand tees, hickory shafts, and bogey as a measure of a golfer's score. The rules of the game continued to change after Ralph put down his sticks for the final time. Changes instituted in 1960 allowed golfers the ability to finally clean their ball on the green. Ralph's near "hole-in-one" back at the Meadow Brook course in Rhode Island would not have been scored a bogey had he hit it today under rule 17–4, although it appears he got the ruling wrong in 1931, as well (under rule 32, which was in force at the time). Ralph said that he checked with the USGA and that his four on the hole was correct. Looking at the rules in effect in 1931, however, he misinterpreted the rules, and it should have counted as either a birdie or a hole-in-one then, as well (as the USGA has confirmed).

Although the rules and conventions of the game moved ahead, advances for black golfers in the twentieth century were slow and painful. Charlie Sifford brought a legal challenge against the PGA Tour's Caucasian-only policy and was victorious in having it removed in 1961, allowing non-whites to compete on tour without restriction.

When Ralph was trying to arrange his round at St. Andrews with Francis Ouimet, Winged Foot president James Shields wrote a letter on his behalf. In the letter Shields received back from the renowned child prodigy, Ouimet wrote, "This is one of the most remarkable performances I have heard of. As a matter of fact, I knew Charlie Fletcher who also had a habit of playing strange courses, and at the time I thought it would be difficult for anyone to beat his record. However, Ralph Kennedy is certainly that champion, a title he should hold forever."

Were Ouimet's comments prescient? Does Ralph Kennedy indeed hold the world record for most courses played? It is clear that Ralph surpassed Fletcher's total early in his travels, but there are other contenders for the title. The most notable is Joe Kirkwood, although as Ralph repeatedly stated, Kirkwood's record was not attested to, and it is not known if he actually played all of the courses where he held exhibitions. In his 1949 letter to the *Golfer's Handbook,* Ralph wrote that Kirkwood had played 1,200 courses but didn't keep any accurate records and therefore, his achievement should not be validated. Kirkwood's own posthumous autobiography, *The Links of Life*, published in 1973, claimed he was the record holder, but without offering proof. The Donovan and Jerris bibliography of golf books gives validity to his claim and states that Kirkwood was *estimated* to have played on 6,500 different courses. Perhaps he did, although he did not leave either the legacy or the documentation that Ralpho of the Iron Arm left.

Others golfers receiving an honorable mention for most courses played are Alex H. Findlay (with 2,388), as well as Robert Trent Jones Jr. and Gary Player, both of whom are widely traveled and have played a lot of courses. Walter Hagen mentions in passing in his autobiography that he played "well over 2,500 courses," although the place where the Haig undeniably gets first prize is at the nineteenth hole, where he mentions that he had the occasion to "bend an elbow . . . and line up with the boys at some three thousand courses." Dwight Eisenhower's playing record also gets kudos based on how much he loved to play, although he is unlikely to have played a higher number of unique courses.

In the same way Ralph wrote RAK on the player line on each of his scorecards, there are also thousands of scorecards in the Far Hills archives from a golfer who only wrote "J. B. R." on the top of his. Many card files in the USGA archives that contain a Kennedy scorecard also have one from J. B. R., as well. The stealth golfer played many of the same courses Ralph did between the 1930s and the 1960s, and he also played many courses overseas. The real dark horse in the race to play more unique courses than any player in history is in fact J. B. R. An adept player, his cards show that he usually shot under eighty. In a funny turn of events, J. B. R. combined two traits of Ralph's frequent rivals: like Charles Fletcher, he was in vaudeville at one time; and, like Joe Kirkwood, he was a trick-shot artist.

Jack B. Redmond was indeed Ralph's stiffest competition. An accomplished player, Redmond was a PGA professional, served at one

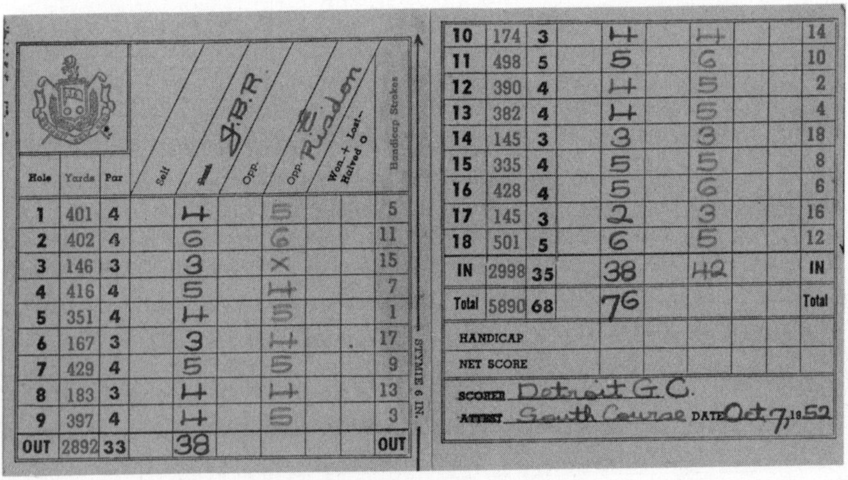

Hole	Yards	Par	Self	J.B.R.	Opp.	Opp. E. Riordan	Won + Lost – Halved 0	Handicap Strokes
1	401	4		4		5		5
2	402	4		6		6		11
3	146	3		3		X		15
4	416	4		5		4		7
5	351	4		4		5		1
6	167	3		3		4		17
7	429	4		5		5		9
8	183	3		4		4		13
9	397	4		4		5		3
OUT	2892	33		38				OUT

10	174	3		4		4		14
11	498	5		5		6		10
12	390	4		4		5		2
13	382	4		4		5		4
14	145	3		3		3		18
15	335	4		5		5		8
16	428	4		5		6		6
17	145	3		2		3		16
18	501	5		6		5		12
IN	2998	35		38		42		IN
Total	5890	68		76				Total
HANDICAP								
NET SCORE								

STYMIE 6 IN.

SCORER Detroit G.C.

ATTEST South Course DATE Oct 7, 1952

Jack Redmond's scorecard from the Detroit Golf Club. *(Photo courtesy of USGA)*

time as a golf coach at Yale University, and played in the 1927 British Open. Born in New Haven, Connecticut, in 1893, Redmond traveled far and wide playing golf, including visits to India, Hawaii, Egypt, Pago Pago, Papua New Guinea, Australia, and throughout Europe and South America. A veteran of the First World War, he had played 2,800 unique courses in forty-one countries as of 1951, as documented in the *Golfer's Handbook*. During 1945 alone, he did a six-month, 45,000-mile USO trip entertaining the troops. Redmond never had the media coverage that Ralph did, although, unlike Kirkwood, his record *is* documented, since he also donated his cards to the USGA.

Known as "Golf's International Clown Prince," Redmond made a living touring the world, entertaining people with his mastery of unusual golf shots. Among the celebrities he played with were Babe Ruth, the Aga Khan, Harry Vardon, Ted Ray, Bobby Jones, "Babe" Zaharias, Jack Nicklaus, Lee Trevino, Charlie Chaplin, Cary Grant,

Jack Redmond hitting a trick shot atop the Whitehall Building in Lower Manhattan. *(Photo courtesy of Corbis Archive)*

and Ben Hogan. He also appeared on the *Ed Sullivan Show*, the *Jack Parr Show*, and the *Mike Douglas Show*. In 1942, he appeared in a short film produced by Warner Brothers with Ronald Reagan and Jane Wyman titled *Shoot Yourself Some Golf*, where the pair watched Jack hit trick shots. Later in his career, Redmond performed in the "19th Hole Revue," which featured his golf entertainment coupled with a troupe of dancing girls. By the time he completed his career in the 1970s, he had played golf in 104 different countries. There is no final count of the number of unique courses Redmond played, and he did not number his cards, but given the fact that he lived to be over ninety years old and played for another twenty years beyond the 2,800 courses he had completed in 1951, it is likely that he is the record holder. As Ralph said, his record was out there waiting to be broken. Like Cal Ripken Jr. was to Lou Gehrig, Jack Redmond was to Ralph Kennedy, likely breaking his course total.

Ralph was surely aware of Jack Redmond, as both their bios and records were submitted to the *Golfer's Handbook* in parallel. Their paths came close to crossing directly; during the summer of 1940, both men played the Kittansett Club on Cape Cod within thirty days of each other. Despite Ralph's inability to retain the record for a long period of

Jack Redmond's own illustration of his golf travels. *(Author's Collection)*

time, his achievement is still striking. After all, as a professional, Jack Redmond played golf for a living, whereas for Ralph it was merely a hobby.

A meaningful part of Ralph's legacy is the record he preserved; his scorecards, documentation, and stories provide a valuable record. The USGA could not have planned it any better if they had a traveling historian on staff to capture and preserve the early history of the game and to record what amateur golf was like in the first half of the twentieth century. In particular, Ralph's documentation provided an especially important record of early golf in the Big Apple that is historically significant.

Many of the courses he played no longer exist, and his scorecards are in some instances all that remain to document their existence. In total, more than 30 percent of the courses Ralph played are gone. Savvy clubs figured out how to survive through tough economic times, using such unorthodox techniques as generating revenue from slot machines. Others were not as fortunate. As was evidenced by the courses in New York City, there were three primary reasons that many of the courses he played did not survive: tough economic times brought on by the Great Depression and the Second World War; the relentless expansion of the suburbs; and the building of the Interstate Highway System beginning in 1956.

Consider a sample of the courses he played that are now gone. Among the great courses lost to history, the Macdonald-Raynor Ocean Links in Newport would rank high. It survived for only ten years, ceasing to exist in 1931. T. Suffern Tailer was the only member of the club, and he suffered an untimely death, leaving the course to his heirs. His wife and son chose not to maintain it and let it go fallow, with portions eventually sold off to build homes. Other private courses were also lost, including the Vanderbilt private course on Long Island.

The history of the Green Meadow Country Club in Westchester (of which Bob Hope was a member, and where Gehrig took lessons) offers a good microcosm of how a golf club's fortunes rose and fell with the difficult times of the thirties and forties. When it ran into financial problems, it closed as a private club and reopened as the Green Valley Country Club in 1941, a public facility. World War II subsequently took a heavy toll on the course's viability, and it closed shortly thereafter. It reopened again in the late forties as the Hasty Brook Country Club, which had a lifespan of less than five years, being re-formed in 1950 as the Willows Country Club. The string of bad luck continued for Willows, when in 1953 it was again reconstituted as the Harrison Country Club. Years later, the course was redesigned by Pete Dye, and it survives today as the Willow Ridge Country Club.

Grassy Sprain, a course Ralph played in 1921, would not survive through 1938; the land it occupied had become more valuable to developers, and the course was sold. The Mount Tom Golf Club that Ralph and Mary Alice played back in 1919—a Donald Ross design—was sliced in two in the mid-1960s when Interstate 91 was built. Now called the Wyckoff Golf Club, only five of the original Ross holes remain. The demise of the Englewood Golf Club in New Jersey, host of a U.S. Open, began in 1960 when Interstate 95 was routed through the heart of the course; it finally closed in 1976. In 1943, the U.S. Army took over the ritzy Glen Oaks Club on Long Island; after the war, it became a public golf course, and in 1971 the land was sold to build a thirty-two-story apartment building. The Salmon Brook Country Club in Granby, Connecticut, closed in 1943 because wartime gas rationing made travel to the club impractical.

Disappearing courses were not a phenomenon limited to the United States. The Hudson's Bay Company's Prince Rupert Golf Course in Edmonton was sold to the city in 1950, and it no longer exists. All but one of the courses the Kennedys played on Prince Edward Island are gone, although the sport thrives there today. The Gatun and Radio Golf Clubs in Panama were also both lost to history. It is not surprising that the Talara and Negritos courses in Peru, and the Guayaquil course in Ecuador disappeared, since they barely existed to begin with. From his South American trip, only the opulent Country Club of Lima clubhouse he spoke so highly of survives, as a luxury hotel.

The Country Club of Havana, later called Cubanacán, survived until 1961, when it was nationalized and turned into an academy of arts. Fidel Castro tried the sport of the "idle rich and exploiters of people" and denounced it as a bourgeois hobby. Castro criticized President Dwight Eisenhower, saying he "was incapable of managing a government and could only play with the little ball." Although Castro only played once (wearing military boots, a beret, and his signature olive-green uniform), he boasted that he could beat Kennedy—John Fitzgerald, that is, not Ralph Anderson.

Although the Kennedy Indoor Golf Club no longer exists, the Kennedy building still stands in Tulsa at the same location. The Coleman Theatre in Miami, Oklahoma, starting point of Ralph's four-states-in-one-day stunt, still exists in prime condition and is listed on the National Register of Historic Places. Three of the four courses he played in his feat are gone: Rockdale, Bella Vista, and Baxter Springs have disappeared, making a repeat impossible; Schifferdecker is the only course that remains.

Many of the company-owned courses Ralph played met their demise or changed ownership over time. Standard Oil of Kentucky survived longer than their golf course did. In 1961, the company was acquired by Standard Oil of California; their nine-hole course disappeared several years after Ralph played it. The Pennsylvania Railroad course disappeared in 1945 as houses were built on its land, and the Kentucky Wood Preserving course no longer exists. The old Union Bag Golf Course in Savannah survives as the Mary Calder Golf Course; it is still nine holes, playing 2,900-yards. Union Bag eventually became part of Union Camp, which is today International Paper, and they still operate a paper mill near the course. The Goodyear Allweather Golf Course in Alabama no longer exists.

Long Island was hit particularly hard with course closures and modifications. In an act of golf vandalism, Charles Alison's Timber Point was modified in the 1970s as it converted to a 27-hole facility, although some holes, including the famous Gibraltar, survive. One of Ralph's favorites, Meadow Brook, was lost in 1954 when Robert Moses requisitioned the land for the construction of the (ironically named) Meadowbrook Parkway. That same year, the Long Island Expressway was routed through a portion of Deepdale, destroying the course. The Deepdale Golf Club remains in a different location, with a course by a different designer, although the club retains its original strong pedigree and has a large membership among those on Wall Street. The only one of Devereux Emmet's Salisbury courses that survives today is No. 4, which has been renamed the Red Course at Eisenhower Park.

Golf course closures are not only a phenomenon of the past. The Macdonald-Raynor Links Golf Club on Long Island survived into the mid-1980s and was then sold for development. The last course Ralph played in Massachusetts, Petersham, was sold in 2013 to Harvard University, which added it to their large "Harvard Forest" holdings in the town.

The last course of Ralph's epic journey, the nine-hole Hamilton Inn Golf Club, did not survive, although not all nine-hole courses have gone the way of the dinosaur. One of the important lessons of Ralph's quest was to remind us that nine-hole golf courses played an important role in the history of the game. The U.S. Open was held twice on nine-hole courses, and they are alive and well: there are still approximately 4,700 in the United States, nearly 30 percent of all courses. Nine states, including Maine and Alaska, still have more nine-hole courses than eighteen-hole courses. Surviving nine-hole courses that the golf nomad king played are numerous: the Hamilton College Golf Course and Lowell Thomas's course in New York; Wawona in Yosemite National Park; the Norfolk Country Club and Fenwick in Connecticut; the Wawashkamo Golf Club on Mackinac Island, as well as the Grindstone Neck Golf Course and the Great Chebeague Golf Club in Maine. For a history lesson in nine-hole courses designed by the best practitioners the game has ever seen, you can still play Marion (George Thomas Jr.) and Whitinsville (Donald Ross) in Massachusetts, the Northwood Golf Club in California (Alister MacKenzie), and the Castine Golf Club (Willie Park Jr.) in Maine; all are worth seeking out.

Throwback courses still exist, as well, including nine-hole courses with sand greens, predominantly in Kansas, Nebraska, and Colorado, though nine-hole courses don't only exist in rural and rustic locations. Golfers in the densely populated state of New Jersey can still roam the nine-hole links of the Lawrenceville School and the Madison Golf Club. A modern-day renaissance man of the golf world, Mike Keiser, built the nine-hole Dunes Club in New Buffalo, Michigan, as recently as 1990.

There is no doubt about Ralph's stamina and achievements, but did our good natured golfer boast a bit? It looks like he did. He talked about how he was able to play in 185-degree temperatures in Yuma, although the highest temperature ever recorded in the state is far lower, and the day he played, a high of 105 was predicted in Phoenix. Exactly how he "played" in Death Valley is unknown. His counting skills were also a little off. He counted the Gotham, Queensboro, and Woodhaven Golf Clubs as unique courses even though they were not, and he counted his round at Amherst College and several other courses twice by mistake. He in fact did not play all the courses in New York, even though multiple news sources reported that he did. He never played several courses in the Rochester area, including Genesee Valley and the Irondequoit Country Club. No cards from Mexico with the RAK notation were found in Far Hills, although Ralph commented on more than one occasion that he played there. In one article, he even talked about how fond he was of the huevos rancheros he ate while visiting. Other anomalies, such as the missing cards from Chile and Colombia, remain an enigma. In the grand scheme of his overall accomplishment, however, these are minor inconsistencies.

In a syndicated Associated Press article published in April 1957, Will Grimsley referred to the elderly and retired golfer as "a globe-girdling enthusiast." Echoing Robert Browning's comments, Ralph told him that he thought the modern game was being drained of creativity, with the emphasis on low scoring: "There is no longer any thrill in executing a great golf shot. Golfers don't want to play golf anymore; all they want to do is score. We are cultivating a new breed—mechanical men with precision tools who swing at almost every shot alike and let the club do the work. We don't have thinkers any more. We have no more imagination in the game." In his day, Ralph used plenty of imagination manufacturing different swings for different shots, especially when he would go around a course using only one club.

He told his confidant George Trevor back in 1935, "Golfers stick too close to their own diggings. They can get mentally fed up with their home course. As a midsummer tonic I prescribe a vagabonding golf trip to nowhere in particular. Just stick your bag in the old bus, find a congenial companion, and start off on a series of one-day golf stands."

So what can we learn about golf—and life—from Ralph Kennedy? Foremost, we can learn the value of serendipity. One's direction in life often comes more out of chance encounters and happenstance than it does from careful planning. Exhibit A was the persistence of Michael Burke to push him to take up the game. Exhibit B was Ralph's meeting Charles Fletcher; it was an unexpected way for him to find his calling. Exhibit C was his fluke relationship with the Newspaper Golf Club and how it blossomed into such an advantageous network.

The road warrior accumulated a lot of wisdom on his long journey and understood many things that have been forgotten in the half-century since he died. Perhaps going back to understand what worked in early twentieth-century golf can help us to better understand our own future. There are several lessons in Kennedy's odyssey. First, nine-hole courses are an important part of the game's history and deserve more respect than they actually receive. Raising the stature and profile of nine-hole courses would help change the perception that eighteen holes of stroke play is the best way to enjoy the sport.

Second, the game doesn't have to be an endurance test. Playing a match at a quick pace is as much fun—probably more fun—as spending five hours or more in a slow eighteen-hole stroke play round. Ralph highlighted what those in the British Isles have never forgotten: the fact that medal play, or playing your own ball for a full eighteen holes, is the exception, rather than the norm. When he noted that their scorecards only have a space for how a match stood, he was onto something. Rather than spending endless time as golfers line up every last putt on every green, the game is more fun and the round is faster in a match, where balls are picked up if a golfer is out of the hole. The wise golfer said in 1935, "I've played them all from the back tees. And I played them quickly. All this fussing, fuming, and stalling that's done today is silly. I can get around Winged Foot in an hour and three-quarters without rushing."

Third, as Ralph also reminded us, golf is a walking game. Carrying a small golf bag, or even one or two clubs, is a delightful way to enjoy the game.

For those who think the game is broken and needs modification, some of the answers are right before our eyes, highlighted in the rules of the courses Ralph played. Pine Valley had no rakes when Ralph played it, and it still has no rakes; overly manicuring bunkers and waste areas are not essential to the game. Every lie doesn't have to be perfect, nor every trap well groomed—rub of the green, they used to call it. In Scotland, the long-standing traditions are a beacon to look at and potentially emulate: Muirfield plays only foursomes (alternate shot) with rare exceptions, and Royal Dornoch only lets out two-ball matches in the early mornings to speed up play. Bandon Dunes didn't exist when Ralph was alive, but their philosophy of walking-only golf (with caddies) has been warmly embraced and enhances the golfing experience. Sitting in a golf cart for over five hours waiting for the group ahead to hit each shot is not enjoyable golf. Walking at a brisk pace in the fresh air is.

It would also be interesting to see the revitalization of match play, with stymies back in force as homage to Bobby Jones; as would playing in a match using the Augusta National format, allocating strokes based on the same old-school methodology the landmark club uses.

What else can we learn from all the scorecards Ralph left? Quite a bit, it turns out. We can learn about the history of the game, its traditions, how the rules have changed, how our mores have changed, and how much the landscape has changed. Think about the record

Kennedy left. What golfer would be attentive enough to save every unique scorecard they ever used and to store them in a safe deposit box because he thought they were valuable? Ralph was wrong when he told reporters that what he did would not make the world a better place. Ralph's cards did turn out to be valuable, but for a different reason than he originally thought. It is not necessarily his Iron Horse record of playing over 3,000 courses that is his most important feat. It is his record of determination and his preservation of a key part of the game's history.

Ralph once said, "If you want to study a man's id, play eighteen holes of golf with him." I suspect if the modern reader could play golf with him, they would find his id very agreeable. In a USGA article about Ralph, they made a most poignant comment, noting that "He and his wife always wanted children but were never blessed with any. Instead they found a mutual and lasting interest in golf." Golf was their life's passion.

Lou Gehrig is honored in Cooperstown, New York, for his achievements. As an early committee member of *Golf House,* why isn't Ralph Kennedy remembered with at least a small display in Far Hills, or in the World Golf Hall of Fame in St. Augustine? As the Executive Director of the USGA said in 1957, "We shall do our best to create a display which will do justice to you and your most interesting hobby." It would be a fitting tribute to honor the earnest man for his accomplishments.

Epilogue

IF RALPH COULD RETURN TODAY, what would his impressions be? He told *Golfing Magazine* in 1952, "Van Cortlandt was immaculate, the players were gentlemanly, and there were no loose sods." After his death, the course's history continued to be a tale of destruction and renewal. The cycle of poor conditions H. B. Martin described in 1936 would be repeated throughout Van Cortlandt Park's history. During the 1970s, the course and the park—like many in the city—became run down and were a hangout for prostitutes and drug dealers. In 1979, the city considered closing some or all of its thirteen courses due to budget shortfalls. During this era of fiscal problems—famously remembered by the 1975 *Daily News* headline, "Ford to City: Drop Dead"—Gordon J. Davis, the parks commissioner, was quoted as saying, "We don't need thirteen golf courses." Given the blighted status of the Bronx during this time, Van Cortlandt was among the courses the city considered closing. Fortunately, the crisis was averted, and the course was saved by turning over operations to a private company. During the administration of Rudolph Giuliani in the late 1990s, the city invested four million dollars to make improvements to the course, building new tee boxes and adding new bunkers and two new lakes. Today, Van Cortlandt is a well kept and extensively used golf course. Its original, historic fin de siècle locker room survives and was used as a set in the 1987 movie *Wall Street*.

Although many of the courses he played have been lost, Ralph would no doubt be pleased to see the renaissance of Van Cortlandt

The 18th fairway of the historic Van Cortlandt Park Golf Course today. *(Author's Collection)*

Park. The stylish Victorian subway station Ralph disembarked from to play the course remains and is listed on the National Register of Historic Places.

Despite the fact that the trees have matured and the course is a bit longer, the leafy Winged Foot would look virtually unchanged to the founding member; he would still feel right at home in the dignified stone clubhouse. He would also be pleased that the club's courses have stood the test of time and still give professionals fits, just as its West Course did during the 1929 U.S. Open. The New York Athletic Club's unchanged, elegant building on Central Park South would also provide fond memories to its loyal life member.

Although he would recognize the soaring, uplifting, and majestic Grand Central Station as it stood in his day, Kennedy would be shocked to see that the original Pennsylvania Station has been torn down, and in its place he would find a dark, dirty, dreary, crowded, underground, sorry excuse for a train station to take his trips south and west.

Other fixtures in the great metropolis remain unchanged. Many retailers Kennedy was familiar with are still in the same locations in his home city, including Saks Fifth Avenue, Bloomingdale's, Brooks Brothers, Macy's, and Lord and Taylor. Two old-school eating and drinking institutions, McSorley's Old Ale House (a hangout for Kennedy and Michael Burke) and Keens Steakhouse, are virtually unchanged, as is Tiffany & Co., Radio City Music Hall, St. Patrick's Cathedral, the Waldorf Astoria, and the James A. Farley Post Office.

The collection of world-class, Art Deco skyscrapers that he saw rise over his lifetime would all be familiar, including the Chrysler Building, the Empire State Building, Rockefeller Center, 40 Wall Street, and the RCA Victor Building (now called the GE Building). The 22nd Regiment Armory, where he registered for the draft, still stands in Washington Heights and is now on the National Register of Historic Places. His old apartment building and neighborhood in Upper Manhattan are largely unchanged; the area is still a haven for immigrants and ethnic groups, including Hispanics and Latinos.

The five-story Beaux-Arts townhouse that served as the USGA's *Golf House* is still there, although it serves another purpose today: the USGA moved its entire museum and archives, including Ralph's cards and scrapbooks, to Far Hills in 1972. He would recognize the area they moved to, since it is close to Somerset Hills, the course on whose second hole he recorded a par by hitting his second ball into the hole after losing his first.

Although New York City's more than five hundred miles of shoreline were once dotted with golf courses, some designed by the greatest golf course architects ever to live, today there are only fifteen remaining, including Marine Park, a Robert Trent Jones design that opened in 1964, and the new Ferry Point course in the Bronx. Regardless of where Ralph's overall course-collecting feat ends up in the history books long-term, one record that cannot be broken is in the number of courses Kennedy played in New York City.

It is interesting to reminisce about early golf in the city when stuck in gridlock en route to La Guardia or Kennedy airports. Inching along in bumper-to-bumper traffic through the dense urban jungle, it is edifying to imagine the days when the city—and to a large extent Queens, where the two airports are located—contained world-class golf courses, offering sweeping views of New York's abundant waterways. Looking at the large apartment blocks, the sprawling USTA Tennis Center, the rusting World's Fair site, and the frenetic city, it is satisfying to visualize golfers in their plus fours using hickory-shafted clubs knocking balls around the early urban links courses. As a reflective moment, the nostalgic look back will perhaps remind us how ephemeral golf (and life) is, making the congested journey go just a tiny bit faster.

Golf remains popular in the Big Apple today, and many fairways offer special views of large suspension bridges: the Clearview Park course offers compelling views of the Throgs Necks Bridge; Ferry Point offers commanding views of the Bronx-Whitestone Bridge; and Dyker Beach offers spectacular views of the Verrazano-Narrows Bridge.

By the middle of the century, companies began to move manufacturing out of New York City to more suburban locations. Among them were the National Biscuit Company and Armour & Co., ending an era when Oreos and Saltines were made in Manhattan, and when cattle could still be seen in the streets on their way to the slaughterhouse. Following the trend, in 1958, the Eagle Pencil Company moved to a modern factory in Danbury, Connecticut. Their large plot of land along the East River was sold to the Consolidated Edison Company, which built a hulking power plant on the site that remains there today, providing electricity to Manhattan's 1.6 million residents. In 1969, Ralph's long-time employer changed its name from Eagle to Berol, a shortened version of the founder's surname; however, you can still buy an Eagle No. 2 pencil!

Ralph would still be comfortable using the New York City subway today but would have to learn how to swipe a paper card in an electronic turnstile instead of inserting a metallic token into a mechanical one. Amazingly, he could still ride through the McAdoo Tunnels between

Eagle No. 2 golf pencils. *(Author's Collection)*

New York and New Jersey. The Port Authority operates the 108-year-old tunnels today, and they are known as the PATH. Trains entering and departing Pennsylvania Station no longer have to switch between electric and diesel at the Manhattan Transfer (which was located in Harrison, New Jersey), since the railroad electrified its entire main line in 1933. A nickel doesn't buy what it used to and no longer pays for a subway ride or a dish at an Automat. Despite its old-style format, the last Horn & Hardart survived for a surprisingly long time, as its last location on Forty-Second Street and Third Avenue remained open until 1991.

Touring around the country today would be a different experience for the hearty New Yorker. The *Fraser's* books he used haven't been published in over seventy years, although he could Google to his heart's content to find courses. Augusta National would still look familiar to the early visitor, although it has been lengthened by over seven hundred yards since it opened. Ralph wouldn't be able to see the clubhouse anymore from Amen Corner, as the tall Georgia pines have long ago obscured the view from the lower portion of the course. The course still has a paucity of sand traps, having added only fifteen over the years, for a total of forty-four. The club no longer has to give away Masters tickets as they did in early years to attract fans to their fledgling tournament. It is now widely acknowledged as one of the finest and best run sporting events in the world. The club still has no slope or handicap ratings.

Aside from taking the subway out to Dyker Beach or up to Van Cortlandt, the closest Kennedy could come to recreating one of his early trips would be to take an overnight Amtrak train to New Orleans, which would leave him in the center of the timeless city, a short walk from the heart of the French Quarter. While the Central Business District has more high-rises than it did in his day, the character of the city is largely unchanged. The St. Charles Avenue streetcars still run, and the original Beaux-Arts Orpheum Theatre is still standing, as are all the old department stores, although many have been repurposed. The Vieux Carré itself has the same look and feel, with its historic wrought iron balconies, galleries, carriageways, courtyards, batten shutters, and casement doors. A short taxi ride to either the Metairie or New Orleans Country Clubs would make him feel like he was transported back in time.

A return trip to Scotland would also look familiar to the man of tartan heritage. The hotels he stayed at in Dornoch, St. Andrews, and Pitlochry are all still there, and the countryside is just as idyllic as it was when he visited. Every course he played in the British Isles still exists, although you can no longer use the railroad bridge as your aiming point at the Old Course, as the local train to Leuchars was eliminated several years after Ralph visited.

His journey over the Atlantic would take half the time, although the buttoned-up Kennedy would no doubt be shocked by how little respect his fellow citizens have for themselves traveling on airplanes in T-shirts and sweatpants. Although he would certainly be impressed by the frequency, speed, and reliability of today's air travel, he would be indignant and stunned to see how small the seats are. The Stratocruiser Ralph flew on had sixty inches of legroom between rows; today, the standard is less than half, twenty-nine inches. He would be sad to see that his surname appears on his home city's largest airport, Idlewild having been renamed in 1963 to honor the fallen JFK. Since his early flight across the Atlantic, airline traffic worldwide has increased by a factor of one hundred, to more than three billion passengers a year.

It is easy to look back with sentimentality at the era in which Ralph lived and to reminisce about how romantic it would have been to live in his times. While there are no doubt aspects of living during the Kennedy epoch that would be desirable, it would be difficult to do. Are we really ready to suffer through the summer heat in New York City in a third-floor apartment without air conditioning? Would we attend the U.S. Open at Winged Foot in late June wearing a three-piece suit and a hat? Or live through the Great Depression, in a world without today's understanding of the human body and advanced medicine? In a world where women can't vote and where people of color are second-class citizens? Of course we can't go back; we can only live in our own times. Later in his life, after he left office, the blunt New York City Mayor Ed Koch was reminded about how nostalgic the old days were when a resident told him they wished they could return to the time when he was running the city. His reply was to the effect that it was never as good as they thought it was, summing up nicely the fallacy of romancing the past.

No doubt Koch was right, although many of us probably wouldn't mind being able to travel back in time to put ourselves in the place of Ralph Kennedy and have the opportunity to meet Bobby Jones and to play Augusta National three months after it opened.

APPENDIX

The Golf Courses of New York City, Past and Present

(Italicized courses no longer exist)

The Bronx

Century Country Club
Ferry Point
Mosholu Links
Pelham Bay
Split Rock Golf Course
Van Cortlandt Park
West Chester Golf Club

Brooklyn

Brooklyn School of Golf
Cliff Haven Golf Club
Crescent Athletic Club
Dyker Meadow Golf Club
Dyker Beach Park
Eastern Park Golf Club
Knickerbocker Field Club
Marine Park Golf Club
Marine & Field Club
Old Flatbush
Sunset Park Club

Manhattan

Governors Island Golf Club
New York Municipal Course

Queens

Antlers Golf & Country Club
Bayside Links
Bayswater Golf Club
Belleclaire Golf & Country Club
Clearview Park Golf Course
Corona Park Golf Club
Edgemere Golf Club
Fresh Meadow Country Club
Highland Golf Club
Hillcrest Golf & Country Club
Hollis Field Club
Idlewild Beach Golf Club
Jackson Heights Country Club
Jamaica Golf Club
Kew Terrace Golf Links
Kissena Park Golf Course
Laurelton Golf Course No. 1
Laurelton Golf Course No. 2
Malba Field & Marine Club
North Hills Golf Club (Douglaston)
Oakland Golf Club
Ocean Country Club
Old Forest Park Course (Forest Park)

Pomonok Country Club
Queens Golf Club
Queensboro Golf & Country Club
Queens Valley Golf Club
Richmond Hill Country Club
St. Albans Golf Club
The Old Country Club

Staten Island
Fox Hills Golf Club
Harbor Hill Golf Club
LaTourette
Mayflower Country Club (South Shore)
Richmond County Country Club
Silver Lake Golf Course
Tysen Manor Golf Club
Willowbrook Golf Club

Acknowledgments

MANY THANKS TO MY EDITORIAL assistant and supermom, Karen Sabino. Special praise to Nancy Stulack and Hillary Cronheim at the USGA for helping me retrieve the multitude of scorecards and scrapbooks needed for my research. Thoughtful input from Neil Regan, the historian at Winged Foot, and David Hamilton, a golf historian in Scotland, are also appreciated, as are the efforts of Eileen Crosby, Archivist at the Holyoke Public Library. Additional assistance provided by the Bronx Historical Society and the archivists at Amherst College, The University of Florida, and the University of Wisconsin. Much thanks to Julie Ganz for her expert and professional guidance and sage editorial advice. Kudos to Bob Mitchell for his erudite editorial assistance and knowledge of golf and baseball.

Bibliography

Books

Barclay, James A. *The Toronto Terror*. Sleeping Bear Press. 2000.

Batchelor, Bob. *American Pop: Popular Culture by Decade*. Greenwood Press. 2009.

Barkow, Al. *Golf's All-Time Firsts, Mosts, Leasts, and a Few Nevers*. Taylor Trade Publishing. 2012.

Bremmer, Ian. *Superpower: Three Choices for America's Role in the World*. Portfolio. 2015.

Briggs, Clare. *Golf, the Book of a Thousand Chuckles*. P. F. Volland & Co. 1916.

Brown, Daniel James. *The Boys in the Boat*. Penguin. 2014.

Browning, Robert. *A History of Golf*. Dutton. 1955.

Buford, Kate. *From Hudson to Hilltop: Time, Change and the Ardsley Country Club*. Privately Printed. 1997.

Chalfant, W.A. *Death Valley*. Stanford University Press. 1947.

Chapman, Kenneth G. *The Rules of the Green*. Virgin Books. 1997.

Cluster, Dick and Hernandez, Rafael. *The History of Havana*. Palgrave Macmillan. 2006.

Cornish, Geoffrey S. and Whitten, Ronald E. *The Architects of Golf*. HarperCollins. 1993.

Cortissoz, Royal. *Nine Holes of Golf*. Charles Scribner's Sons. 1922.

Daley, Paul. *Golf Architecture: A Worldwide Perspective*, Volume 2. Pelican Publishing. 2013

Diehl, Lorraine B. and Hardart, Marianne. *Automat: The History, Recipes, and Allure of Horn & Hardart's Masterpiece*. Clarkson Potter. 2002.

Diamonstein-Spielvogel, Barbaralee. *The Landmarks of New York: An Illustrated Record of the City's Historic Buildings*. State University of New York Press. 2011.

Dodson, James. *Ben Hogan: An American Life*. Broadway Books. 2005.

Donovan, Richard and Jerris, Rand. *The Game of Golf and the Printed Word 1566–2005*. Castalio Press. 2006.

Eig, Jonathan. *Luckiest Man: The Life and Death of Lou Gehrig*. Simon & Schuster. 2006.

Fountain, Charles. *Sportswriter: The Life and Times of Grantland Rice*. Oxford University Press. 1993.

Fraser's International Golf Yearbook (various years).

Frost, Mark. *The Greatest Game Ever Played*. Hyperion. 2002.

——— *The Match*. Hyperion. 2009

Gay, Cheri Y. *Detroit Then and Now*. Thunder Bay Press. 2002.

Glaser, Nancy J., Caldwell, Lee Ann, Albertin, Mark, Klaus, Amanda. *Augusta Then and Now*. Arcadia Publishing. 2012.

Grimsley, Will. *Golf: Its History, People & Events*. Prentice Hall. 1966.

Golfdom, *The Golfer's Handbook 1951*.

Gordon, Robert J. *The Rise and Fall of American Growth: The U.S. Standard of Living since the Civil War*. Princeton University Press. 2016.

Hagen, Walter. *The Walter Hagen Story*. Simon & Schuster. 1956.

Hansen, James R. *A Difficult Par Robert Trent Jones, Sr. and the Making of Modern Golf*. Gotham. 2014.

Harper, William. *How You Play the Game: The Life of Grantland Rice*. University of Missouri. 1999.

Harris, Robert L. and Terborg-Penn, Rosalyn. *The Columbia Guide to African American History Since 1939*. Columbia University Press. 2008.

Hilliard, Robert and Keith, Michael C. *Broadcast Century*. Focal Press. 2010.

Hood, Clifton. *722 Miles: The Building of the Subways and how they Transformed New York*. Simon & Schuster. 1993.

Hope, Bob and Netland, Dwayne. *Bob Hope's Confessions of a Hooker: My Lifelong Love Affair with Golf*. Doubleday & Company. 1985.

Hopkins, Frank. *Golf Holes They Talk About*. Privately Printed. 1927.

Jerris, Randon and Mallon, Bill. *Historical Dictionary of Golf*. Scarecrow Press, Inc. 2011.

Johansen, Lisa Tillinger. *Fast Food Vindication*. J. Murray Press. 2012.

Jones, Bobby and Keeler, O. B. *Down the Fairway*, Minton Balch. 1927.

Jones, Robert Tyre. *Golf Is My Game*. Doubleday. 1960.

Keeler, O. B. and Rice, Grantland. *The Bobby Jones Story*. Tupper and Love. 1953.

Kennedy, Ralph, Scrapbooks. USGA Museum, book one 1917–1932; book two 1932–1936; book three 1936–1940; book four 1940–1946; book five 1946–1951; book six 1951–1955.

Kirkwood, Joe. *The Links of Life*. Privately Printed. 1973.

Klein, Bradley S. *Discovering Donald Ross*. Sleeping Bear Press. 2001.

Landau, Peter. *Presidential Lies: The Illustrated History of White House Golf*. Macmillan. 1996.

Lang, Arne K. *Prize-Fighting: An American History*. McFarland & Company. 2008.

Longhurst, Henry. *The Best of Henry Longhurst*. Golf Digest. 1978.

Mandell, Richard. *Pinehurst: Home of American Golf*. T. Eliot Press. 2007.

Martin, H. B. *Fifty Years of American Golf.* Dodd, Mead & Co. 1936.
——— *Great Golfers in the Making.* Dodd, Mead. 1932.
Matthew, Sidney, L. *Life & Times of Bobby Jones: Portrait of a Gentleman.* Sleeping Bear Press. 1995.
Miller, Jeff. *Grown at Glen Garden.* Skyhorse Publishing. 2012.
Morris, Charles R. *The Tycoons: How Andrew Carnegie, John D. Rockefeller, Jay Gould, and J. P. Morgan Invented the American Supereconomy.* Holt's Paperbacks. 2006.
Nash, Eric and McGrath, Norman. *Manhattan Skyscrapers.* Princeton Architectural Press. 2010.
National Golf Links of America. 1927.
Olman, John. *The Squire: The Legendary Golfing Life of Gene Sarazen.* Olman Industries, Inc. 1987.
Owen, David. *The Making of the Masters.* Simon & Schuster. 1999.
——— *My Usual Game.* Main Street Books. 1996.
Ozersky, John. *Colonel Sanders and the American Dream.* University of Texas Press. 2012.
Parkes, Marty. *Classic Shots: The Greatest Images from the United States Golf Association.* National Geographic. 2007.
Peterson, Theodore. *Magazines in the Twentieth Century.* The University of Illinois Press. 1956.
Petroski, Henry. *The Pencil: A History of Design and Circumstance.* Knopf. 1992.
Phillips, Cabell. *From the Crash to the Blitz 1929–1939.* Fordham University Press. 2000.
Pioppi, Anthony. *To the Nines.* Sports Media Group. 2006.
Portraits of Early Augusta Members. Augusta National Golf Club. circa 1962.
Quirin, William. Metropolitan Golf Association. *Golf Clubs of the MGA. A Centennial History of Golf in the New York Metropolitan Area.* Golf Magazine Properties. 1999.
Rafferty, Jeanette Edwards. *Maidstone Club 1891–1941, The First Fifty Years.* Privately Printed. 1941.
Rees, Jonathan. *Refrigeration Nation: A History of Ice, Appliances, and Enterprise in America.* Johns Hopkins Press. 2013.
Revell, Alexander H. *Pro and Con of Golf.* Rand McNally. 1915.
Rice, Grantland and Briggs, Claire. *The Duffer's Handbook of Golf.* The Macmillan Company. 1926, and Ailsa, 1988.
Roberts, Randy. *Joe Louis: Hard Times Man.* Yale University Press. 2010.
Sampson, Curt. *The Masters: Golf, Money, and Power in Augusta, Georgia.* Villard. 1999.
Scotland's SMT Magazine. *The Book of Scottish Golf Courses.* 1947.
Sherman, Adam. *Golf's Book of Firsts.* World Publications Group. 2007.
Siegfried, Andre. *America Comes of Age.* Harcourt, Brace & Company. 1928.
Sifford, Charlie. *Just Let Me Play.* British American Publishing. 1992.

Silverman, Jeff. *Merion The Championship Story.* The Merion Golf Club. 2013.
Simmonds, Gordon G. *The Walker Cup 1922 to 1999 Golf's Finest Contest.* Grant Books. 2000.
Smith, Douglas La Rue. *Winged Foot Story: The Golf, The People, The Friendly Trees.* Winged Foot Golf Club. Mamaroneck, New York. 1984.
Tauranac, John. *The Empire State Building, the Making of a Landmark.* Cornell University Press. 2014.
Thorp, Rosemary and Bertram, Geoffrey. *Peru, 1890–1977: Growth and Policy in an Open Economy.* Columbia University Press. 1978.
Trebus, Robert S. and Wolffe, Richard C. Jr. *Baltusrol 100 Years: The Centennial History of Baltusrol Golf Club.* Baltusrol Golf Club. 1995.
Twomey, Bill and Casey, Thomas X. *Northwest Bronx: Images of America Series.* Arcadia Publishing. 2011.
White, Norval and Wiliensky, Elliot. *AIA Guide to New York City.* Macmillan Publishing. 1978.
Veronico, Nicholas A. *Airliner Tech Series: Boeing 377 Stratocruiser.* Specialty Press. 2001.
Ward-Thomas, Pat. *The World Atlas of Golf.* Gallery Books. 1987.
Waterman, Frederick. *The History of the Newport Country Club.* Newport Country Club Preservation Foundation. 2013.
Wind, Herbert Warren. *The Story of American Golf.* Farrar, Strauss & Giroux. 1948.
Wendehack, Clifford Charles. *Golf and Country Clubs.* Richard Helburn, Inc. 1929.
Wexler, Daniel. *The Book of Golfers.* Sports Media Group. 2005.
———*Lost Links: Forgotten Treasures of Golf's Golden Age.* Wiley. 2003.
———*Missing Links: Americas Greatest Lost Golf Courses and Holes.* Wiley. 2000.
Whigham, H. J. *The New Deal.* G. P. Putnam's Sons. 1936.
Young, Phillip. *Tillinghast Creator of Golf Courses.* Future Classics of Golf. 2005.
Zoglin, Richard. *Hope: Entertainer of the Century.* Simon & Schuster. 2014.

Other sources, including websites, pamphlets, newsletters, and ephemera

30 Minutes with George Hughes, July 1934, publication unknown.
The Acushnet Company.
American Stationer & Office Outfitter.
Ancestry.com for access to birth, death, census, travel and military records.
A Slice of Golfing History: The Development of Golf in Nova Scotia, 1895–1945, Allan Dunlop.
Albuquerque Country Club, Albuquerque, New Mexico.
American Express, Our Story, The American Express Company.
Amherst College Archives & Special Collections.
Announcing the Opening of the New Courses, Winged Foot Golf Club, Mamaroneck, New York, September 8, 1923, The Winged Foot Golf Club.

Baharris.org.
The Borough of Fenwick, Connecticut.
Boston & Maine Railroad, Local Timetable, 1913.
British Overseas Air Corporation Stratocruiser Brochure 55/207/50M/SP.
The Bronx Historical Society, Bronx, New York.
The Centers for Disease Control, *Leading Causes of Death, 1900–1998.*
City of Riverton, Wyoming.
City of Philadelphia archives.
Coleman Theatre, Miami, Oklahoma.
Columbia University Medical Center, New York.
The Commonwealth of Massachusetts, Birth Register.
Department of the Army, General Orders No. 2 (September 26, 1947).
Differential Unemployment and Characteristics of the Unemployed in the United States, 1940–1954, Philip M. Hauser, University of Chicago, 1957.
Dwight D. Eisenhower Presidential Library and Museum, Abilene, Kansas.
Elephant Rocks Golf Course, Williams, Arizona.
Encyclopedia Britannica.
Expansion of Golf Courses in the United States. Napton, Darrell E., Laingen, Christopher R., The Geographical Review.
Federal Reserve Bank of Boston, *Closed for the Holiday, The Bank Holiday of 1933.*
Funding Universe, Acushnet Company History.
Golf Association of Philadelphia (GAP) Magazine, Spring 2011, Jeff Silverman, *Here Today, Gone Tomorrow: The Philadelphia Area Lost Golf Courses.*
Glen Garden Country Club, Texas.
Historical Society of Somerset Hills (New Jersey).
Honorable Order of Kentucky Colonels.
International Air Transport Association.
The Knollwood Country Club, Elmsford, New York.
The Longniddry Golf Club, Scotland.
The Olympia Fields Country Club, Olympia Fields, Illinois.
Pennsylvania Turnpike website.
The Pinehurst Resort, Pinehurst, North Carolina.
Quaker Hill Country Club, Pawling, New York.
Marion Golf Club, Massachusetts.
Minnesota Historical Society, *Caucasians Only*, Thomas B. Jones, 2003.
Moundbuilders Country Club, Newark, Ohio.
New York Athletic Club Newsletter, *The Winged Foot.*
New York State Museum, Albany, New York.
National Park Service, Washington, D. C.
PBS.org *The Golden Age of Golf Course Architecture in America.*
Pennsylvania Railroad, New York and South schedule, 1942.
Playing Fair: The fight for interracial athletics in Baltimore, Sara Patenaude, Georgia State University, 2001.

Publications.newberry.org.
Royal Society of Chemistry.
The Savannah Golf Club, Savannah, Georgia.
Starwoodhotels.com.
St. Andrew's Society of New York, *Pibroch* Newsletter.
Smithsonian.com, *Meet Me at the Automat*, August 2001, Carolyn Hughes Crowley.
Social Security Bulletin, Volume 10, December 1947, Number 12.
The Tufts Archives, North Carolina.
United States Golf Association.
US Department of Agriculture, *1986 Surgeon General's Report*.
US Department of the Interior, National Parks Service, *National Historic Landmark Nomination, Baltusrol Golf Club, 2013.*
US Patent and Trademark Office.
Weatherbase.com.
Willow Ridge Country Club, New York.
The Winged Foot Golf Club, New York.
The Winged Foot Golf Club Newsletter, *Putt Putt.*
The Worcester Country Club, Massachusetts.

Newspapers and Periodicals

Aberdeen Press Journal (Scotland), *Adelaide* (Australia) *Advertiser, American Annual Golf Guide* (various years), *American Hebrew and Jewish Tribune, The American Golfer, American Magazine, The Atlanta Constitution, Atlanta Journal, The Atlantic, The Atlantic City Press, The Baltimore Sun, Berkeley Daily Gazette, Berlin Register, Birmingham News Eagle, Bluefield Daily Telegraph, Boston Post, The Bradford Era* (Pennsylvania), *Brisbane Telegraph, Brisbane Courier-Mail, The Brooklyn Daily Eagle, Chicago Daily News, The Chillicothe Constitution-Tribune* (Missouri), *Coeur d'Alene Press, Collier's Weekly, Courier-Journal* (Louisville), *Daily Capital Journal* (South Dakota), *Daily Gleaner, Daily Republican* (Pennsylvania), *Dallas Morning News, Desert Sun* (Arizona), *Dundee Courier Advertiser* (Scotland), *Dziennik DLA Wszystkich* (Polish Language), *Elks Magazine, Elmira Advertiser, El Telegrafo* (Ecuador), *Esquire, Evansville Courier and Journal, Evening Independent, The Evening Standard* (Pennsylvania), *The Evening Sun* (Pennsylvania), *Examiner* (Launceston, Tasmania), *Florence* (Alabama) *Times-News, Florida Times Union, Forbes, Ft. Smith Southwest American, Free Press Ontario, Gazette and Colonist* (Bermuda), *Gettysburg Times, The Glasgow*

Herald (Scotland), *The Globe and Mail* (Canada), *Golfdom, Golf Digest, Golf Illustrated, Golfing, Greensboro Daily News, Green Book* (Golf), *Greenwood* (South Carolina) *Index Journal, Harper's Golf Guide* (various years), *Harper's Round Table, The Hartford Courant, Havana Evening Telegraph* (Cuba), *Herald and News* (Oregon), *Herald-Post* (Louisville), *The Herald Tribune, The High Point Enterprise* (North Carolina), *Holyoke Daily Telegraph, Irish Independent* (Ireland), *Joplin Globe, Kentucky New Era, The Key West Citizen, Kingsport Times* (Tennessee), *La Grange Daily News, Las Vegas Review-Journal, The Lewiston Daily Sun, The Lincoln Star* (Nebraska), *London Times* (England), *The Los Altos News, The Los Angeles Times, Louisville Courier, L & N Magazine, Louisville Times, Mackinac Island News, Macon Telegraph, Masters Journal, McClure's Magazine, Medicine Hat Weekly* (Canada), *Milwaukee Journal, Minneapolis Star, Minnesota Star, Minnetonka Herald, Muskogee* (Oklahoma) *Phoenix, Nashville Tennessean, Nassau Daily Review* (Long Island), *National Geographic, National Greenkeeper, Newark News, The Newark Star-Ledger, The New Haven Register, The New Yorker, New York Daily Mirror, New York Daily News, New York Evening Post, New York Evening World, New York Journal-American, New York Sentinel, New York Sun, The New York Times, New York Tribune, New York World-Telegram, The News* (Frederick, Maryland), *Nova Scotia* (Canada) *Spectator, Omaha Bee, Omaha World-Herald, Ottawa* (Canada) *Citizen, Ottawa* (Canada) *Journal, Pampa* (Texas) *Daily News, Philadelphia Inquirer, Philadelphia Public Ledger, Pittsburgh Press, Portland Herald, Providence Journal, Raleigh News Observer, Rapid City Daily Journal, The Reading Eagle, Richmond Times-Dispatch, Roanoke Beacon, Robesonian* (North Carolina), *Rochester Times, Salt Lake Tribune, San Antonio Express, San Diego Union, San Francisco Chronicle, San Francisco News, Santa Cruz Sentinel-News, The Saturday Evening Post, Savannah Morning News, Scottish Daily Herald* (Scotland), *Springfield Daily News, Springfield Daily Republican, Springfield Daily Transcript, South China Morning Post, Sports Illustrated, St. Louis Globe-Democrat, St. Petersburg Times, Standard Herald American, Staten Island Advance, Stratford Beacon Herald, Stockton Record, Sudbury Daily Star, Sunday*

Times (Perth, Australia), *The Sydney* (Australia) *Mail, Syracuse Herald-Journal, The Times-Picayune, True Citizen* (Georgia), *Tweed Daily* (New South Wales), *USGA Bulletin, USGA Journal and Turf Management, The Victoria Advocate, The Wall Street Journal, The Washington Post, Westchester Magazine.*

Author's note: Ralph's scorecards are stored in the USGA library in alphabetical order by state, Canadian province, and country. If he kept a chronological list of the courses he played, he did not donate it to the library. Thus, it is difficult to put together an exact complete list from the beginning of his journey to the end in meticulous fashion. In addition, because he appears to have numbered the cards after the fact using a pen, and in many instances was doing so decades after the fact, the dates and his course numbers don't always fall into place in exact order. Because of this, in some cases I have had to piece together the correct information using a combination of the original dates on the cards (which take precedence, since they were written contemporaneously) and newspaper articles, where available. To give one example, the front of his Old Course scorecard at St. Andrews says 14/9/51, and on the rear it is dated 17 Sep 1951. The proper date of the 17th was established by verifying against the USGA article *The Dr. Livingstone of Golf* and because he said he played the New Course at St. Andrews on the same day, which was the 17th. If there was no additional supporting material available, I used my best judgment.

The author was drawn to Ralph Kennedy because, having played a lot of golf around the world myself (although nowhere near the level of RAK), I fully appreciated the scope of his accomplishments. Along the way, I found that I had a lot in common with him: I enjoy an occasional cigar, don't wear a glove when I play, and am not particularly long off the tee. I have worked a good part of my life in New York City and know the neighborhoods he frequented well. Ralph and I also share a love of Shinnecock Hills, Yale, Mid Ocean, Pine Valley, the Los Angeles Country Club, Cypress Point, Pebble Beach, and Winged Foot, although I appreciate the National Golf Links of America more than he does and have a strong disdain for the current Pennsylvania Station and leaf blowers.